Cook More, Waste Less

D1211025

Cook More, Waste Less

Zero-Waste Recipes to Use Up Groceries,
Tackle Food Scraps, and Transform Leftovers

CHRISTINE TIZZARD

Copyright © 2021 Christine Tizzard

All rights reserved. The use of any part of this publication, reproduced,
transmitted in any form or by any means electronic, mechanical, photocopying,
recording or otherwise, or stored in a retrieval system without the prior written
consent of the publisher—or in the case of photocopying or other reprographic
copying, license from the Canadian Copyright Licensing Agency—is an
infringement of the copyright law.

Appetite by Random House® and colophon are registered
trademarks of Penguin Random House LLC.

Library and Archives of Canada Cataloguing in Publication is available upon request.
ISBN: 9780525610656
eBook ISBN: 9780525610663

Cover and book design by Kelly Hill
Food photography by Reena Newman
Food styling by Christine Tizzard
Food styling assistants: Leah Wildman, Andrea Lane and Cara Wallach
Prop styling by Andrea McCrindle
Zero-Waste profiles photography and photos on pages 3 and 250 by Lindsay Duncan
Photo on page 88 by Ryan Hegarty
Printed in China

Published in Canada by Appetite by Random House®,
a division of Penguin Random House LLC.

www.penguinrandomhouse.ca

10 9 8 7 6 5 4 3 2 1

appetite
by RANDOM HOUSE

Penguin
Random House
Canada

To the wonderful
world we live in
and to all of you
who strive to
keep it that way.
Respect.

Contents

Pantry-Inspired Staples

Stocks and Condiments

Sweeter Stuff

Beyond Meals

INTRODUCTION

Growing up, I would often see my dad hunched over the kitchen table with a plate of odd bits from the fridge. A little mustard, a few pickled goods, some bread. "Cleaning out the fridge," he would say. Our Monday meals of Spam and leftover veggie hash patties came from Sunday's supper, served with ketchup. Was it the healthiest approach? Probably not. But it did make me think about using leftovers, reducing food waste, and eating on a budget from an early age.

As I got older and started cooking and enjoying my time in the kitchen more and more, I turned my obsessive love of cooking into a career. When I first started as a food stylist, I couldn't believe how much food was thrown away. After securing that perfect burger advertisement or filming a favorite food TV challenge, my colleagues would chuckle as I loaded up my work bins with left-over scraps from shoots to bring home.

I spent weekends pawning off food, which my colleagues didn't claim, on family and friends, making one too many fruit pies or huge batches of soups with those leftovers. I found it so difficult to throw out food. And so I developed a simple practice of batch cooking week to week, using it as the opportunity to clean out my fridge and freezer, and experiment. And, over the years, my favorite recipes became those that were most adaptable to the ingredients I had kicking around the kitchen. Fancy Fried Rice (page 165), for example, combines leftover rice, with whatever bits of this or that I had on hand. Then I can use the leftovers into Packed Peppers (page 70) the next day. After developing these and more food waste solutions in my own kitchen, I realized there *need*s to be a book that shares these kinds of practical, everyday solutions for using up the food we typically toss aside. And *Cook More, Waste Less* was born.

As I have been writing this cookbook, food waste has become an increasingly hot topic, and a global one at that. Globally, 1.3 billion tons of the total food produced is lost before it even reaches the market because of poor farming infrastructures. I don't even want to tell you how much money that is (spoiler alert: it's over 1 trillion dollars!). And currently one-third of all the food produced in the world is wasted (while sadly over 800 million people are suffering from malnutrition, 1 in 4 households have encountered food insecurity in the US, while 1 in 8 households have experienced food insecurity in Canada). We all play a part: on average we unwittingly throw away one in every four bags of groceries we buy.

The problem with food waste is multi-fold: when we toss aside perfectly edible food rather than using it, not only are we creating needless waste and negatively impacting the environment by adding more methane into the atmosphere (not to mention, wasting our own valuable dollars), but we are perpetuating the demand for more food to be produced overall; and the more food that is produced, the more detrimental the impact on the environment. Consumer expectations for ever-more perfect produce also causes food waste as retailers reject what they don't think they'll sell before it even hits shelves. You could write a whole book about global food waste (and yes, there are whole books written on this subject). I'm not here to make you feel guilty. I don't want to cram facts and food politics down your throat. I know I get overwhelmed by these startling facts. As much as I would love to change food policies and technologies to reduce the carbon footprint of our food systems, it takes a village to make changes and it's going to take time.

During COVID-19, farmers and food systems have been hit hard, making many of us reflect even more on our own food and consumption habits. Lots more people have chosen to take the time and effort to grow their own food as a result, yet sometimes struggle to use up all the bounty from their garden, facing a different challenge about waste. Along the way I have learned there is only one thing we have immediate, direct control of: our own consumption habits, i.e., how we buy, store, eat, and dispose of our food.

My hope with this cookbook is to show how you can make small changes and work toward minimizing your food waste. Even simple, small shifts in how we buy, cook, and eat food can make a significant difference to the amount of food waste we produce. And if going zero waste feels unattainable, remind yourself regularly, as I do, that it is a goal and not a hard target. Included in these pages are some basic strategies and tools to help you start this zero-waste journey and get you thinking about new ways of planning your meals, and buying and preparing food. The recipes demonstrate creative ideas to use up what is already in your fridge, freezer, and pantry, as well as how to transform leftovers, and how to use the often-overlooked parts of food (from onion skins to banana peels) we might usually throw away.

We won't solve the world's problems all at once, and you don't have to change your life overnight, but we can begin with simple, actionable steps focused on what you'll eat next—and what you *won't* throw away. Whether you are an environmentally or socially conscious eater, someone working with a tight food budget, or just looking for new ideas for what to cook, I hope you enjoy this journey towards zero waste.

Christine

PART I

Zero–Waste Kitchen Basics

Zero–Waste Shopping Strategies

Let's start at the beginning: how we buy the food we eat. We all have our routines, budgets, and preferences. Some love that big, bulk Costco run, while others shop day to day. My biggest challenge, personally, is that I buy too much food. My eyes are all aglow strolling food markets, and I have fairytale fantasies about all the wonderful recipes I will create with the bright and beautiful food I see. Then things pop up, life happens, and food gets left behind. So I consistently have to avoid the temptation to buy items (especially perishable ones) just because they are appealing, or because they are on sale! Here are some ways to make shopping easier while also reducing your food waste.

FRIDGE FIRST

Look in your fridge before you head to the store. What needs to be used up first? Cross-reference this with the staples you have on-hand, and decide what meals you want to make. Then decide what's missing. That's what you shop for, along with any other day-to-day essentials you have run out of. This is how I shop for the week; I find this advance-planning (although not sexy!) makes sure that I use up everything I have, and saves money in the process. Tip: always keep an efficient food pantry stocked up with simple, common ingredients that can turn a few leftovers or spare ingredients into something spectacular (read more on page 9).

WHEN YOU'RE ON THE GO

Wait, what if you're on your way home from work and you forgot to make a list? Solution: at the grocery store, buy one fresh item that is easy to mix and match with other ingredients, say . . . trout. When you get home, before unpacking the groceries, open your fridge and take out the things you need to use up most. Then, figure out a way to incorporate them with your trout (see my whole fish recipe on page 109).

WHERE TO BUY

GROCERY STORE CHAINS

Some people think grocery store chains are the enemy, but many have been making headlines with promises of becoming zero food waste within the next few years. Did you know that report cards are now being given to grocery stores by the Center for Biological Diversity? Only one major chain, as of now, has received a B—but with more stores offering sales on "ugly" produce, reducing excess inventory, increasing food donations, and embracing zero-waste packaging, they are at least heading in the right direction. Don't overlook the ugly or discounted produce available—but, on the flip side, don't just buy it because it's on sale unless you are really going to use it otherwise you're just creating more waste. To reduce impulse purchases, only go down aisles where there is something you actually need. And remember that shopping at deli counters, and for unpackaged produce, lets you control exactly the amount of something you buy, which helps prevent overbuying and unnecessary waste later.

BULK STORES

These stores are convenient, but when shopping there, plan out how you are going to use your bulk buys before you get to the checkout counter and be sure to store the food properly when you get home (and, be confident before buying that you have room for it in the first place!). For example, I buy bulk nuts and seeds because my family goes through them like crazy. However, since they go rancid quickly, I only store small amounts in the pantry and freeze the rest. Try not to get excited by the low prices and buy more than you need, especially with something you have never tried before. Just because something is on sale doesn't mean you will eat it all. I have to remind myself of this regularly. On a side note, big-box stores are also making headlines with their plans to phase out plastics and/or reach zero food waste over the next few years, which is great.

GROCERY DELIVERY

It's convenient and cheap (sometimes free), but it's an acquired taste. Some people just like shopping for groceries in person. Grocery delivery has saved my life at times, like when I just couldn't bear the thought of packing up a screaming infant and wandering toddler in the middle of winter. It is also a great alternative for things that are just no fun to shop for, those nonperishable everyday household items like toilet paper, cleaning supplies, dog food, and cat litter. It also reduces your likelihood of impulse buying. The big issue with delivery services is all the packaging that's left behind. So when ordering these services, see if there is a sustainable grocery delivery in your area. They tend to offer reusable packaging (mesh bags and mason jars, for example) that they pick up on your next order. And, as always, order only what you need, and resist the temptation to buy more.

SPECIALTY STORES

Visiting your neighborhood specialty food stores supports your community and supplies you with the best of the best ingredients. Whether it's the aromatic spice store, the smells inside my favorite French bakery, or the neighborhood Italian fine foods store where the olives make me drool, I have to tame my impulse buying and stick to my meal plan in mind or my list in hand.

FARMERS' MARKETS

Every time I travel somewhere new, the first thing I ask is where and when is the local farmers market? A jaunt to your local farmers' market supports community agriculture, farmers, and your neighborhood in a big way. It is where you begin to understand what fresh, seasonal, and local really means, and it can inspire you to cook what is in season. Once again, you will want to buy and eat everything, but stick to what you need. Most farmers' markets have already hopped on the zero-waste train and have more and more waste-free packaging. Just be sure to bring your own egg cartons to get refilled and other reusable shopping bags and containers.

COMMUNITY SUPPORTED AGRICULTURE SERVICES

With local community supported agriculture (CSAs), you are buying seasonal food directly from your local farmer with the added bonus that most will drop your food-box order at your door or have it ready at a designated local pickup area, in a reusable bin with no food packaging. If you haven't tried one before, give it a shot! They come in all shapes and sizes and deliver everything from fresh seasonal produce to milk, dairy, and meat. Subscriptions can be weekly or monthly. There are many resources online as to how to find one. In Canada, there is www.csafarms.ca,

BUY FOOD AND NOT PACKAGING

Try to avoid buying food with unnecessary packaging, like cauliflower wrapped in plastic. Also, be sure to have the following handy:

REUSABLE BAGS AND SHOPPING BINS When grocery shopping I try to avoid single-use plastic bags. I toss my food in one large reusable bag and my produce into one large reusable shopping bin (or even used milk crates). For smaller items, I always carry a small reusable bag in my purse. Having an accessible (which means finding a way that works for you so don't forget them) collection of reusable bags is especially great for smaller fruit and veggie items.

REUSABLE PACKAGING My teenage daughter and some of her friends got their first jobs at a local grocer in the deli section. According to them, customers are bringing in their own reusable packaging for their deli cuts and portioned cheese chunks. Amazing to hear since this not only eliminates single-use plastics, but by buying from the deli (rather than with pre-packaged options) you only buy what you need for the week, preventing food wasted in your fridge. Also, it keeps people employed behind those deli counters. When shopping, have your reusable containers ready to go.

and in the US, there is www.ams.usda.gov. By using CSAs you are instantly supporting local farmers and seasonal produce, plus you cut out the middleman, which leads to a less wasteful model.

ZERO-WASTE RETAILERS

There have been a sprinkling of zero-waste grocery stores popping up (not to mention zero-waste bulk stores, coffee shops (where you can bring your own mug), and retailers) that tackle waste in general. When it comes to reducing *food* waste specifically, zero-waste retailers are great because you can pick and choose the quantities of foods that you need. Plus they give monetary incentives for bringing your own reusable containers. It's definitely easier to change your habits when you get instant rewards. I look forward to seeing more of these over the coming years.

What to Buy

The importance of having a few key things on hand, in constant rotation, helps when planning your meals. Here is a quick overview of how to stock your pantry and fridge with the essential building blocks you will need to make a recipe while reducing your kitchen waste.

PANTRY

CANNED, JARRED OR DRIED FOODS Only you know what you like here, but having a reasonable selection of canned, jarred or pantry items makes cooking more convenient. Canned beans, tomatoes, or coconut milk, jarred nut butter, honey, or jam, or dried legumes, dried fruit, cereal or nuts and seeds, are just some of the items in constant rotation at my house. To feed the two adults and two teenagers in my house, I usually buy two to three kinds of each because I know they will be used up before I do a big grocery run. More unique items, like clam juice, may not be a must-have unless you are going to make something that week with it. Observe what pantry items are the most (and least) popular in your house and stock accordingly.

GRAINS Have a few grains you know you like and will get eaten, whether that's quinoa, brown rice, or your favorite brand of pasta. In the past, my pantry had more than six different types of rice alone. Not anymore. Now I buy two kinds of rice as I know they will be used up. This book is filled with different ways to use up your grains and make day-olds new again.

SPICES There's nothing like a kitchen with a spectacular spice rack. I cannot express how important spices are to me. This is instant flavor! However, there is no point in having all those spices unless you are going to cook with them. Spices should have a best before date stamped on them. They will typically last a few years, but their flavor diminishes over time. Avoid buying large packages of ground spices—buy amounts that make sense for you. Bulk food stores are great for buying smaller quantities.

ESSENTIAL DRIED SEASONINGS CHECKLIST

If you're starting your spice rack from scratch, here are my suggestions for essential dried herbs and spices to have on hand. Since these are in use regularly in our home, I know they will always be used up! This list may vary depending on your palate and how you like to cook.

Allspice

Bay leaves

Black peppercorns

Chili powder, sweet

Cinnamon, ground

Coriander, whole or ground

Cream of tartar

Cumin, whole or ground

Curry leaves

Curry powder

Garam masala

Garlic powder

Ginger powder

Nutmeg, whole

Onion powder

Oregano

Paprika, smoked

Rosemary

Savory

Sumac, ground

Thyme

Turmeric, ground

Vanilla extract, pure (not a dried spice, but you know . . .)

BAKING STAPLES As I am an avid baker, I always ensure the following baking essentials are stocked: flours (all-purpose and alternatives), cornstarch, baking powder, baking soda, cane and brown sugar, oats, and cocoa powder. If you bake once in a blue moon, buy the quantities you need for that recipe at a bulk store.

FRIDGE

VEGETABLES AND FRUIT Buy only what you can eat before produce goes past its prime. Seasonal produce will always be cheaper and healthier. And buy produce whole, not precut, since cutting into produce raises its "respiration rate." (In lay terms, cutting reduces or removes a fruit or vegetable's protective "skin." The more of its flesh is exposed to the air, the more nutrients get lost. It also spoils more quickly.) You will also reduce your plastic use by avoiding most packaged precut items. Check out my food storage table (page 16) for more specifics on how to properly buy and store individual types of produce. In general, the recipes in this book assume you will have garlic, onions and some other basic veggies (like carrots and celery) on hand.

MEAT, POULTRY, AND SEAFOOD Only buy proteins you know you will need and, if possible, buy cuts on the bone. Bones add flavor, and cuts with bones are generally cheaper: whole chickens cost less than boneless skinless breasts, for example, and you can make stock (page 188), soup, sauce, and more with all the bits and pieces left over.

DELI AND CHEESE The good thing about deli meats and cheeses is that they are typically sold in smaller packages, or you can order the exact portions you need from the counter. These can be pricey, so buy what you need. If you are putting cheese out for guests, serve it in smaller portions and replenish if needed to avoid leftovers. Once cheese is out, uneaten portions should be back in the fridge within four hours. However, softer cheeses will look weepier than, say, a wedge of Parmesan after two hours, so use your own judgment (page 19).

CONDIMENTS AND SAUCES Is your fridge door overloaded with old jars and bottles? Oh, and when was the last time you looked at their best before dates? Declutter that mess! Buy one great mustard, one hot sauce, and a few extra condiments if you know you will use them regularly. Use them up, then buy more. Stop collecting them, for goodness' sake. Better yet, try making your own condiments from scratch (page 185). Tip: if you buy a salad dressing and you aren't fond of it, try it as a marinade to use it up.

Essential Kitchen Tools

There are so many kitchen gadgets and tools out there you just don't need, believe me. I have worked with them all throughout my career, but when it comes to my home kitchen, what I use regularly is minimal. For me, a decluttered kitchen means less to clean up. It does pay off to buy reputable, long-lasting appliances—they will yield much better results.

THREE GOOD-QUALITY KNIVES You need a chef's knife, paring knife, and bread knife. A knife sharpener (called a steel) would be a bonus as well. My knife kit for work typically stays in my car, but I have had some of my knives for 18 years. I sharpen them regularly with my steel and drop them off at my local kitchen appliance store for professional sharpening a few times throughout the year.

TWO CUTTING BOARDS One for meat, poultry, and seafood that can easily go in your dishwasher or can be washed regularly without warping. Another large, thick wooden cutting board with little rubber "legs" on one side for everything else. People always buy wooden cutting boards thinking they are going to use both sides, but if you use your cutting board multiple times a day, as I do, and have kids or guests in and out, it is constantly getting wet or wiped down, not dried properly, and one side eventually gets moldy or starts to warp. The little legs will keep the air circulating underneath. If your board doesn't have legs, you can buy them at the local hardware store and screw them in. Oh, and please don't forget to oil the board regularly. This will prevent it from drying out and cracking. A dry board absorbs liquids, so a well-oiled board also prevents bacteria from growing in those little cracks. Do not put wooden cutting boards in the dishwasher. Too much water and steam may cause them to warp.

A REALLY GOOD SET OF POTS AND PANS I use Lodge cast-iron and All-Clad at home (and no, they did not pay me to say this). Most nonstick pans will have a limited life-span, unless you buy one that has a lifetime warranty. When purchasing any pot or pan, look for warranties and see if you can learn anything about the brand's efforts in sustainability. All-Clad, for example, has a line called Encore that recrafts old pots and pans and sells them at a cheaper price, instead of sending them to the landfill.

A HIGH-PERFORMANCE BLENDER Try for one that can also take whole-grains and turn them into flour (like oats to oat flour). You can count on a blender like this to grind nuts into butters and make your own nut, seed, or grain milks (page 105). It will also take the place of a food processor and make everything from creamy soup to salad dressing.

A CHEAP LITTLE COFFEE GRINDER This is for grinding spices, nuts, and seeds, and helps my food budget immensely. I like to buy whole spices, since they have more flavor and are cheaper. I can also grind my own flax, chia, and other small seeds I like to add to baking.

SILPATS OR REUSABLE SILICONE BAKING MATS These reduce the need for parchment or aluminum foil to line pans. I have quite a few, and I use them all the time; one of them has lasted me over 10 years. If you need to wrap or cover food while baking, and want to avoid aluminum foil, you can also use silicone lids or pots (upside down) or their lids to cover them. Or, to avoid it altogether, try cooking things in enamelware, cast-iron, or stoneware with lids.

Food Storage 101

The good, the bad, and the reheated. How do you store fresh produce for optimal freshness? How do you properly store and reheat leftovers? How can you really tell if those half-eaten meals in the fridge or freezer are safe to eat? The smell test? The taste test? We have all done them. Most of the time, we are so concerned about food safety, it's easier to toss it than to question it. But more education about food safety means that we can start making more informed decisions as to what to toss and what to keep a little longer. And learning how to store food so that it lasts longer in the first place makes weekly cooking at home less stressful and, of course, creates less waste.

The food preparation and storage techniques that I have learned over the years have now become instinctive, since my job depends on them, and in this section we cover it all. Avocados not quite ripe? Store them on the counter next to your bananas to ripen faster. Not sure you can eat all those apples before they go mealy? Pop them in the fridge! The charts on pages 16 to 22 are designed to help you buy and store food so it lasts as long as possible—with some tips on buying the best-quality food in the first place—allowing you to enjoy every last bite!

ZERO-WASTE STORAGE SOLUTIONS

Environmentally friendly, reusable food storage solutions are important, and new ideas are popping up everywhere!

CLEAR STORAGE CONTAINERS I don't know how much stuff gets thrown away because some people, not naming names, cannot be bothered to open a container and look inside. Even worse, it gets pushed to the back of the fridge for me to discover later. Out of sight, out of mind. But if you can see that vibrant, lovely fruit salad, it may have a fighting chance of getting eaten. This is why clear storage containers, mason jars, and bowls are great. In a pinch, reuse your glass or plastic food containers. If you are looking to buy some, try your local thrift store first. They always have a good selection of canning supplies (don't forget that canning seals cannot be reused for canning and preserving) and old glass containers.

RELIABLE FREEZER-SAFE CONTAINERS There is nothing quite like air-tight storage for freezer foods, which is why folks who freeze a lot may splurge on a vacuum sealer. While such equipment helps us with our food waste by freezing food more efficiently, it adds to our plastics dilemma. For food safety issues, you should never reuse plastic bags that have already been used for freezing meat, poultry, and seafood. You can use reusable, dishwasher-safe, food grade silicon bags instead. Glass or metal containers and paper bags are other great sustainable ways to freeze. And some food items like bananas, tomatoes, and peaches, even come with freezer packaging built in—with their peels and skins!

REUSABLE WRAPPING Plain old waxed paper is an easy and affordable alternative to plastic wrap and can be wiped and reused a few times. Reusable food wraps like beeswax wraps (which come in the coolest patterned fabrics), silicon stretchy covers and suction lids, are the best option, and also great for transporting food on the go.

REUSABLE DRINK CONTAINERS To avoid the copious waste created from to-go coffee cups, always have a re-usable drinkable container on hand! I have a lot of gear to bring to work and those not-so-cheap bottles tend to vanish as soon as I bring them into the house. They have legs, I swear. So I recommend you store them in the car, on your bike, or in your bag at all times.

These are just some examples. Find reusable ways to store food items that make sense for you and your family.

STORING FRESH FOOD

Fruits and veggies ripen faster at room temperature, not as fast in the fridge, and stop ripening completely in the freezer, and you can use that to your advantage. Produce can be stored in the fridge in a mesh produce bag or open bin/container or wrapped in damp towels. Generally, once you've cut into something, wrap it well before storing it. Store fresh meat and seafood in the lowest compartment of your fridge in a leak-proof container to avoid cross contamination. Live seafood, like lobsters or mussels, need to be kept alive before cooking, so store in the fridge in a shallow pan with moist tea towels overtop. If you know you are not going to eat fresh animal or seafood protein within a few days, make the decision to cook and/or freeze it. If you decide to freeze it when raw, thaw from frozen in a sealed container in the fridge before using.

STORING FROZEN FOODS

Your freezer can seriously extend the shelf life of foods. There was a time when I thought everything I cooked needed to be fresh, but freezing seasonal produce at its peak actually locks in their key nutrients. You can then use these frozen items throughout the year to supplement a meal or build out a dish. For example, I love wild blueberries (see my taco recipe on page 135), but can only get them fresh for a few weeks of the year. Freezing means I can cook with them year round. That said, keep in mind that over time frozen foods can lose flavor and texture, especially with produce with higher water content. Most often, freezing produce works best when you're planning to cook or blend the food after. Here are some tips on properly freezing your food at home.

BLANCH BEFORE FREEZING Some vegetables require blanching first, such as broccoli and asparagus. This is where you plunge foods into boiling salted water for a very brief period of time (30 seconds to a few minutes), then cool them quickly in an ice bath or under cold running water (shocking) to prevent overcooking and lock in texture and color, then freeze accordingly. When you're ready to use them, add them directly to the recipe or defrost them if necessary.

PORTION OUT Smaller things freeze faster and maintain their quality better. Portion out bulk quantities of foods you want to freeze, so you can thaw what you need when you need it.

FLAT FREEZING This is best for small items, for example, berries. Just lay them flat on a baking sheet and partially freeze first before transferring to a freezer-safe container. This prevents them from freezing into one big clump.

LEFTOVERS SHOULD BE FROZEN WITHIN TWO DAYS

USE FREEZER-SAFE CONTAINERS Cardboard, foil, and milk cartons don't freeze well.

SOMETIMES YOU CAN RE-FREEZE If a frozen raw product has been defrosted and used in a recipe, say thawed chicken made into chicken soup, then you can refreeze your new soup creation.

HAVE A "FREEZER WEEK" EVERY FEW MONTHS See how much stuff in your freezer you can use up.

STORING PACKAGED FOOD

When it comes to shelf life, manufacturers use a bunch of different terms, and those can get confusing. Here is what you need to know about date labeling on packaged food and ways to store it:

BEST BEFORE DATE OR BEST IF USED BY This means that any unopened package will be of the highest quality before this date. This is not for food safety; it is for optimal freshness. As such, it is legal to sell certain products after their best before date (BBD), and it's not necessarily unsafe to eat foods after this date, but only if the packages have been unopened and they have been stored properly. After the BBD has passed, a product can lose flavor, nutrients, or texture but can still be safe to eat. Once you've opened the package, the BBD will change depending on how well you are storing the product, and every product will be different. For instance, if your kids leave the milk on the counter for the afternoon, it may go bad earlier. How do you tell if a product is still safe to eat after BBD? This is a tough one. Mold can be cut off cheese, canned goods can last years past their BBD, eggs can be checked with the water test (if they sink in water you are good to go, if they float, compost them), cookies, crackers, and cereals just start to taste stale, etc. (but can be turned into delicious Crispy Coatings, page 183). You really do have to use your own judgment and Google when you are unsure. The bottom line is to buy only what you need and start to curb overpurchasing.

EXPIRATION DATE Yes, sadly, this is the day your food expires, and it should be discarded after this date. Very few grocery store items have these, so we don't come across it often. Some products that do are baby formula and meal replacements.

PACKAGED ON Foods with a "packaged on" date are packaged by the retailers: for example, larger cuts of meat that your grocer has broken down into smaller ones and then sealed. These should always have a BBD also listed on the package. Retailers are only allowed to package items that last 90 days or less.

STORING NON-PERISHABLE FOODS

Store dried foods (such as legumes) in sealed containers in dark, dry places for the best results. Many of these foods won't truly go bad, but they will lose flavor and potency over time.

Food Storage Glossary

Produce	Counter	Fridge	Freezer	Tips
Apples	3 days	1 month	6 months	Apples will continue to ripen on the counter but will eventually turn mealy—and one apple can spoil the bunch. Store the apples separate from the other produce. Toss cut apples with lemon juice to prevent them from browning (also good to do before freezing cut apples).
Apricots	2 days	5–7 days	1 year	To ripen apricots faster, store them in a paper bag.
Asparagus	N/A	3–5 days	1 year	Look for firm stalks and closed, compact tips. In the fridge, store asparagus upright in a jar in 1 inch of cold water. If freezing, blanch for 2 minutes first.
Avocados	4–5 days or until ripe	3–4 days	6 months	Ripe avocados have a slight give when pressed. To ripen them faster, store in a paper bag.
Bananas	2–6 days to desired ripeness	2–7 days	1 year	Banana skins will brown in the fridge, but the insides will still be good.
Beets	N/A	1 month	> 1 year	Look for firm, smooth beets, with the tops attached if possible. Cut the tops off before storing (they'll last 2–3 days in the fridge in an airtight container). Store beets in an open container in the fridge with a damp towel overtop. If you freeze them, cook until fork-tender first.
Berries	N/A	2–7 days	1 year	Remove any mushy, moldy fruit before storing since the spores will spread across your berries. Transfer berries into a roomier container lined with a tea towel. They like to breath, so loosely cover with a lid. To freeze them, spread them on a baking sheet, then transfer to a freezer bag for storage (this will prevent them from sticking together).
Broccoli	N/A	3–5 days	12–18 months	Look for firm, compact florets, not flowering. Store as a whole head, if possible, either in a bag or wrapped in a damp towel in an open container. If you freeze the florets, blanch them for 3 minutes first.
Brussels sprouts	N/A	3–5 days	1 year	You can freeze Brussels sprouts raw, or blanch them for 3 minutes first.
Cabbage	N/A	3 weeks–2 months	1 year	Buy whole heads rather than precut, and look for heavy heads with tightly packed leaves. To freeze, chop and blanch for 90 seconds first.

Produce	Counter	Fridge	Freezer	Tips
Carrots	N/A	4–5 weeks	6 months	Store root vegetables in a cool, dark place (no tight plastic bags). If you freeze them, peel, cut, and blanch for 3–5 minutes first.
Cauliflower	N/A	1 week	8 months	Look for packed florets free from large spots, and cut off any small brown spots. If you freeze them, cut into florets and blanch for 3 minutes first.
Celery	N/A	3–4 weeks	1 year	Look for crisp, firm stalks with the leaves on. Don't store in plastic bags. Wrap celery in aluminum foil. Freezes for 3 months raw, or 1 year blanched for 3 minutes.
Cherries	N/A	1 week	1 year	Best kept cold and dry. Store unwashed and wash as needed.
Citrus fruits (such as lemons, limes, grapefruits, and oranges)	1 week	3 weeks	6 months	When it comes to most citrus fruits, larger means juicier. Note that color isn't necessarily a sign of quality. Look for a firm and fragrant fruit that has a good weight and size. Freeze them whole, peeled, or cut into sections in a sealed bag, or freeze the zest and juice.
Corn	No	3–5 days	1 year	Look for firm corn, with kernels filling the cob from end to end. More color isn't necessarily better. You can freeze either whole cobs or cut kernels, blanched for 3 minutes.
Cucumber	2 days	Up to 10 days	No	Wrap cucumbers tightly in reusable wrap and store in the crisper drawer of your fridge and away from moisture. Cut cucumbers dry out quickly so store in a sealed airtight container.
Eggplant	2 days	1 week	1 year	Store loose in the crisper. Freeze after chopping and blanching for 4 minutes.
Garlic	Up to 6 months	No	1 year	Look for firm, dry bulbs, and store in a cool, dark, dry place. Sprouted garlic is still fine to eat, but may be more bitter. Peeled or chopped, it lasts up to 2 weeks in a sealed container.
Ginger and galangal	1 week	2–3 weeks	6 months	Look for smooth, firm with no wrinkles. In the fridge, store in paper or reusable bag. Once frozen, just grate off what you need when you need it.
Grapes	No	1–2 weeks	1 year	Discard any moldy grapes before storing. Store unwashed in cloth produce bag, and wash as needed.
Green onions	No	5 days	6 months	In the fridge, wrap the roots in a damp towel or place in a jar with 1 inch of water. To freeze, chop and seal in an airtight container.

Produce	Counter	Fridge	Freezer	Tips
Greens (lettuce, spinach, bitter greens, etc.)	No	1 week	6 months	Look for crisp, colorful leaves. Wash and dry well before storing in an airtight container with a few damp paper towels. You can freeze greens to use in cooked dishes or smoothies.
Guavas	1 week	4 days	8 months	Guavas are ripe when they smell sweet and give slightly when pressed. The rind is edible, too!
Herbs	No	2–3 weeks	1 year	Wash and dry herbs well before refrigerating, and wrap the ends in wet paper towel or place them in a jar with 1 inch of water. If you freeze them, chop first and freeze in small batches. Ice cube trays work well; just push the chopped herbs in with a little water.
Kiwi	2 days	1–2 weeks	9 months	Look for plump kiwis with no wrinkles.
Mangoes	Up to 5 days or to desired ripeness	4 days	6 months	Use green mangoes in savory recipes and ripe mangoes in sweet ones. Mangoes are ripe when they smell sweet and give slightly when pressed.
Melons	4 days	3–5 days	1 year	Look for melons that smell sweet and are heavy for their size.
Nectarines	2 days	5–7 days	1 year	To ripen nectarines faster, store them in a paper bag.
Onions	1 month	2 months	8 months	Look for onions with firm, dry, shiny skins. Store in a cool, dark, dry place—no plastic bags.
Papayas	2–4 days	1 week	> 1 year	Look for firm, smooth papayas—freckles on the skin are OK! The seeds are edible, too.
Parsnips	No	4–5 weeks	6 months	Store root vegetables in a cool, dark place (no tight plastic bags). If you freeze them, peel, cut, and blanch for 3–5 minutes first.
Peaches	2 days	5–7 days	1 year	To ripen peaches faster, store them in a paper bag.
Pears	1 week	3 days	6 months	Look for firm pears with no bruising.
Peppers (sweet and hot)	No	1 week	9 months	Look for firm peppers, and use them before the skin starts to wrinkle.
Pineapples	4 days	1 week	1 year	The yellower the pineapple, the better it will taste. They are ripe when they smell sweet and give slightly when pressed.
Plantains	To desired ripeness	1 week	1 year	Use green plantains for cooking and frying, yellow for frying and steaming; eat super ripe or black plantains raw or cooked.
Plums	2 days	5–7 days	1 year	To ripen plums faster, store them in a paper bag.
Pomegranates	1 week	1 month	6 months	Look for large, heavy, smooth pomegranates. Once you've opened them, the seeds (arils) keep 5–7 days in the refrigerator. Seal them well before freezing.

Produce	Counter	Fridge	Freezer	Tips
Potatoes (baby)	Cold and dark storage only.	2 weeks	1 year	Avoid wrinkled or green potatoes, and eat sprouting potatoes ASAP. Don't store them in plastic bags! If you freeze them, blanch for 2 minutes first.
Potatoes	2 weeks on counter or up to 3 months in cold and dark storage	No	1 year	Avoid wrinkled or green potatoes, and eat sprouting potatoes ASAP. Store in a cool, dark, well-ventilated place. To prevent your potatoes from sprouting, do not store them next to onions and instead store them with an apple. If you freeze them, blanch for 3 minutes first.
Squash	1 month	3 months	6–8 months	Look for heavy, firm squash with stems intact, rich color, and matte skin. Cook before freezing.
Sweet potatoes and yams	2 weeks	N/A	1 year	Look for firm, smooth, heavy sweet potatoes or yams, and store in a cool, dry, dark place.
Tomatoes	4 days	N/A	> 1 year	Tomatoes taste so much better when they ripen on the vine! Smell the stem to check for a sweet, earthy odor.
Turnips	N/A	4–5 weeks	6 months	Store root vegetables in a cool, dark place (no tight plastic bags). If you freeze them, peel, cut, and blanch for 3–5 minutes first.
Watermelons	1 week	1 week	1 year	If buying whole watermelons, look for a yellow navel, not green or white. Whole watermelons are best when stored on the counter until cut.
Zucchini	N/A	1–2 weeks	3–6 months	Look for smooth, firm, unwrinkled zucchini.

Protein and Dairy	Counter	Fridge	Freezer	Tips
Bacon	N/A	Check BBD, around 1 week	1 month	See page 33 for my tips on repurposing bacon fat.
Broth	N/A	3–4 days	6 months	Use ice cube trays for freezing small portions; once frozen, transfer to a freezer-safe container.
Butter	3–4 days, salted will last longer at room temperature.	Check BBD. Salted butter up to 5 months; unsalted butter up to 3 months	6–9 months	You can use butter up to 1 month after the BBD. Use a butter bell to keep butter at room temperature for up to a month.
Cheese (fresh) (e.g., ricotta)	N/A	2 weeks after opening	N/A	Store in a reusable clean container or original packaging.
Cheese (hard aged) (e.g., Parmesan)	About 4 hours	Up to 6 weeks	N/A	Wrap in reusable beeswax wrappers, wax or parchment paper, then place in a reusable bag, once opened.

Protein and Dairy	Counter	Fridge	Freezer	Tips
Cheese (hard and semi-hard) (e.g., cheddar)	About 4 hours	2–4 weeks	N/A	Rub oil on cut surfaces and place in sealed container. Reminder: if you find a little mold on the edge, just cut and discard 1 inch around the perimeter of the mold. The rest is perfectly fine to eat.
Cheese (semi-soft, soft, and blue cheese) (e.g., brie)	About 2 hours	Up to 3 weeks once opened	N/A	Store in a sealed container.
Eggs	2 hours	Whole: 5 weeks Yolks and whites: 4 days Hard-boiled eggs: 1 week	Beaten raw eggs: 1 year Yolks do not freeze well.	Check for cracks before buying. Store eggs in egg carton, not in fridge door. Egg whites store in sealed airtight container. Yolks store in an airtight container with a little water overtop.
Deli meat	N/A	Check BBD date; 3–5 days once opened	N/A	Since there are so many types of cured meats out there, I find it's best to just ask the deli how long (if no BBD is listed on package) and how best to store their products.
Dry cured meats	Depends.	Check BBD; 1 week once opened	4–6 months unopened; 2 months opened and sliced	Dry cured meats can last months if stored properly: some can be stored at room temperature, wrapped in a paper bag in the bottom of fridge, or hung in a cold room. Thaw from frozen in sealed container in fridge.
Ground poultry and meats (raw)	N/A	Up to 2 days	4 months	Avoid buying discolored meats. Best eaten ASAP or frozen in sealed container and thaw in bottom of fridge before use.
Ground poultry and meats (cooked)	N/A	4 days	6 months	Store in bottom of fridge. Thaw from frozen in sealed container in fridge.
Hot dogs	N/A	Up to 2 weeks unopened; 1 week once opened	2 months	Hot dogs are pre-cooked but it's best to reheat until they are steaming in case of any contamination at the processing plant.
Red meat (uncooked) (e.g., beef, veal, pork, lamb, wild game meats)	N/A	4 days	1 year	Store in bottom of fridge. Thaw from frozen in sealed container in fridge.

Protein and Dairy	Counter	Fridge	Freezer	Tips
Red meat (cooked) (e.g., beef, veal, pork, lamb)	N/A	4 days	3 months	Best eaten ASAP or frozen in sealed container and thaw in bottom of fridge before use.
Sausages	N/A	2 days	2 months	
Poultry and rabbit (raw)	N/A	2 days	1 year	Store in bottom of fridge. Thaw from frozen in sealed container in fridge.
Poultry and rabbit (cooked)	N/A	4 days	6 months	
Fish	N/A	2 days	Fatty fish: 3 months Lean fish: 8 months	Store on ice, covered to make sure fish doesn't dry out. Store in bottom of fridge. Thaw from frozen in sealed container in fridge. Frozen seafood can be thawed in its sealed bag by quickly immersing the bag in cold water.
Shellfish	N/A	3 days	Can freeze fresh live seafood, and cooked seafood	Eat ASAP. Do not cook live seafood if dead. Keep live seafood in shallow pan covered with moist tea towels. Live lobster should be cooked ASAP. Frozen seafood can be thawed it its sealed bag by quickly immersing the bag in cold water.
Tofu	N/A	Check BBD; 1 week once opened	3 months	Cover tofu with water in a sealed container in the fridge, changing the water daily to keep fresh. Store in a sealed container in the freezer; some prefer texture of tofu after it's frozen as tofu's high water content freezes inside the block of tofu, pushing the curds apart.

Nonperishables	Counter	Fridge	Freezer	Tips
Beans and legumes (dried)	Forever, but best up to 3 years	N/A	N/A	Best stored in a sealed container.
Breadcrumbs (fresh)	1 week	N/A	3 months	Best stored in a sealed container.
Coffee (ground)	5 months	N/A	2 years	Store in an opaque sealed container away from heat, moisture, and light.

Nonperishables	Counter	Fridge	Freezer	Tips
Coffee (instant)	20 years	N/A	Forever	Instant coffee never goes bad but does loose flavor. Store in opaque sealed container away from heat, moisture and light.
Coffee (whole)	9 months	N/A	3 years	Store in an opaque sealed container away from heat, moisture, and light.
Dried fruit	6 months	1 year	1 year	Best stored in a sealed container.
Flour	Check BBD	> 2 years	> 2 years	Gluten-free flour has a shorter shelf life—about 6 months in the freezer.
Herbs (dried)	1–3 years	N/A	N/A	Store in sealed containers, away from heat, moisture and light.
Nuts and seeds	Up to 3 months	6 months	N/A	Whole, raw nuts and seeds will keep fresh longer. Rancid nuts become bitter and can upset your stomach.
Oils (artisanal) (e.g., hazelnut, sesame, or pumpkin seed)	N/A	3–12 months	1–3 years	Best stored in the fridge.
Olive oil	2 years, unopened 1 year, opened	1–3 years	2 years	Olive oil may harden and go cloudy in the fridge, but this won't affect the taste.
Spices (ground)	2–3 years	N/A	N/A	Store in sealed containers, away from heat, moisture, and light.
Spices (whole)	4 years	N/A	N/A	Store in sealed containers, away from heat, moisture, and light.
Tea (black)	2–3 years	N/A	N/A	Store in an opaque sealed container away from heat, moisture, and light.
Tea (green and herbal)	1 year	N/A	N/A	Store in an opaque sealed container away from heat, moisture, and light.

A NOTE ON STORAGE TIMES: Something to keep in mind when using leftovers in a recipe is that the storage life of a meal produced with leftovers will likely be diminished. For example, three-day-old cooked chicken turned into a chicken salad won't last you another three days in the fridge. The fridge storage guidelines for all of these recipes are approximate and should be adjusted accordingly when using leftovers.

Waste 101

Unfortunately, even with all the zero-waste strategies you try, some food waste is inevitable, so here are some guidelines for disposing of the food we DO have to discard. Regulations are constantly changing on what and how we can discard food, and they also vary depending on where you live. To simplify things, here is a general breakdown.

SHARING AND DONATING

Whether it's because you bought too much food or grew too much produce in the backyard, there are many ways you can donate surplus food. Look for food sharing programs and initiatives in your community. Some resources take it a step further by harvesting your produce for you, such as Not Far from the Tree (not-farfromthetree.org) in Toronto, if you need someone to pick those apples growing in your backyard. In Canada there is also www.foodrescue.ca, a division of Second Harvest, which rescues food from small businesses (as a food stylist working with small independent businesses, I think this is genius) and donates it to those who need it. They aim to make sure no food goes unused—no matter the donation size—and rescuers will even walk or bike to collect. In San Rafael, California, extrafood.org has volunteers to pick up excess food of any type (prepared, fresh, packaged, you name it) and delivers it to a nonprofit in under 30 minutes. Check out the resources guide (page 254) for more ideas.

COMPOSTING

Composting food waste is a great idea and common place now for many of us. To start composting, get a small indoor compost bucket for your kitchen where you can pitch compostable food scraps. Keeping it on the counter is the most convenient for me (since I have teenagers who need visual reminders), but if you have space, in the freezer is also a good option and reduces smell.

Then there are several different things you can then do with those scraps. First, you could use them as compost for your own backyard or outdoor space (read more about that on page 26), or many regions have compost pick-up free of charge (just like with your garbage or recyclables.) Then there are all sorts of community composting initiatives: every spring I get a community newsletter with free compost drop-off times at the local park, and there are grassroots organizations that collect compost—at farmers markets, for example. If you don't already know, check out the local services available in your area. Many cities have a program, and some even have an app. For example, in Toronto we have the TOwaste app with a Waste Wizard that tells you how to properly sort your waste. Also check the local guidelines for *what* can be composted, as this varies from one region to another. In addition to your everyday food scraps, you can usually add plants, soiled tissues and napkins, animal waste, meat scraps, coffee grounds, and tea bags too, but check the policies in your local municipality.

NON-FOOD WASTE

While this book focuses on food waste, there are other types of waste involved in buying and preparing food that I wanted to highlight, such as packaging.

AT A GLANCE: WHAT FOOD PACKAGING CAN I RECYCLE?

The best way to recycle is to avoid buying things that need to be recycled in the first place, which is why there has become a strong (and hopefully not too late) initiative to eliminate single-use plastics. What packaging we can and cannot recycle changes as technology evolves. Generally, rinsed glass containers or bottles can be recycled. Black plastic and coffee cups, however, cannot. But it isn't always black and white. Check your city's guidelines to see if and how plastic bags, frozen-food packaging, take-out containers, heavier glass jars, and plastic utensils, to name a few, can be recycled in your area. One thing I found interesting in my region, is that if I have cardboard or paperboard takeout containers that are greasy or dirty, they should go in with my food scraps rather than the recycling.

JUST PLAIN GARBAGE

The garbage is the last place your waste should go after you finish donating, recycling, and composting. Decreasing what gets thrown away can be a slow and sometimes frustrating learning process, so don't be too hard on yourself as you work toward making this pile smaller and smaller.

Zero-Waste Tips from Carson Arthur

Since I am far from being a composting expert, I decided to call up Carson Arthur—Canada's go-to home and garden expert, author, and owner of the beloved Garden + Market in Prince Edward County—to pick his brain. He helped me weed through my many queries about home composting and threw in some other ideas too.

HOME COMPOSTING

According to Carson, these are the main ways to compost at home:

DIG A TRENCH This is Carson's favorite approach, and also the easiest and most economical. Digging a hole to put your food scraps into allows direct contact with the soil and makes the composting process up to three times as fast. This works best for families with larger backyards. If you have grass and can dig a hole close to a tree, roll up a section of the sod, dig the hole, and roll the sod back overtop. The deeper the hole, the better to prevent rascal rodents and other critters from getting into your compost. Once you toss in your scraps, chop them up with the end of a shovel and mix them around. If it has been really rainy for a few days, toss a bit of soil on top. During cold and snowy winters, you can set up a covered bin closer to the house and transfer it to the trench when weather permits.

BUY A COMPOST TUMBLER These sealed containers (drums) come in many sizes to suit any family's needs. They rotate, and being able to turn over and mix the materials speeds up the process with less smell, less mess, and fewer critters—but they're definitely more expensive than digging a hole. These are the best solution for small backyards, city backyards, and apartment and condo patios. I bought one for my backyard since I have a dog and cat that both like to dig, and as Carson pointed out, I can easily toss our backyard dog poop in there (cat poop, because of toxoplasmosis, no). Just check your city's guidelines first.

START A WORM BIN (VERMICULTURE) This was Carson's least favorite, but if you have a small condo or apartment with no access to a garden or balcony, it is probably the only solution. All you need is a couple of bins, shredded paper, a little dirt, food scraps, and of course worms. The worms eat your food scraps, producing compost that settles at the bottom that you can harvest every few months. Do worms make you squirm? Don't worry, there are some pretty sweet-looking modern vermiculture bins for sale, and the worms won't escape. You can even turn it into some DIY furniture: turn your bin into an extra seat, store it under a cabinet, or make it into a small side table. Worms require more maintenance and generally last for about a year, and like that pet hamster or lizard you bought your kid, the novelty may wear off. You can't see them or hear them, so they get forgotten. More waste. If you still are queasy about them being so close, place the bin on your deck or front porch, although not when it's too hot or too cold, since, well, they may perish. No cruelty to worms needed! To open up another can of worms, there has also been increased concern that composting worms, if released into the wild, can become an invasive species if not native to the area.

How These Recipes Work

The recipes in this book are designed to be flexible and encourage you to make use of the ingredients you have on hand. Try cooking with a fridge first approach, and follow the basic first in, first out rule (page 33) to avoid good food going to waste.

For maximum flexibility with this, I have kept lots of the ingredients in the recipes deliberately vague where there are lots of options that will suffice. For example, why go out and buy Parmesan when another "hard cheese" you already have will suit just as well? And don't worry about buying that expensive organic kale, when the Swiss chard overflowing in your planter box is just as perfect a "hardy green" to try. The Taco Tuesday tacos (page 136) will be just as tasty with whatever cooked protein (tofu, chicken, pork etc.) you have on hand. And if you don't have as much broccoli as a recipe calls for, just add another type of cruciferous vegetable into the mix rather than running to the store to buy more.

There are often many substitution possibilities for a recipe—that's one of the joys of cooking with a zero-waste approach: you will constantly discover new and new-to-you ways to cook with what you have. I have tried to include specific substitutions where it makes the best sense, and have also put together the cheat-sheet substitutions table on pages 30 to 32 for you to reference as needed.

In addition, you'll see throughout, that some recipes have optional add-ins and garnish suggestions to help use up even more of the food in your fridge, freezer, or pantry. These suggestions are by no means essential to the recipe, so you can safely assume, that an "any, all, or nothing" mix and match approach to the options will work equally well with these! And finally, you'll notice an occasional flavor variation suggestion in the recipes; these are not only to help you satisfy specific cravings or cater to the fussy eaters in your family, but also to provide options to use up those fresh or dried herbs or spices you have at home.

RECIPE ICONS

At the top of each recipe page you'll find one or more of the icons below that identifies why and how that particular recipe is in-line with my zero-waste approach to food:

M MAIN MEAL These are the showstopping recipes where you cook a big protein (and deliberately some extra) and then reap the rewards of the leftovers in many ways for many days to come (see Mapped-Out Meals on page 34 for more on this).

F FRIDGE FIRST Recipes that use up the vegetables, fruit, protein, dairy etc. that you already have on-hand. Open your fridge, figure out what has to be used up first, then turn to one of these recipes for ideas and inspiration.

P PANTRY FIRST As above, in Fridge First, but this time with your pantry!

L LEFTOVERS Love your leftovers! These are the recipes perfect for using up leftovers from previous meals—be it a roast chicken, cooked quinoa, or mashed potatoes, get ready for the transformation.

S SCRAPS These recipes make use of the food scraps you would normally toss aside, with ideas for repurposing tops, stems, roots, peels, and even bones in creative and tasty ways.

GENERAL HOUSEKEEPING NOTES

Here are the ingredient basics for you to keep in mind as you cook through the recipes. Please note, unless otherwise specified:

- Broth = stock
- Butter = unsalted
- Cooked vegetables = blanched or cooked tender crisp
- Eggs = large
- Heavy cream = 35% cream
- Oil = any (see page 32)
- Olive oil = extra-virgin
- Salt = kosher or sea salt

And, in addition to the recipes, I have also included:

- ZERO-WASTE SHOPPING STRATEGIES (PAGE 6): Breaking down the buying habits ingrained in us over generations and advice on how you can make small changes.
- FOOD STORAGE 101 (PAGE 12): Myth busting on our fears about food gone bad and ways to properly store your food.
- MAPPED-OUT MEALS (PAGE 34): My favorite feature, showing how far you can stretch a meal.
- ZERO-WASTE TIPS: Aiming to help you save precious food dollars and reduce packaging (which—bonus!—helps the environment), all while eating delicious foods.
- ZERO-WASTE PROFILES: Featuring advice and recipes from chefs, restaurateurs, and other experts who are all making positive changes by reducing their food waste.
- BEYOND MEALS (PAGE 245): Tips and tricks to use up food scraps in other ways from making dog treats to face masks to cleaning your home.

Cooking with a zero-waste approach can seem like a bit of a leap at first, but once you get into the swing of it, I promise you'll find yourself a much happier and confident cook. And proudly producing a whole lot less waste!

SUBSTITUTIONS CHART

Ingredient	Use or Substitute	Use It In (for example)
PRODUCE		
Cabbage	Green, red, Savoy, Napa, Brussels sprouts	Custom Coleslaw (page 49) Brussels Fried Hash (page 55)
Chili peppers	Jalapeño, finger, habanero, Thai, Scotch bonnet (every chili packs a different amount of heat, so add to taste)	Hawaiian Chili Water (page 195) Chili Yogurt Cornbread (page 69)
Citrus	Orange, grapefruit, lemon, lime, mandarin, clementine, blood orange, cara cara orange	Pucker Pie (page 229) Moroccan Preserved Lemons (page 204)
Cucumber	Zucchini	Bong Bong Chicken (page 128) Chunky Squash Raita (page 68)
Greens (bitter)	Radicchio, endive, chicory, dandelion, arugula, frisée	Stem Au Gratin (page 45) Charred Asparagus Niçoise (page 50)
Greens (hardy)	Kale, Swiss chard, turnip greens, cabbage, callaloo, collards, cabbage, Brussels sprouts, sometimes spinach	Glorious Golden Green Soup (page 80) Callaloo (page 153)
Greens (leafy)	Lettuce, watercress, arugula, spinach, baby kale, beet greens, microgreens, celery leaves	Curried Feta and Hardy Greens Galette (page 174) Curried Chicken and Grape Salad (page 131)
Herbs (fresh)	Any hardy or soft herb; 1 tablespoon chopped fresh herbs = 1 teaspoon dried or ½ teaspoon ground	Zero-Waste Herbs (page 58) Vegetable Stock (page 187)
Herbs (hardy)	Oregano, rosemary, sage, thyme, savory, sometimes basil (any kind)	All-Purpose Brine Spice Mix (page 192) Meat Stock (page 188),
Herbs (soft)	Chives, basil (any kind), dill, parsley (+ stems), cilantro, tarragon, chervil, mint, green onions, fennel fronds (as a garnish)	Put it in a Pesto (page 74)
Onion	Shallot	Stone Soup (page 79) Poultry Stock (page 188)
Peppers	Bell, field, cubanelle, or poblano peppers (if you like a little spicy)	Packed Peppers (page 70) Roasted Vegetable Frittata (page 41)
Potatoes	Cassava, taro, jicama, sweet potato, unripe green or yellow plantain	Nan's Fish Cakes (page 117) Sour Cream and Chive Potato Biscuits (page 59)
Pumpkin	Any variety; squash, parsnip, sweet potato, celery root, potato, winter squash	Grand Gnocchi (page 65) Dog Treats (page 251)
Spinach	Beet greens, chard, sorrel, turnip greens, baby kale	The Great Risotto (page 160) Glorious Green Soup (page 80)

Ingredient	Use or Substitute	Use It In (for example)
Squash	Acorn, Hubbard, buttercup, red kuri, kabocha, pumpkin	Stuffed Pumpkin with Shrimp (page 61) Chunky Squash Raita (page 68)
Tomato purée	Tomato passata	Marvelous Minestrone (page 81) Smashed Strawberry and Maple Barbecue Sauce (page 197)
Tomato sauce	Marinara (page 77), tomato purée or an equal mix of tomato paste and water	Ragù (page 78) Crispy Fried Pasta (page 159)
Tomatoes	Any variety; 1 pound fresh tomatoes = 1½ cups canned, 3 tablespoons tomato paste, or 6 to 8 sun-dried (reconstituted in water)	Marinara (page 77) Bouillabaisse (page 112)
Vegetables (cruciferous)	Broccoli, cauliflower, Brussels sprouts, romanesco, cabbage, rapini, kale, broccolini	Custom Coleslaw (page 49) Creamy Cauliflower Mac and Cheese (page 66)
Vegetables (mixed)	Any variety e.g., asparagus, celery, broccoli, carrots, cauliflower, rapini, green beans, Brussels sprouts	Chow Chow (page 199) Freestyle Paella (page 164)
Vegetables (root)	Potatoes, sweet potatoes, carrots, turnips, Jerusalem artichokes, yellow or green plantains	Rustic Coconut Fish Stew (page 110) Sunday's Rosti Pot Pie (page 173)
Vegetable Scraps	Any variety e.g., carrot ends, beet greens, kale stems, onion skins, celery stumps, leek greens, limp herbs, ginger knobs	Stone Soup (page 79)
DAIRY		
Cheese (hard)	Parmesan, Manchego, Asiago, pecorino Romano	Parm Broth (page 191) Meatballs 101 (page 144)
Cheese (semi-soft)	Mozzarella, cheddar, Swiss, Gruyère, Gouda, Monterey Jack	Ham and Cheese Hand Pies (page 174) Creamy Cauliflower Mac and Cheese (page 66)
Cheese (Parmesan)	Nutritional yeast (vegan)	Meatballs 101 (page 144) Put it in a Pesto (page 74)
Cream	Heavy, double, half and half, light, or a combination of cream with whole milk; unsweetened vegan cream; coconut cream; cashew cream (some swaps affect the fat content and therefore creaminess of final product)	Endless Ice Cream (page 211) Maritime Seafood Chowder (page 114)
Milk	Whole milk, nut milk, seed milk, oat milk, coconut milk, soy milk, rice milk	Curried Feta and Hardy Greens Galette (page 174) Pumpkin Pie Lost Bread Pudding (page 236)
Yogurt	Kefir, sour cream, quark, buttermilk, silken tofu, sometimes mayo	Chili Yogurt Cornbread (page 69) This Bread is Bananas (page 217)

Ingredient	Use or Substitute	Use It In (for example)
PROTEINS		
Beans	Dried, cooked, or canned	A Pot of Chili (page 141) Greek Chickpea Salad (page 47)
Lentils	Dried, cooked or canned (all colors), pigeon peas, split peas, split black-eyed peas	Armenian Lentil Stew (page 98) Apple Curry Dal (page 95)
Poultry	Chicken, capon, Cornish hen, duck, goose, guinea fowl, pheasant, turkey	Curried Chicken and Grape Salad (page 131) Quinoa Meatballs (page 146)
Protein	All meats e.g., beef, bison, deer, game meat, game bird, ham, moose, poultry (see above); tofu, vegan protein	Savory Pies: 3 Ways (page 173) Taco Tuesdays (page 136)
Ground meat	All varieties e.g., turkey, beef; crumbled extra-firm tofu or other veggie meat replacement	A Pot of Chili (page 141) Meatballs 101 (page 144)
PANTRY		
Breadcrumbs	Crispy Coatings (page 183), gluten-free breadcrumbs, Panko	Croquettes (page 56)
Broth	Stock or combination of stock or broth of choice	Very Celery with(out) Chorizo Soup (page 82)
Chili oil	Any oil with a pinch of cayenne or a few dashes of hot pepper sauce	Bong Bong Chicken (page 128)
Chili paste	Harissa, sambal oelek, Szechuan chili paste, red pepper flakes, whole chili + chopped garlic, hot sauce	Noodles with Spicy Peanut Sauce (page 170)
Flour	All-purpose, organic, gluten-free, or whole-grain flour mix	Pancakes: 3 Ways (page 240) CBZ Cake (page 215)
Grains	Pasta of choice, rice, quinoa, riced cauliflower, barley, farro, sorghum, couscous	Quinoa Meatballs (page 146) The Great Risotto (page 160)
Oil	Olive, extra-virgin olive oil, coconut, canola, vegetable, avocado	
Oil (finishing)	Nut oils, high-quality extra-virgin olive oil, pumpkin seed oil, sesame oil	Marvelous Minestrone (page 81)
Oil (high smoke Point)	Vegetable oil, grapeseed, avocado, peanut oil, canola	
Pasta	All varieties e.g., penne, spaghetti; zucchini noodles, spaghetti squash, Asian wheat and egg noodles	Crispy Fried Pasta (page 159) Neptune's Pasta (page 119)
Sugar	Brown sugar, cane sugar, honey, maple syrup, agave syrup, date syrup, or coconut sugar (may change flavor profile). Do not use alternative sweeteners like stevia or erythritol at 1:1 ratio in recipes. One cup sugar = ¼ teaspoon liquid stevia.	
Vanilla extract	Scraped seeds of vanilla bean	100% Pure Vanilla Extract (page 212) My Weekly Iced Steep (page 246)
Vinegar	White wine vinegar, red wine vinegar, leftover white wine, any combinations of vinegars, lemon, or lime juice	Chow Chow (page 199) Hawaiian Chili Water (page 195)

My Top Zero–Waste Tips to Get You Started

There are many tips scattered throughout this book to help you reduce your food waste on the daily. To get your creative juices flowing, let's kick-start you off with these:

FIRST IN, FIRST OUT A simple food rotation system where you eat up what was bought earliest and has the shortest shelf life remaining. In other words, most perishable foods gets eaten first. This is one of the first rules you learn in chef school.

REVIVE BENDY VEGETABLES Firm up limp veggies like celery or broccoli in a five-minute cold water bath or cook them up ASAP.

RETHINK OVERCOOKED VEGETABLES Don't despair if you overcooked the carrots again, overly soft vegetables make for an easy and tasty mash or purée.

GET SOUP- AND SAUCE-ING Leftover vegetables make great soups and sauces. Just blend them with a cup of liquid, like coconut milk, along with some stock and a little seasoning.

PEELING IS OVERRATED Edible thin peels like on potatoes really just need a good scrub. And you can add more fiber and nutrients to your diet by leaving these on.

THINK BIG PICTURE Use the overlooked tops, stems, peels, skins, and rinds of fruits and vegetables as they have many uses! See page 42.

RE-CRISP STALE CHIPS AND CRACKERS Just pop them in your oven at 350°F for a few minutes until toasty.

SAVE THE BONES Gather up leftover bones and store them in a container in the freezer until you have enough to make a big batch of stock. The bones are already roasted, which means more flavor, and you can quickly rinse any heavily seasoned (hot and spicy) bones first. If eating others' scraps sounds icky, remember that the bones end up being boiled for hours. Why toss such a valuable source of essential amino acids, minerals, and collagen?

UTILIZE FAT Store leftover bacon fat or pan drippings in a sealed container in your fridge for use throughout the week. Bacon fat or schmaltz (rendered chicken fat) can be used instead of oil or butter.

PLAN YOUR PORTIONS Knowing how much to buy and cook can be daunting, but it goes a long way to reduce waste. There are many free online portion planning tools and other helpful resources, such as from Love Food Hate Waste Canada (www. lovefoodhatewaste.ca)

Mapped-Out Meals

If you haven't guessed already, I'm a planner who lives for lists, charts, and diagrams—anything that makes my life easier. And that planning comes in handy when approaching food from the zero-waste perspective. Here are a few ways to help you get more mileage out of your meals.

MEAL PLAN Meal planning is a classic approach to making food go as far as it can. Not only does it help balance my family's hectic schedule, it's great for the family budget. Your planning doesn't have to be a cookie-cutter plan printed out weekly, though it does help. As you plan your meals, look at the ingredients in one recipe and try to find commonalities with others, so the produce you buy, for example, gets two kicks at the can.

LOOK FOR LEFTOVERS Think about your main meals, and then brainstorm the possibilities for the leftovers from those meals. Cooking this way can save you waste, money and—sometimes most importantly!—time. Try stretching Sunday's roast beef dinner to Wednesday's beef stir-fry; or turning leftover roast chicken into a chicken salad that looks as good as new for the kids. As you approach each meal, ask yourself, "How can I prep this food so that it can be easily repurposed?" A little planning can go a long way. Even simple things like having everyone toss their own portioned-in salad dressing so that salad leftovers aren't soggy helps transform them into a new salad (page 46) the next day.

MEAL PREP If you aren't a fan of cooking after a long work day, and are tempted to order in even with a packed fridge, try picking two or three meals you've planned for the week to prep all in one go on the weekend. That way you will be less inclined to let the food you have (and the food you order in) go to waste.

Opposite are some handy meal road maps to help you start navigating your week. Sometimes the main dish can be repurposed, sometimes the side can be transformed; sometimes even the leftovers of the leftovers can be whipped up into something new!

NOTE: If you have enough leftovers, you can make a new recipe in full, or you can scale it down to match the amount you have left to use up. Do what's best for your pantry and fridge. On your mark, get set, go!

Marinated Tofu Steaks (page 91):

- A Pot of Chili (page 141)
- Wrap It Up Fresh Spring Rolls (page 171)
- Packed Peppers (page 70)

Whole Fish (page 109):

- Taco Tuesdays (page 136)
- Maritime Seafood Chowder (page 114)
- Nan's Fish Cakes (page 117)
- Fish Stock (page 189)

Two Roast Chickens (page 127):

- Bong Bong Chicken (page 128)
- Freestyle Paella (page 164)
- Curried Chicken and Grape Salad (page 131)
- Noodles with Spicy Peanut Sauce (page 170)
- Poultry Stock (page 188)

Perfect Roast Ham (page 139):

- Brussels Fried Hash (page 55)
- Croquettes (page 56)
- Easy Peasy Soup (page 96)
- Crispy Fried Pasta (page 172)
- Ham and Cheese Hand Pies (page 174)

Mexican Spiced Pork Tenderloins (page 140):

- Packed Peppers (page 70)
- Fancy Fried Rice (page 165)
- Pipian Verde (page 63)

Pot Roast (page 149):

- Savory Pies (page 173)
- A Pot of Chili (page 141)
- Meat Stock (page 188)
- Beefy Black Lentil Stew (page 150)
- Packed Peppers (page 70)

PART II:

Zero-Waste Recipes

Produce

Vegetables are the number one most wasted food out there. Falling close in second place are fruits. What should be our closest companions are the ones getting left behind, going limp in the back of our fridges after starring in just one dish. Well, no more! The recipes in this chapter take everyday produce staples—whether raw or cooked leftovers—and turn them into something extraordinary. You'll also find easy and delightful ways to use an ingredient up from root to tip. The parts—whether it's the stems, leaves, or even peels—we often toss away can actually taste amazing.

Simple Roasted Vegetables ▣F

This recipe is the perfect way to use up those vegetables—like broccoli, Brussels sprouts, zucchini, or bell peppers—that are languishing in your fridge. Roasted vegetables make for a perfect side dish or as the star of the meal served with the grain of your choice; scale up or down depending on what you have on hand and/or how many people you need to feed. Make some extra veggies and use them in a delicious Roast Vegetable Frittata (opposite) later in the week. And keep any leftover stems for Stem Au Gratin (page 45) or pop them in the freezer to use in future vegetable soups and stocks.

Chopped vegetables (1 cup per person; see note)

Oil to coat

Salt and pepper

Optional Seasonings

Balsamic or red wine vinegar

Condiments (hot sauce, Hawaiian Chili Water (page 195), harissa paste, or mustard)

Hard cheese, grated, or nutritional yeast

Honey or maple syrup

Fresh or dry herbs, e.g., thyme, rosemary, or oregano

Garlic cloves

Spices (paprika, chili powders, curry powder, cumin, mustard seed etc.)

1. Preheat the oven to 425°F. Line or grease a baking sheet.

2. Toss the vegetables in just enough oil and, if using, any of the other liquid optional seasonings to lightly coat. Then season with salt and pepper and add any other optional seasonings to taste. Transfer to the baking sheet and space out the vegetables so there is no overcrowding.

3. Roast until the vegetables are tender and golden, about 20 minutes.

USES UP vegetables

SERVES 1

TOTAL TIME about 20 minutes

KEEPS FOR up to 4 days in the fridge

Zero–Waste Tip   Buy the ugly produce. Almost a third of produce wasted is because we think it is too unattractive to buy despite it being just as healthy and delicious on the inside.

Food 911 We don't typically think about making a tray of *mixed* roast vegetables because different vegetables roast at different temperatures and different times. But, you can roast almost any vegetable or root vegetable together, whether it's potato, sweet potato, broccoli, carrots, radishes, bell pepper, or beet. How do you do it? Chop them properly. First, prepare the most tender items (say tomato or zucchini chunks) you plan on roasting as these will roast the fastest. From the size of these, you can then judge the size to chop the hardest vegetables (potatoes, carrots etc.). You want these chopped smaller than the tender vegetables as they will roast faster the smaller they are cut. Then, cut any medium-firm vegetables (broccoli, eggplant etc.) so everything can roast evenly. Just be sure to keep an eye on the vegetables and pull them out when they are tender and golden.

Roasted Vegetable Frittata `F` `L`

If you've got eggs, you've got a meal. A frittata is a genius way of taking eggs and combining them with bits and pieces of other foods that got lost throughout the week. Here I take leftover roasted veggies and bake them up in a frittata—a fine travel companion that you can eat morning, noon, and night. If you don't have a couple of cups of roasted vegetables hanging around, try roasting some up (see left), or using stemmed, blanched or sautéed vegetables instead. I toss some cooked protein into my frittatas—whatever I have to hand—but that's completely optional.

2–3 Tbsp oil or melted butter

3–4 cups sliced and chopped
mixed roasted vegetables
(see substitutions)

½ cup chopped cooked protein
(optional)

6 eggs

1 cup milk or cream

1 Tbsp Dijon mustard

2 Tbsp chopped fresh soft herbs

Salt and pepper

½ cup grated cheese

1. Preheat oven to 350°F.

2. Preheat a large ovenproof cast-iron pan or skillet over medium heat. Add the oil to coat the bottom and sides, a heatproof pastry brush is good for this. Arrange the roasted veggies and cooked protein evenly in the bottom of the pan and cook for 3 to 5 minutes to heat through.

3. In a large bowl, whisk the eggs with the milk, mustard, herbs, salt, and pepper. Pour over the veggies. Reduce the heat to medium-low and cook until the edges just start to set, about 5 minutes. Sprinkle the grated cheese overtop.

4. Transfer to the oven to finish cooking for about 10 minutes or until the center is just set. Cool for 10 minutes before serving.

USES UP vegetables, eggs

SERVES 6

TOTAL TIME
30–35 minutes

KEEPS FOR up to 3 days in the fridge

CAN SUBSTITUTE
Roasted veggies with steamed or blanched vegetables like green beans or asparagus, spinach, kale, or other hardy greens (squeezed and drained well of water)

Root to Tip

There are so many parts of fruit and vegetables that get tossed away, but they can actually do wonders for a dish. Here are the most commonly tossed away parts that have more value and flavor than you think.

TOPS Celery, radish, beet greens, turnip, carrot, and fennel fronds are just some of the tops screaming to be eaten. Besides saving tops for a soup or stew (see page 82), think of tossing chopped tops into a salad, blending them into your next pesto (page 74) or chimichurri sauce, or folding them into a holiday stuffing.

STEMS AND STALKS Mushroom, fennel, and woody herb stems can easily be used as an aromatic flavoring in earthy broths and stocks (page 187). Stems from tender herbs like parsley or cilantro are wonderful finely chopped and stirred into your next salsa, dip, sauce, or dressing. Beefy broccoli, cauliflower, chard, and kale have stems that can eat like a meal. Save them for a quick garlicky sauté or stir-fry or Stem Au Gratin (page 45). Or use kale and chard stems for a morning smoothie.

PEELS Peels can not only lock in nutrients as you cook produce but can also add nutritional value (like fiber) to your meals. You can set aside peels, like carrot peels, to help flavor a stock (page 187). Then there are the peels that you may never have thought of using, like banana peels (page 217), just boil them first. Try my Crispy Veggie Skins (see right) with peels from beets, carrots, parsnips or potatoes.

COBS AND SILKS These can be simmered in a simple broth to make it subtly sweet and milky. So it makes sense to throw them into say a Fish Stock (page 189) that's then used in a Maritime Seafood Chowder (page 114). Just discard them before serving.

SKINS The woody inedible dark-green parts of leeks and unused green tops (which have most of the nutrients) of scallions are a wonderful addition to stocks and broths (page 187). Onion skins can add flavor and a lovely caramel color to stocks and broths. Some other skins that deserve to be left *on* and eaten are kiwi skins, and the cooked skins of squashes and pumpkins.

RINDS There are many rinds, besides pork, that can be used in cooking. Cheese rinds (natural ones) can be added to a stock or broth for flavor (page 191). Citrus rinds can be grated and steeped to add extra flavor to a recipe (page 243). Store in the freezer until you're ready to use.

Crispy Veggie Skins `s`

Baked or fried, crispy potato skins are a great treat. So, why not transform other types of vegetable skins or peels? That's right, we're taking potato skins on a ride with some other veggie friends. Use these veggie crisps as a snack, garnish, or salad topping.

1 cup peels from washed vegetables
   (e.g., carrots, beets, potatoes,
   parsnips)
High smoke point oil (see note)
Salt and pepper

Optional Seasonings
Balsamic or red wine vinegar
Condiments such as hot sauce,
   Hawaiian Chili Water (page 195),
   harissa paste, or mustard
Fresh or dry herbs
Garlic cloves

Hard cheese (e.g., Parmesan), grated,
   or nutritional yeast
Honey or maple syrup
Spices (e.g., paprika, chili powders,
   curry powder, cumin, mustard
   seed etc.)

1. Using a salad spinner, dry the vegetable peels. You want them dried well.

To Fry:

1. In a large Dutch oven or high-sided heavy-bottomed pot, heat 2 inches of oil to 350°F to 375°F. Measure the temperature with a thermometer or test the oil by submerging the back of a wooden spoon into the oil. If the oil bubbles around the wood, it is ready. In the meantime, line a plate with paper towel.

2. Fry the peels, in batches if necessary to avoid overcrowding, until crispy, 2 to 3 minutes. Place on the paper towel–lined plate and while still warm, season with salt and pepper and any optional seasoning. Serve warm.

Or, To Roast:

1. Preheat the oven to 400°F. Line a baking sheet.

2. Drizzle the peels with a little oil. Season with salt and pepper and any optional seasonings.

3. Transfer to the prepared sheet and roast until crispy, about 15 minutes. Serve warm.

Food 911 Since they brown easily, potato peels should be used ASAP. Other peels can be stored in the fridge for up to 5 days. Avocado oil is great for frying and searing, with its neutral taste and high smoke point of 520°F, compared to grapeseed at 420°F and olive oil at around 400°F.

USES UP vegetable skins and peels

TOTAL TIME 15 minutes

MAKES 1 cup

KEEPS FOR the moment, these are best eaten ASAP

Stem Au Gratin S F

This old-school technique for baking potatoes can be used for any root vegetable stems, hardy greens, and/or their stalks, or even chopped vegetables. Last time I made it, I ran out of cream and used a combination of whole milk and coconut milk. It was still fantastic. A crispy, creamy, herby vegetable side dish, and just perfectly zero-waste.

Stems of 1 large head of broccoli, trimmed and sliced into ½-inch spears (see substitutions)

1 bunch Swiss chard, stems removed and reserved, leaves roughly chopped (see substitutions)

2 Tbsp oil or butter (+ extra for greasing)

1 onion or 2–3 shallots, diced

3 cloves garlic, finely chopped

2 cups cream (see substitutions)

1 bay leaf

½ tsp ground or freshly grated nutmeg

1 Tbsp fresh or 1 tsp dried thyme leaves

Salt and pepper

1 cup (3 oz) grated semi-soft cheese

¼ cup Breadcrumbs (page 182)

¼ cup grated hard cheese

1. Preheat the oven to 350°F and grease a baking or casserole dish with oil.

2. Bring a large pot of salted water to a boil. Add the broccoli and Swiss chard stems and simmer until tender-crisp, about 3 minutes. Drain well. Layer the stems with the Swiss chard leaves in the prepared dish.

3. In a heavy-bottomed saucepot over medium heat, heat the oil. Sauté the onions and garlic until softened, about 3 minutes. Add the cream, bay leaf, nutmeg, and thyme, and season with the salt and pepper. Simmer for a few minutes.

4. Lower the heat and stir in the semi-soft cheese until melted. Pour the cheesy sauce over the vegetables, tilting the dish to make sure it gets into all the nooks and crannies.

5. Combine the breadcrumbs with the hard cheese and sprinkle on top to make a gratin. Bake for 15 minutes or until bubbling and golden brown on top.

Food 911 Edible vegetable stalks and stems can be just as nutritious as their tops, especially with broccoli. Broccoli stems take a little longer to cook than the florets, but they taste just as good and can be eaten raw as well as cooked.

USES UP vegetable stems

SERVES 6 as a side

TOTAL TIME 35 minutes

KEEPS FOR up to 3–4 days in the fridge

CAN SUBSTITUTE
- Swiss chard and broccoli with hardy or bitter greens (and stems), grilled, steamed, or blanched mixed vegetables, or very thinly sliced root vegetables such as potatoes (will need to cook longer, since potatoes need to cook through)
- Cream with alternative plant milk (page 105), taking into account that the thinner the milk, the thinner the sauce

Salad for Days

A salad is the perfect vehicle for using up a wide array of ingredients you have on hand, and can be served as a side dish or a main, or even as an edible bed to round out other food items. During my culinary training, I learned there are five categories of salads, which I have described below. This is followed by a list of all the ways to make a salad. Mix and match depending on what you have on hand.

THE GREEN: Fresh, clean, and crisp simple salad greens tossed with a light dressing; typically served as a side or as a base for other foods.

THE FARINACEOUS: Chopped raw or blanched vegetables tossed or topped with a cooked starch. Protein or cheese is a welcome addition, as seen in the Quinoa Surprise (page 169).

THE BOUND: Cooked starches, proteins, and vegetables bound together with a thick emulsified or a mayonnaise-based dressing, like my Curried Chicken and Grape Salad (page 131). Perfect for a sandwich filling, or a topping on other salads, like the Green.

THE COMPOSED: A combination of cooked or raw ingredients layered on a plate or platter rather than tossed. Great for using up leftover cooked proteins or grilled, cooked vegetables, like in my Charred Asparagus Niçoise (page 50).

THE FRUIT: An all fruit salad or a salad that uses fresh or dried fruit as an accompanying ingredient. Can also enjoy as a quick dessert or with yogurt and granola for breakfast. Any excuse to eat more fruit!

FIRST STOP: BUILD YOUR BASE
Custom Coleslaw (page 49); cooked grains, pasta, beans and/or legumes; greens: lettuce or bitter; raw vegetables, chopped; sprouts

SECOND STOP: EAT YOUR VEGETABLES
Assorted vegetables: raw, blanched, steamed, and/or grilled, or frozen and thawed (peas, corn etc.), chopped; greens: lettuce or bitter; raw sprouts or microgreens

THIRD STOP: ADD THE PROTEIN BOOST
Canned fish or seafood (tuna etc.); cooked legumes; cooked protein (any meat, seafood, tofu etc.); cured deli meats, e.g. ham; Nan's Fish Cakes (page 117); falafels; hard-boiled eggs; meatballs (page 144 or page 146); smoked/cured seafood

THE DETOUR: FRUITY TWIST
Apples and/or pears, sliced; berries; citrus wedges; dried fruit and/or berries; grapes; papaya, mango, pineapple, and/or peach slices

THE SCENIC ROUTE: ADD MORE FLAVOR!
Anchovies; avocado or guacamole; capers or caper berries; cheese, grated, chopped, or crumbled; crispy fried onions or legumes; Croutons (page 183) or I'm Feeling Crackers (page 181); dried coconut; fresh herbs, chopped; green onions, sliced; hummus or other dips (pages 100 and 101); kimchi; marinated or pickled vegetables; nori; nuts (candied or not), chopped, and/or seeds; olives; sundried tomatoes; salsas; sprouts; Vegan Crackling (page 84)

FINAL DESTINATION: DRESS IT UP
Bong Bong Dressing (page 128); combination of oil, vinegar, and herbs; French Vinaigrette (page 50); Greek-Style Dressing (page 47); Lemon Dill Buttermilk Dressing (page 166); Not-So-Creamy Coleslaw Dressing (page 49); Simple Vinaigrette (page 53); Sumac-Lime Vinaigrette (page 168); Turmeric Aioli (page 72); Vietnamese-Style Dressing (page 137)

Greek Chickpea Salad F P

Recipe pictured on page 148

Everyone needs a go-to recipe for a crunchy chopped salad, it's the perfect way to use up cruciferous vegetables. Your typical Greek salad with its iceberg lettuce won't yield great leftovers, but this one with chickpeas keeps you chomping for days. Chopped salads made of crunchy veggies like this one won't get all wilted, so they hold up exceptionally well. I never use up a whole package of feta in one recipe, so this salad has become my go-to for using up leftover feta. Paired with a simple Greek-style dressing, you will want to make this again and again—and the dressing is just as good tossed with any bean or grain bowl.

Salad

One 14 oz can chickpeas, drained
    and rinsed
1 cup chopped (small florets) broccoli
1 cup chopped (small florets) cauli-
    flower
1 large carrot, peeled and chopped
2 stalks celery + tops, chopped
1 bell pepper, cubed
1 bunch (4–5) radishes, diced
½ cup diced fennel bulb
4½ oz diced feta (see substitutions)
1 Tbsp chopped fennel fronds

Optional Add-Ins

2 Tbsp chopped Moroccan Preserved
    Lemons (page 204), to taste
Canned or marinated artichoke hearts,
    chopped
Olives, sliced or whole
Sun-dried tomatoes, chopped

Greek-Style Dressing

½ clove garlic, finely chopped
1 tsp dried oregano; Greek or moun-
    tain oregano is best
¼ cup fresh lemon juice
Pinch salt
½ cup olive oil
Pepper

USES UP vegetables,
chickpeas, feta

SERVES 4–6

TOTAL TIME 20 minutes

KEEPS FOR up to 3 days
in the fridge

CAN SUBSTITUTE Feta
for Halloumi

1. For the Salad: In a large bowl, combine all of the salad ingredients and optional add-ins.

2. For the Greek-style Dressing: Add all of the dressing ingredients into a jar with a lid. Shake well. Pour over the salad and toss.

Custom Coleslaw F S

Any vegetable (or their stems), such as broccoli, kohlrabi, fennel, daikon, colorful beets, or even tart apples can be chopped into ribbons to make a coleslaw. So get crazy with it, because coleslaw never gets boring. For example, radishes can add a peppery heat while carrots can add a sweetness; Brussels sprouts add texture and up the ante on nutrients while raw beets add an earthy crunch. A coleslaw is probably one of the only salads that actually gets better after it's all dressed up and hanging around for a bit. It is also the perfect base for last night's leftover protein, like in the Spicy Vietnamese Cabbage and Duck Coleslaw (page 137).

Not-so-Creamy Coleslaw Dressing

¼ cup oil

2 Tbsp vinegar

2 tsp mustard or Dijon mustard

1–2 tsp sugar

½ clove garlic, finely chopped

¼ tsp celery seeds or dill seeds, or a handful of chopped celery tops/ leaves

Salt and pepper

¼ cup chopped chives or green onions (optional)

1–2 Tbsp chopped fresh soft herbs (optional)

Custom Coleslaw

8 cups shredded vegetables and/or their stems

USES UP vegetables (and stems), hardy greens, cabbage, apples

SERVES 6

TOTAL TIME 15 minutes

KEEPS FOR up to 3 days in the fridge

1. For the Not-so-Creamy Coleslaw Dressing: In a small bowl, whisk all of the dressing ingredients. Taste and adjust seasoning.

2. For the Custom Coleslaw: In a large bowl, add the shredded vegetables.

3. Pour the dressing over top and toss well.

4. Taste and adjust the seasoning with salt and pepper.

Charred Asparagus Niçoise with a French Vinaigrette `F` `P` `L`

You can't beat a good Niçoise salad, a French favorite that brings out the best of simple Mediterranean ingredients. It's my go-to when dining out if I just can't decide what I want. Besides the tuna, you get an additional protein boost from the hard-boiled eggs, a gratifying vegetable fix, and just enough potatoes, and it's all tossed with salty and sour Niçoise olives and capers . . . It satisfies all my food cravings. This is a great salad for using up canned or fresh tuna and pre-cooked potatoes (save some from Sunday's supper!), and then feel free to adapt to what you have on hand, like subbing the asparagus for green beans (page 75) for a more classic take.

French Vinaigrette

½ clove garlic, finely chopped

2 tsp Dijon mustard

1½ Tbsp apple cider, or red or white wine vinegar

1 Tbsp chopped fresh or 1 tsp soft dried herbs

3 Tbsp extra-virgin olive oil

Salt and pepper

Niçoise Salad

½ bunch asparagus, trimmed (see substitutions)

1 Tbsp oil

Salt and pepper

4 oz tomatoes, halved or quartered

Few handfuls torn leafy greens

4 oz cooked or roasted potatoes, cut to your liking (new or baby potatoes are great for this)

One 6 oz can of tuna, drained and flaked (see substitutions)

2 peeled hard-boiled eggs, halved or quartered

1½ oz (about 12) olives (Niçoise are my favorite)

2 Tbsp drained capers, for garnish

Optional Garnishes

4 anchovies, whole or finely chopped

2 chopped green onions or ¼ cup finely sliced red onions, to taste

1. For the French Vinaigrette: Place all of the ingredients in a sealed jar and shake or place in a small bowl and whisk until emulsified. Taste, and adjust the seasoning if desired.

2. For the Niçoise Salad: Preheat a grill or skillet over high heat. Meanwhile, toss the asparagus with a little oil and season with salt and pepper. Char the asparagus in the skillet until tender-crisp, turning occasionally. You can also slightly char your tomatoes, if desired.

3. To arrange the salad, start by placing the lettuce on plates, divvying up the veggies and proteins, and assembling to your liking. Drizzle with vinaigrette. Garnish with the anchovies or green or red onions.

Zero–Waste Tip Looking for sustainable tuna? Check out Seafood Watch at www.seafoodwatch.org. Also, don't forget to rinse those cans before recycling.

USES UP lettuce, vegetables, potatoes, tuna, eggs

SERVES 2, makes about ¼ cup of dressing

TOTAL TIME 25 minutes

KEEPS FOR tossed and dressed salad is best eaten ASAP; but salad and dressing can be stored separately for up to 3 days

CAN SUBSTITUTE
- Tuna with 6–8 oz seared or charred fresh tuna, grilled mackerel, or other cooked fish
- Asparagus with 2 fistfuls of trimmed green beans or pole runner beans

Zero-Waste Tips from Allison Day

Meet Allison Day. Allison is a food writer, blogger at Yummy Beet, and author of Modern Lunch *and* Whole Bowls. *She cooks a lot at home and has developed some tried and true ways to curb food waste.*

Q. Since you work in the food industry, does this change how you shop and/or cook at home?

A. With my home cooking, I always try to shop my refrigerator, freezer, and pantry before heading out to buy more food. Even when it looks like "there's nothing to eat," a magical meal is made with this and that. I always shop with a rough meal plan for the week and a list. If I go into the week with a loose idea of a make-ahead lunch that will last Monday to Friday (usually a big-batch of soup, stew, grain salad, or a bunch of grain bowl components) and weeknight dinners, I shop smarter and use up what I purchase.

Q. What is the toughest part about wasting food?

A. Throwing away vegetables, herbs, and fruits that are past their prime but still completely edible is my food waste pet peeve. Freeze a container with chopped carrots, celery, and onions (ends, skins, and all!) for making stock (page 187) in the future. Turn herbs into a green goddess salad dressing for the week, or make and freeze a batch of pesto (page 74). And my favorite way to "save" older fruits is to turn them into a crumble.

Q. Do you have any food shopping/prep/storage tips that people may not know about?

A.

- I recommend a good salad spinner to thoroughly wash and then dry dark greens and herbs. If you put them in a container after washing and drying well, they should last all week.
- If I'm making a big batch of beans, I freeze them in 2-cup portions in the freezer for use in soups, stews, hummus, salad, chili, and more.
- Embrace the quick pickle (page 193). Quick-pickled red onions, for example, keep in the refrigerator for ages and can be used to dress up tacos, bowls, chili, sandwiches, roast meats, salsa, and more. I also use the onion-infused pickling liquid in salad dressings for a mellow allium kick.
- Kitchen sink salads (see below!) are one of my go-tos for using up what I have. I roast different vegetables and combine them with fresh ones, toss them with a sturdy green like kale along with a cooked grain, like quinoa, and dress them in something zippy, like a lemon vinaigrette.
- Crowdsource. Check out online food communities (pressure cooker groups, meal planning groups, baking groups, etc.) if you have a mountain of a specific ingredient you aren't sure what to do with. Ask and you shall receive a deluge of enthusiastic suggestions to use it up, a lot of the time including links to a tried-and-true recipe. I've done this, and it's really helpful.

Q. What is your biggest everyday hurdle in reducing your food waste?

A. Boredom. I am happy to eat the same thing every day for lunch with a few little tweaks to make it feel fresh and new, but I prefer a different dinner every night, meaning leftovers have to be transformed into something almost "brand new" for me to be happy (except lasagna—I will eat that every day). So although it can be a hurdle, it does push me to become more creative with my meals.

Q. What do you think our biggest challenge is going to be in reducing food waste globally?

A. We are told to eat more produce, fish, grains, beans, etc., but aren't shown how to actually enjoy them. Teaching people how to cook simple recipes with everyday ingredients will reduce food waste, because if you don't know what to make with something, you'll eventually throw it out. When you learn to cook, you gain the confidence in the kitchen to transform raw ingredients into a meal.

Beet, Fennel, and Radicchio Salad with Feta and Pine Nuts F

Pleasingly bitter radicchio, refreshing fennel, sweet beets, creamy feta, and pine nuts are tied together with a simple, vibrant vinaigrette for a texturally exciting, ultra-colorful salad. This recipe uses less common, more head-scratch-inducing vegetables that often pose a kitchen challenge. Together, the ingredients sing.

Salad

1½ lb whole beets

1 small or ½ large head radicchio, roughly torn (see substitutions)

1 small bulb or ½ large bulb fennel, cored and thinly sliced or shaved into strips

⅓ cup pine nuts or chopped walnuts, toasted

½ cup crumbled feta cheese

Pea shoots and/or fennel fronds, to serve

Vinaigrette

⅓ cup olive oil

¼ cup avocado oil or grapeseed oil

¼ cup apple cider vinegar

1 tsp grainy Dijon mustard

½ tsp maple syrup

½ tsp fine-grain sea salt

Pepper, to taste

⅛ tsp dried onion powder or ½ tsp dried onion flakes

USES UP vegetables, nuts

SERVES 4 as a main, 6 as a side

TOTAL TIME 1 hour, 40 minutes

KEEPS FOR the day of (for tossed salad), but salad and dressing can be stored separately for up to 3 days

CAN SUBSTITUTE
- Radicchio with bitter greens

1. For the Salad: Preheat the oven to 375°F. Place whole beets and a splash of water in a large Dutch oven or oven-safe pot with a tight-fitting lid. Cover and roast until beets are tender, about 40 minutes for small and 1 hour and 30 minutes for very large beets. When cool enough to handle, peel and slice into wedges, rounds, or a mixture of both. Add to a large bowl.

2. For the Vinaigrette: Make the dressing by shaking all dressing ingredients together in a glass jar. Add about 2 tablespoons of the dressing to the beets and toss to coat.

3. To assemble the salad, on a platter or individual plates, layer radicchio, fennel, beets, pine nuts, feta, and pea shoots and/or fennel fronds and drizzle generously with dressing. You will have dressing left over for another salad this week; keep sealed in a jar in the refrigerator for up to 1 week. Serve immediately.

Zero-Waste Tip Save the fennel core for stock or soup and fronds for an herby garnish to add a fresh, bright character.

(Recipe contributed by Allison Day)

Brussels Fried Hash F L

Growing up, my folks made fried hash during the week to use up leftover cooked root veggies from Sunday's supper. I believe it is a custom that migrated from the old British recipe for "Bubble and Squeak." However, we never had it with the cabbage (the squeak). Instead, we East Coasters reached for the Spam. I have adapted this recipe many times based on my leftovers, and I change up the seasonings depending on my mood. Sometimes I want them spicy, or I crave a tablespoon or two of chopped fresh herbs for brightness. Try this as a side dish or a main with some Hawaiian Chili Water (page 195) or Lemon Dill Buttermilk Dressing (page 166).

2 cups cooked diced potatoes or about 1½ cups mashed (see substitutions)

1 tsp sweet chili powder

1 tsp smoked paprika

1 Tbsp chopped fresh or 1 tsp dried oregano

1 cup finely chopped cooked Brussels sprouts (see substitutions)

½ cup finely chopped cooked ham or cooked ground meat (optional)

Salt and pepper

2–3 Tbsp oil

1. In a large bowl, mash the potatoes if they are diced. I like to keep them a little chunky.

2. Fold in the chili powder, smoked paprika, and oregano.

3. Stir in the Brussels sprouts and ham. Season with salt and pepper.

4. Portion out ¼ cup of the mixture, and use your hands to flatten it into a patty about 2½ inches in diameter. Repeat with the rest of the mixture.

5. In a large skillet or cast-iron pan over medium-high heat, add the oil. Once the pan is hot, fry the patties in batches until browned on both sides, about 4 minutes per side.

Food 911 If you start out with previously mashed potatoes, it may be easier (and just as yummy) to fry the hash like a scramble instead of in patties.

USES UP cooked potatoes, cooked vegetables, cooked protein

MAKES about eight 2½-inch patties

TOTAL TIME 30 minutes

KEEPS FOR up to 2 days in the fridge

CAN SUBSTITUTE
- 1 cup of potatoes with 1 cup cooked root vegetables or cooked mashed plantains
- Brussels sprouts with cabbage, collards or other hardy greens

Croquettes ▪F▪ ▪L▪

This recipe is an indulgent way to use up leftover mashed potatoes. Traditionally these Spanish tapas are filled with ham and a creamy béchamel sauce; however, as long as you can roll them into balls and fry them, you can sneak in almost whatever you like. Serve them up with my Marinara Sauce (page 77).

Béchamel Sauce
2 Tbsp butter
½ onion or 1 shallot, finely chopped
¼ cup flour
1 cup milk or cream (any fat % will do)

Optional Add-Ins
½ cup finely chopped mushrooms
¼ cup shredded cheese
Soft herbs, chopped
Handful of chopped baby spinach

Filling
1½ cups mashed or riced potatoes
    (about 2 medium-size potatoes)
1 cup diced cooked protein
Pinch ground nutmeg
Salt and pepper

Crust
1 egg
¾ cup Breadcrumbs (page 182) or
    Crispy Coatings (page 183)
¼ cup shredded hard cheese
High smoke point oil, for frying

1. For the Sauce: In a saucepot over medium heat, melt the butter. Add the onion and cook for about 3 minutes to soften. Stir in the flour until it absorbs the butter and let cook for 2 to 3 minutes.

2. While stirring, slowly pour in the milk until it fully incorporates and forms a smooth sauce. Reduce the heat if needed, and cook the sauce until it is thick and creamy.

3. For the Filling: Stir in the mashed potatoes, protein, and nutmeg and season with salt and pepper. Stir in any optional add-ins. Transfer to a bowl or dish, cover, and refrigerate until cold, a minimum of 2 hours. You can prepare the recipe up to this step the day before.

4. With floured hands, shape 1 heaping tablespoon of the mixture into a football-like round, and place on a tray or plate. Repeat.

5. For the Crust: In a small bowl, beat the egg. In another bowl, combine the bread-crumbs and cheese. Dip each croquette in the egg, then roll in the coating, pressing the crumbs in. If not frying right away, you can set them in the fridge for up to 12 hours.

6. To fry, in a skillet over medium-high heat, preheat 1 inch of oil to 350°F. Measure the temperature with a thermometer or submerge the back of a wooden spoon into the oil. If the oil bubbles around the wood, it is ready.

7. Fry the croquettes in batches to avoid overcrowding the pan (which reduces the temperature of the oil) until golden brown, 3 to 5 minutes on each side. Place on a paper towel-lined plate and serve warm.

USES UP cooked potatoes, cooked protein

MAKES 15–20 croquettes, serves 6 as a side

TOTAL TIME 2 hours, 15 minutes (including chilling)

KEEPS FOR up to 6 months in the freezer uncooked; just thaw for 15 minutes before frying

CAN SUBSTITUTE
• Béchamel sauce with Creamy Cauliflower Sauce (page 66)

Zero–Waste Herbs

A common food waste that many lament is throwing out wilted fresh herbs. Whether you're growing your own or buying from the store, surplus herbs happen to us all! To extend the lifespan of fresh herbs, store them in the fridge with their roots submerged in water, the same as you would a bouquet of flowers. Another method is to wrap their stems in a wet tea towel. And when you know you're not going to get to them in time, freeze them—that way the freezer locks in their flavor and you can use them when you next need. Here are some different ways to freeze your herbs:

ON THE STEM Hardy herbs (like rosemary, thyme, bay leaves, lime leaves, winter savory, and chopped lemongrass) freeze well on their stems. Form a log with your stemmed herbs then roll it up tight in an airtight reusable freezer bag. Use as needed. These herbs thaw and release their flavor very quickly once added to cooked dishes.

IN CUBES Wash, dry, chop, and portion herbs into ice cube trays. Pour water, oil, stock, or melted butter over top, depending on the intended use, until two-thirds full (for example you wouldn't want to use herbs stored in stock for a thick dip or pesto, but they're great for soups). Freeze, and once frozen, pop out and store in a labeled freezer bag or container. Note: flavor holds better in an oil base.

AS PESTO Why not use the simple pesto method (page 74) for any greens and herbs? I am constantly making and freezing batches of pesto with leftover herbs and greens from work, so much so that my daughter's friends have gotten into the habit of asking me if I have any stashed in the freezer for them. Portion into your regular meal-sized-portions and freeze in containers (or use the ice cube method above).

Sour Cream and Chive Potato Biscuits ▪F ▪P ▪L

Recipe pictured on page 151

Leftover mashed potatoes? How about some steamy warm potato biscuits with dinner? You will be surprised how easy these biscuits are to make and you will be happy to have them all warm and steamy with dinner, or even as a savory treat at brunch or during afternoon tea.

5 Tbsp melted butter

¼ cup sour cream (see substitutions)

½ cup milk

1 Tbsp sugar, honey, or maple syrup

1 tsp baking soda

1 tsp salt

1 cup mashed potatoes

2½ cups flour

1 cup grated cheese (optional)

¼ cup chopped chives

1. Preheat the oven to 325°F. Grease or line a baking sheet.

2. In a large bowl, whisk together the melted butter, sour cream, milk, sugar, baking soda, and salt. Stir in the mashed potatoes, flour, and cheese, if using, until combined. Fold in the chopped chives.

3. Transfer the dough to a floured surface and knead, adding more flour if it is too sticky. Roll out dough lightly with floured hands or a rolling pin until it is about 1-inch thick. Cut the dough into individual biscuits with a floured round cutter or a floured knife.

4. Place on the baking sheet and bake for 20 minutes (depending on size of biscuits) or until puffed and golden brown.

USES UP mashed potatoes

MAKES 8 biscuits

TOTAL TIME 35 minutes

KEEPS FOR the day of, or can be stored up to 6 months in the freezer

CAN SUBSTITUTE
• Sour cream with full-fat plain yogurt

Stuffed Pumpkin with Shrimp F

This recipe is my take on a Brazilian dish known as Camarão na moranga, and it is freaking fantastic. Here, a whole pumpkin is the star of the show and the coolest serving bowl ever. Its tender roasted flesh is scooped and served with spoonfuls of creamy spiced prawns and melted cheese. And we even keep the seeds, to roast and use as a garnish. Add a side of cooked grains, like rice or quinoa, to round out the meal, and serve this at your next dinner party for something that everyone will rave about.

One 3 lb pie pumpkin (see substitutions)

2 lb (medium to large) shrimp, peeled and deveined

Zest and juice of 2 limes

2 cloves garlic, finely chopped

Salt and pepper

3 Tbsp oil

1 onion, finely chopped

1 Tbsp fresh or 1 tsp dried thyme

1 Tbsp fresh or 1 tsp dried oregano

1 Tbsp curry powder (optional)

½ tsp ground coriander

1 tsp ground cumin

1 finely chopped jalapeño (optional)

1 bay leaf

Dash of hot sauce (optional)

2 cups chopped tomatoes or 1 cup tomato sauce (page 77) or store-bought

2 bell peppers, chopped

1 Tbsp cornstarch

2 Tbsp water

½ cup coconut milk

4½ oz cream cheese at room temperature

Optional Garnishes

2 Tbsp chopped fresh parsley

Perfectly Roasted Pumpkin Seeds (page 62)

1. Preheat the oven to 350°F. Wash the pumpkin and cut a circle in the top to make a lid, the same as you would a jack-o'-lantern. Scrape out all of the seeds and set aside to roast for the garnish (see Perfectly Roasted Pumpkin Seeds, page 62). Wrap the pumpkin, lid on, with foil and place on a baking sheet. Cook until tender, about 40 minutes. Set aside.

2. While the pumpkin is cooking, in a large bowl, marinate the shrimp with the lime zest and juice and garlic, and season with salt and pepper.

3. In a large sauté pan over medium heat, heat the oil. Sauté the onion until softened, about 3 minutes. Stir in the thyme, oregano, curry powder, coriander, cumin, jalapeño, bay leaf, and hot sauce, and sauté for 1 minute. Add the tomato and bell peppers and let simmer for 5 minutes. Add the shrimp and continue to simmer until the shrimp are cooked through, about 5 minutes.

4. In a small bowl, mix cornstarch with water until dissolved, set aside.

5. Stir the coconut milk into the shrimp mixture. Season with salt and pepper. Whisk in the cornstarch mixture. Bring the shrimp mixture to a simmer to thicken, about 3 minutes. Take off the heat and set aside. Remove the bay leaf.

6. Take the pumpkin out of the oven and carefully remove the lid. Let cool slightly, then with a spoon, spread the cream cheese onto the pumpkin's inside wall until it is about ⅛ to ¼ inch thick. If this is too tricky, you can also make little cream cheese cubes and add them together with the shrimp mixture. Pour the shrimp mixture into the pumpkin.

USES UP whole pie pumpkin, shrimp, cream cheese

SERVES 4–6

TOTAL TIME 2 hours

KEEPS FOR up to 3 days in the fridge

CAN SUBSTITUTE
- Pumpkin with winter squash or 4 mini pumpkins (see note)

7. Place the pumpkin back in the oven, top on, wrapped in aluminum foil and bake for an additional 15 minutes.

8. Serve family style with the whole pumpkin on the table and a big spoon. Start scooping the creamy shrimp mixture, making sure to get chunks of silky sweet pumpkin and cream cheese into the bowls. Garnish with the parsley and roasted pumpkin seeds, if using.

Food 911 For a different take, try using 4 mini pumpkins instead. You can prepare the bulk of this recipe ahead of time and pour the shrimp sauce into the pumpkin 15 minutes before serving time.

Perfectly Roasted Pumpkin Seeds `S`

Never toss perfectly good pumpkin, acorn, or other squash seeds again! Instead turn them into a tasty snack, salad topper (see page 46), or soup garnish (page 61). You can keep them plain, or try one of the two spice variations listed below.

Pumpkin seeds (from 1 or more
    pumpkins) (see substitutions)
Oil
Salt and pepper

Flavor Variation

Spicy 2 parts sweet chili powder to
    1 part garlic powder + pinch cayenne

Curry 2 parts curry powder to 1 part
    ground cumin + ground coriander

USES UP pumpkin seeds

SERVES Varies: the bigger the squash or pumpkin, the more the seeds it makes

TOTAL TIME 10 minutes

KEEPS FOR Best eaten ASAP

CAN SUBSTITUTE
- Pumpkin seeds with acorn or other squash seeds

1. Preheat the oven to 325°F.

2. Dunk the seeds in a large bowl of water and pull off the guts with your hands. The seeds will float to the top. Place seeds on a clean tea towel and pat dry.

3. Transfer the seeds to a bowl and drizzle with a little oil, just enough to coat. Using your hands, massage the seeds with the oil, salt, pepper, and desired flavor variation.

4. Bake for 10 minutes, remove from the oven and stir, and bake again for 8 to 10 minutes or until slightly golden. Seeds will get crisper as they cool.

Food 911 Pumpkin and squash seeds are full of fiber, protein, and potassium.

Pipian Verde aka Mexican Pumpkin Seed Stew F P

Recipe pictured on page 148

A stew made from pumpkin seeds (aka pepitas) that is adaptable to any protein. Genius! This recipe stems from the Puebla region of Mexico. It can be served as is, with simple sides, or used as a filling for enchiladas, tacos, burritos, or Packed Peppers (page 70). In a pinch, you can make the Pipian Verde Sauce on its own and pour it over a leftover cooked protein from the night before.

Pipian Verde Sauce

1 cup shelled pumpkin seeds (aka pepitas)

½ cup chopped onion

½ cup chopped jalapeño or serrano chilies (see substitutions)

1 clove garlic, chopped

1 Tbsp fresh or 1 tsp dried oregano (Mexican if you can find it)

½ tsp ground cumin

4 cups Vegetable (page 187), Poultry (page 188), or Meat (page 188) Stock, divided

1 tsp salt

2 Tbsp oil

½ cup chopped cilantro stems (see substitutions)

Zest and juice of 1 lime

Pipian Verde Stew

1½ lb protein, diced into 1-inch cubes

Optional Garnishes

Cilantro, parsley, or basil, chopped

Lime wedges

Warm tortillas, cooked rice, cooked rice and beans, or cooked grains, for serving (optional)

1. For the Pipian Verde Sauce: Preheat the oven to 350°F and place the pumpkin seeds on a baking sheet. Toast for 5 to 8 minutes or until lightly browned and puffed. Keep a close eye on the seeds since they burn easily. Transfer the pumpkin seeds to another dish to cool.

2. Place the onion, chilies, garlic, oregano, cumin, 1 cup of the stock, and salt in a blender or food processor. Pulse a few times to incorporate. Once the seeds have cooled, add them to the blended ingredients and purée until smooth.

3. Preheat a large heavy-bottomed saucepot over medium heat. Add the oil and pumpkin seed mixture. Swirl ½ cup of the stock into blender to get out all of the sauce and add to the mix. Bring to a simmer and cook, lowering the heat if necessary, for 10 minutes, stirring occasionally. Cook until the sauce is thick enough to coat the back of a spoon. Add more stock if necessary.

4. In the same blender, purée the cilantro stems and an additional ½ cup of stock until smooth. Add to the sauce. Taste and adjust the seasoning with salt, lime zest, and lime juice.

5. For the Pipian Verde Stew: Add the chopped protein and let it simmer on low until cooked through, about 20 minutes for large proteins like chicken breasts or 10 minutes for cubed proteins.

6. Serve warm with garnishes and sides or use as a filling for warm tortillas.

USES UP pumpkin seeds, jalapeños, protein

SERVES 4, makes about 4 cups of sauce

TOTAL TIME 45 minutes

KEEPS FOR up to 4 days in the fridge or 3 months in the freezer for the sauce. The stew keeps up to 4 days in the fridge

CAN SUBSTITUTE
- Hot chilies with poblano pepper, or green bell peppers for a mild version
- Cilantro stems with parsley stems

Grand Gnocchi P L

Since we never seem to eat a whole cooked or roasted pumpkin or squash in my house in one sitting, we tend to have leftovers, which are perfect for making gnocchi the next day. Gnocchi is not like other pasta. It's way easier to make from scratch— and that's been a great food activity to do with my kids. Serve it with tomato sauce (page 77) or pesto (page 74).

2 cups well-mashed cooked pumpkin or squash (see substitutions)
1 egg yolk (reserve white for egg white recipes (see page 224) or store for later use)

1 cup "00" or all-purpose flour (+ extra for dusting)
1 Tbsp finely chopped fresh or 1 tsp dried herbs
Pinch salt
Your favorite sauce

1. To make the dough, in a large bowl, combine the mashed pumpkin and the egg yolk and stir until combined. Add the flour, herbs, and salt and continue to stir until you have a fairly dry dough. Depending on how wet or dry your mash is to begin with, you may need to add more flour.

2. To form the gnocchi, transfer the dough to a lightly floured surface and divide into 4 portions. Using your hands, roll a portion into a long snake until it is about ½ inch in diameter. With a floured knife, divide it into approximately 1-inch-long gnocchi. If you like, you can press each gnocchi lightly with the back of a fork to create lines.

3. Bring a large pot of salted water to a boil and simmer the gnocchi until they rise to the top, 3 to 5 minutes.

4. Drain and toss with your favorite sauce.

Zero-Waste Tip While freshly cooked pasta is wonderful, sometimes it's even better the next day. One of my favorite ways to serve pasta is fried up in a really hot pan so some of its bits and pieces get nice and crispy (see page 159).

Food 911 "00" or double zero flour is a finely milled Italian flour that is considered one of the best for pasta making because of its high protein content and silky texture.

USES UP cooked root vegetables

SERVES 2 as a main or 4 as a side

TOTAL TIME 25 minutes

KEEPS FOR up to 2 days in the fridge, cooked, or up to 6 months in a sealed container in the freezer, uncooked and lightly tossed in flour.

CAN SUBSTITUTE
• Pumpkin with winter squash, other root vegetables or celery root

Creamy Cauliflower Mac and Cheese F L

A magical sauce made of cauliflower. No flour, no cornstarch, no roux, and nobody can tell the difference. Use it in place of cream in soups, baked pasta dishes, or even as a replacement for butter in mashed potatoes. Here I serve it with pasta to make a delicious, healthy alternative to mac and cheese, as well a great vehicle for using up all kinds of leftovers. Got some bacon leftover from breakfast? Toss it in! Maybe some extra cooked protein from lunch? Toss that in, too! How about some fresh veggies you need to use up? Yup, in they go!

Creamy Cauliflower Sauce

1 head cauliflower, chopped (about 5 cups)

1 clove garlic, peeled and chopped

2–3 cups Vegetable Stock (page 187), or Stone Soup (page 79) or Parm Broth (page 191), divided

1½ cups grated semi-soft cheese (optional)

Pinch ground nutmeg

Pinch cayenne or ¼ tsp chili flakes

Salt and pepper

Mac

8–10 oz dried macaroni or pasta

Optional Add-Ins

1 cup cooked protein

1 cup chopped fresh tomatoes

1 cup sautéed hardy greens

1 cup sautéed mushrooms

1 cup sautéed onions

½–1 cup crispy bacon bits

½ cup chopped fresh basil

Garnish

Crispy Coatings (page 183) (optional)

1. For the Creamy Cauliflower Sauce: In a saucepot, simmer the cauliflower and garlic in 2 cups of the broth until the cauliflower is tender, about 20 minutes, depending on the size of the florets.

2. Carefully pour the mixture into a blender and blend on high for 1 to 2 minutes until silky smooth.

3. Return the blended sauce to the saucepot. If sauce seems too thick, stir in a little more broth. Over medium heat, stir in the grated cheese (if using) and the nutmeg, and cayenne. Cook until the cheese is melted. Taste and season with salt and pepper.

4. For the Mac: In the meantime, preheat the oven to 350°F. Bring a pot of salted water to a boil and cook the pasta according to the package instructions. Grease a casserole dish.

5. Drain the pasta, transfer to a large bowl and fold in the cauliflower sauce and any optional add-ins. Toss to coat.

6. Transfer to the casserole dish, sprinkle with the Crispy Coatings (if using), and bake for 20 to 30 minutes or until golden brown on top. Serve immediately.

USES UP cauliflower, cooked protein, cooked vegetables

SERVES 4–6

TOTAL TIME 40–50 minutes

KEEPS FOR sauce can be stored for up to 1 week in the fridge or 6 months in the freezer; cooked mac and cheese for up to 3 days in the fridge; unbaked for up to 6 months in the freezer (just bake from frozen covered for 1 hour to 1 hour, 10 minutes for large dishes, 40 minutes for medium to small)

Chunky Squash Raita F L *Recipe pictured on page 94*

I pretty much, year-round, always have plain yogurt and cucumber in my fridge. So with a few additional flavorings, I often enjoy this chunky take on the classic Middle Eastern yogurt and cucumber raita, which is a great way to use up leftover cooked squash. This is a great side paired with a spicy stew, like the Apple Curry Dal (page 95).

1 cup plain yogurt

½ tsp ground cumin

½ tsp ground coriander

½ Tbsp finely diced chili pepper (optional)

¼ cup chopped fresh cilantro (see substitutions)

½ cucumber, finely chopped or coarsely grated

1 cup cubed cooked or roasted winter squash

Salt and pepper

Zest and juice of half a lime

1. In a large bowl, mix the yogurt with cumin, coriander, chili, and cilantro.

2. Gently fold in the cucumber and squash into the yogurt mixture, leaving the mixture chunky and mashed.

3. Season with salt and pepper and add lime zest and juice to taste.

Food 911 Winter squash skins can be a pain to peel, especially if you don't have a good sharp knife. The good thing is that while the skins are not edible raw, they can be eaten cooked. The thinner the skin, the more palatable they will be.

USES UP yogurt, cooked squash, cucumber

SERVES 4 as a side

TOTAL TIME 10 minutes

KEEPS FOR up to 3 days in the fridge

CAN SUBSTITUTE
- Cilantro with basil or mint

Chili Yogurt Cornbread P L *Recipe pictured on page 162*

Cornmeal is another item that seems to get lost in the back of my pantry. So now whenever there is leftover cooked or grilled corn, I use it as an opportunity to make a batch of cornbread. It's a welcome change from bread at dinner and a way to use up any extra fresh herbs, chunks of cheese, or hot chili peppers.

1 cup whole-grain cornmeal

1 cup flour

1 tsp baking powder

1 tsp baking soda

½ tsp salt

2 eggs

⅓ cup honey

4 Tbsp melted butter

½ cup plain yogurt

½ cup milk

1 cup cooked, canned, or thawed frozen corn kernels (the corn from about 2 cobs)

1–2 finely chopped chili peppers

Optional Add-Ins

½ cup shredded semi-soft cheese

¼ cup chopped chives or green onions

2 Tbsp fresh or 2 tsp dried thyme

1. Preheat the oven to 425°F. Grease a square 8- or 9-inch pan with butter or oil.

2. Combine the cornmeal, flour, baking powder, baking soda, and salt in a medium-size mixing bowl.

3. In a large mixing bowl, combine the eggs, honey, melted butter, yogurt, and milk.

4. Stir the dry ingredients into the wet ingredients and mix until combined. Stir in the corn kernels, chili peppers, and any optional add-ins. Pour into the greased pan and level with a spoon (the batter will be very thick).

5. Bake for 20 to 25 minutes or until the cornbread is golden brown on the top and a cake tester comes out clean.

USES UP corn, cornmeal, yogurt

SERVES 9

TOTAL TIME 40 minutes

KEEPS FOR up to 3 days at room temperature or 6 months in the freezer

Zero-Waste Tip   It's rare to find a grocer where you can buy just one or two hot chili peppers, especially smaller Thai chilies, which seem to always be sold in packages with way more than you really need or can use up in the course of a week. I like to dry my left-over hot chilies by stringing them together with a needle and thread like garland and hanging them in a dry well-ventilated area. After a few weeks, you have made your own dried chilies that you can grind into a powder.

Packed Peppers ⬛F ⬛L

Peppers make a vibrant lifeboat for your leftovers, and can totally transform last night's stew, chili, roast chicken or pulled pork, as just a few examples, into a whole new taste experience. There are so many varieties of fillings that work well with peppers, it's hard to settle on one version, so here I have provided you with one simple method to use for anything you want to pack your pepper with. My personal favorite is stuffing smoky spicy poblano peppers with leftover Jambalaya (page 163).

4 bell peppers (see substitutions)
½ lb cooked protein
1 cup cooked grains
1–2 cups sauce such as a homemade
    tomato (page 77) or cream
Salt and pepper
½ cup (or more) grated cheese or
    a few Tbsp of nutritional yeast
    (+ extra to garnish), divided

Optional Add-Ins
2–3 green onions, chopped
Fresh herbs, chopped, or a few tsp
    dried herbs
Hot sauce, to taste

1. Preheat the oven to 375°F and grease a baking dish big enough to hold the peppers with oil or butter.

2. Cut the tops of the bell peppers off, as you would a jack-o'-lantern. Discard the seeds and membranes. Remove the stems from the tops and discard, reserving the tops for the filling. Dice the tops.

3. Place the peppers cut side up in the prepared dish. If the peppers won't stand up, you can slice some of their bottoms off to even them out.

4. In a bowl, mix the protein, grain, sauce, and any optional add-ins with the diced pepper tops and season to taste with salt and pepper. Mix in the cheese, reserving a little to use as a garnish. Spoon the stuffing into the peppers and sprinkle cheese over top.

5. Pour just enough water in the baking dish to cover the bottom. Cover the peppers loosely with compostable parchment, a silicone baking mat, or the top of a pot or pan.

6. Bake for 20 minutes, then uncover and bake for an additional 5 to 10 minutes to brown the tops. The filling should be heated through and the peppers softened.

Food 911 I have also made this recipe with jalapeños stuffed with a little leftover stew or chili and grated cheese, perfect served as a spicy appetizer for parties.

USES UP peppers, cooked protein, cooked grains, cheese, tomato sauce

SERVES 4

TOTAL TIME 30 minutes

KEEPS FOR up to 3 days in the fridge

CAN SUBSTITUTE
- Bell peppers with field or poblano peppers cut in half lengthwise; amount of filling may change depending on the size of the peppers

Avocado Boats with Turmeric Aioli F L

I had been meaning to try stuffed avocados for some time—since half an avocado with a squeeze of lemon and a sprinkle of salt and pepper is my quick go-to snack—so I always have a half left over! It wasn't until I demolished them in a little bar in San José, Costa Rica, that I was like . . . why am I not doing this all the time?! In this recipe they are simply stuffed with chopped grilled shrimp and veggies, then drizzled with fresh turmeric aioli. Honestly? If you love avocados, you can easily stuff them with almost any leftover chopped protein, grains, or mixed veggies and serve them with your favorite dressing or sauce for an instant dinner or snack. Here's my interpretation from San José.

Turmeric Aioli

¼ cup mayonnaise or 1-Minute Mayo (page 196)

1 Tbsp lemon juice, apple cider vinegar, or white wine vinegar

½ clove garlic, minced

1 Tbsp fresh finely chopped turmeric or 2 tsp ground turmeric

Salt and pepper

Avocado Boats

1 cup chopped grilled shrimp (see substitutions)

1 cup chopped grilled or roasted veggies (page 40) (see substitutions)

½ cup chopped fresh tomato

Zest and juice of half a lime

2 Tbsp extra-virgin olive oil or avocado oil

Salt and pepper

2 just ripe avocados, cut in half and pit removed

4 leaves of leaf lettuce

Optional Garnishes

2 Tbsp chopped cilantro, basil, or parsley

2 Tbsp seeds or chopped nuts

1. For the Turmeric Aioli: In a medium-size bowl, combine all of the ingredients.

2. For the Avocado Boats: In a medium-size bowl, combine the shrimp, veggies, tomato, lime zest and juice, and oil. Then season with salt and pepper to taste.

3. Take each avocado half, and with your fingers carefully peel off the skin. Avocados that are just ripe will still be a little stiff and not too soft, so this will be easy. If your avocado is fully ripe and possibly a little on the mushy side, you can simply scoop out the avocado half with a large spoon.

4. Portion the stuffing on top of each avocado boat (it may be overflowing) and place each boat on a lettuce leaf. Garnish, if desired.

5. Serve with the Turmeric Aioli or drizzle with your favorite salad dressing or a few dashes of hot sauce.

USES UP avocados, cooked protein, cooked vegetables

SERVES 2 as a main, 4 as a snack

TOTAL TIME 35 minutes

KEEPS FOR the day of

CAN SUBSTITUTE
- Grilled shrimp with cooked chicken, fish, meat, or vegan protein
- Mixed veggies with cooked grains or rice

Food 911 Avocados, like apples and pears are subject to oxidation and browning. If you are preparing these items ahead of time, place them in a large bowl of water with the juice of a lemon or lime. The citric acid will help prevent browning. Also when storing these items in your fridge, create an airtight seal directly on their surfaces. For example, store guacamole in an airtight container with some water or a wax wrapper directly overtop to prevent browning.

Put It in a Pesto F

Pesto requires five key ingredients: garlic, Parmesan, nuts and/or seeds, olive oil, and the main event. Classically, basil is the star. But, pesto can really be made with any combination of greens and is an excellent way to use up fresh herbs and/or greens. From watercress or spinach to beet greens (my personal fave), and even jalapenos, pesto is born. Enjoy it over noodles (page 157), as a pizza sauce (page 178), drizzled over roast vegetables (page 40), as a dip, on crackers (page 181), or add it to scrambled eggs, an omelet or frittata (page 41). You can also freeze pesto into perfect little ice cubes to use later.

2 cloves garlic, chopped
¼–½ cup nuts and/or seeds
½ cup grated Parmesan, pecorino
    Romano, or nutritional yeast
    (optional)

2 packed cups of chopped herbs,
    greens or hearty greens
    (see substitutions)
½–⅔ cup extra-virgin olive oil
Salt and pepper
Squeeze of lemon juice (optional)

USES UP greens, hearty green, herbs

MAKES about 1 cup

TOTAL TIME 5 minutes

KEEPS FOR 1 week in the fridge or up to 1 year in the freezer

CAN SUBSTITUTE
- Try any combination of greens, hearty greens or fresh herbs such as basil, arugula, kale, watercress, parsley, beet greens etc. or blanched carrot and parsnip tops (yes, they're delicious and good for you!)

1. In a blender, food processor, or using a mortar and pestle, purée the garlic with the nuts and cheese. Add the greens and continue to process, blend, or mash until the mixture has a smooth consistency.

2. Drizzle in the olive oil while processing, blending or mashing to incorporate.

3. Season with salt and pepper, then taste and adjust seasoning if needed.

Zero-Waste Tip Pesto likes to discolor when exposed to air, so seal it in an airtight container with a drizzle of olive oil on top to protect it, or freeze (see page 58).

Green Beans for Days

There is nothing more gratifying than a vegetable everyone likes and is willing to eat multiple days in a row. Enter green beans. Green beans can be served so many ways over the course of three or four days, all with very little prep. Here is how to make the best of a bunch of green beans.

RAW The first thing I do is portion out enough raw beans to chop and toss in a salad. Sliced into small rounds, they are a welcome crunchy addition to any simple green or chopped veggie salad (see page 46).

BLANCHED Blanch the beans in boiling salted water for two minutes, just enough time for their green color to pop and still leave some crunch.

> **To serve warm:** drain and toss with melted butter or olive oil, and salt and pepper to taste.

> **To serve cold:** drain and shock them in a cold water bath to stop them from overcooking. Toss the cold drained green beans with your favorite salad dressing, or store for up to three days in the fridge.

STEAMED Steam beans in a steamer basket with a couple of inches of boiling water for 5 to 7 minutes, depending how crisp you like them.

SAUTÉED Sauté leftover blanched or steamed green beans with some oil and aromatics and dish them up again. In a large sauté pan over medium heat, add 2 Tbsp of oil, a chopped shallot, and a couple of minced cloves of garlic and cook to soften, about three minutes. Throw in a few handfuls of blanched green beans to heat through. At the end, finish with some additional oil or butter and season with salt and pepper.

STIR-FRIED Add sautéed green beans from the night before to a stir-fry or other pan-fried dish.

SEARED To give them some color and additional flavor, get your skillet or sauté pan super-hot, drizzle in a little oil, and sear those suckers for a few minutes.

Tomato Sauce: 3 Ways F L S

When tomato season rolls around, it can be tricky to use them all up; enter: tomato sauce. I'm giving you three different recipes here, which almost act as building blocks for each other. Marinara sauce may sound fancy by name, but it's in fact the simplest, freshest, and fastest tomato sauce to make from scratch. From there, you can take it to my Basic Tomato Sauce, which adds vegetables into the mix, and then onto Ragù, which can be made as meaty (or not) as you like. Marinara is great paired with my Croquettes (page 56), the Basic Tomato Sauce is lovely in the Crispy Fried Pasta (page 159), and the Ragù is a great addition to your Pasta Night (page 157). The amounts in these recipes are just suggested, so if you only have three or four whole tomatoes on hand, scale the recipe down and make it for two. Or you can scale up—tomato sauce lasts for a year in the freezer, taking you through to next tomato season!

USES UP tomatoes, cooked and raw vegetables, cooked and raw proteins

MAKES about 4 cups

TOTAL TIME 20 minutes (Marinara), 40 minutes (Tomato and Ragù)

KEEPS FOR 5–7 days in an airtight container in the fridge, or in the freezer for up to 1 year

MARINARA

¼ cup olive oil
4–8 cloves garlic, finely chopped

4 lb fresh tomatoes, chopped, or 2 cans (28 oz each) tomatoes
Salt and pepper

Pinch crushed red pepper flakes (optional)
3 Tbsp chopped fresh basil

1. In a large pan over medium heat, heat the olive oil. Add the garlic and cook until softened, about 3 to 5 minutes.

2. Add the tomatoes, red pepper flakes, and a pinch of salt. Bring the sauce to a simmer and let thicken, about 15 minutes. Stir in the basil towards the end of the cooking time. Taste and adjust seasoning with more salt, pepper, or basil. If you like, blend or purée the sauce.

BASIC TOMATO SAUCE

¼ cup olive oil
4–8 cloves garlic
1–2 onions
1–2 leeks, white and light-green parts only (optional), finely sliced
2 cups mixed chopped or grated vegetables (such as carrots or celery)
1 recipe Marinara (above), or 2½ lb fresh tomatoes, chopped, or one (24 oz) jar tomato purée
Salt and pepper

Optional Seasonings
¼ cup chopped fresh or 3 tsp dried basil, parsley, and/or oregano
1 Tbsp sweet chili powder
2–3 bay leaves
A few hard cheese rinds
Pinch chili flakes

Optional Add-Ins
½ cup roasted red peppers
½ cup sun-dried tomatoes
½ cup grated hard cheese
¼–½ cup cream
1 Tbsp capers
Handfuls of hardy greens, chopped
Handful pitted olives
Sprinkle of semi-soft cheese (pulled fresh mozzarella is especially good)

1. In a large pan over medium heat, heat the olive oil. Add the garlic, onion and leek and cook until softened, about 5 minutes, then add the chopped vegetables, and cook until softened, stirring, about 5 minutes.

2. Add the marinara, tomatoes or tomato purée, season with salt and pepper and bring to a simmer. Stir in the optional seasonings and cook, stirring occasionally, for up to 30 minutes or until thickened.

3. Add any optional add-ins, except the dairy and cheese, and cook just until wilted and heated through. Stir in the dairy, if using. Taste, and adjust the flavor and consistency as needed. If you like, blend or purée the sauce.

RAGÙ

1 Tbsp–¼ cup olive oil

Protein (Mix and Match, For How Meaty You Want It)

½–1 lb cured fatty proteins (bacon, chorizo, pancetta etc.)

1 lb raw proteins (ground meat, diced chicken etc.)

1–3 cups chopped cooked protein (pulled pork, ground beef, meatballs etc.)

1 recipe Marinara or Tomato Sauce (above), or 1 bottle (about 24 oz) tomato sauce

Seasonings
See Tomato Sauce (above)

Optional Add-Ins
See Tomato Sauce (above)

1. In a large pan over medium heat, heat the oil and cook the cured proteins (if using) until cooked through, then remove from the pan and set aside. In the same pan, cook any ground raw meats (if using) until browned and cooked through, and set aside. Cook any raw proteins (if using) until just seared or browned (not cooked all the way through), then remove from the pan and set aside. If using multiple proteins, like ground meat and then chicken, cook separately since they may have different cookies time; you may have to add oil in between.

2. In the same pan, add the marinara or tomato sauce and bring to a simmer. Stir in the seasonings.

3. Add the seared raw proteins back to the pan and simmer until completely cooked through, about 10 minutes for chicken and up to 45 minutes for meatballs. Add any of the cooked cured or ground meats and cook until heated through.

4. Add any optional add-ins, except the dairy and cheese, and cook just until wilted and heated through. Stir in the dairy, if using. Taste, and adjust the flavor and consistency as needed. If you like, blend or purée the sauce.

Stone Soup F S

Stone soup refers to the tale of a fantastic meal made from nothing but a fire, pot, water, and a stone, and in this case, vegetable scraps. It's simple: just keep a large freezer-safe container or reusable bag in the freezer. Every time you cook, toss in any leftover vegetable scraps (such as wrinkly tomatoes or mushroom stems), herb stems (such as thyme or rosemary stems), or even leftover liquid from blanching or steaming veggies to replace part of the water. Once it's full, you've got free vegetable stock! Just keep in mind that strongly flavored or colored veggie scraps will influence the taste. For example, beets will make a soup dark and purple, and lots of broccoli will make broccoli-flavored soup.

About 12 cups fresh and/or frozen
vegetable scraps

3 bay leaves

10 crushed peppercorns

Small bunch parsley stems
Small bunch hardy or soft fresh herbs
or 3 Tbsp mixed dried herbs
(except mint)

USES UP vegetable scraps

MAKES about 4 quarts

TOTAL TIME 1 hour

KEEPS FOR up to 1 week in the fridge or 6 months in the freezer

1. Fill a large stockpot with water, about 4 quarts. Add the vegetable scraps, bay leaves, peppercorns, stems, and herbs, and bring to a low simmer. Simmer for 45 minutes.

2. Cool, strain, and use as a base for soups and stews or even for braising vegetables.

Food 911 Certain vegetables have protective outer layers, which can hold more nutrients than their interior. Onion skins, for example, contain antioxidants and anti-inflammatory compounds. So be sure to save these to simmer in stocks, soups, and stews to add nutritional value, flavor, and color.

Glorious Golden Green Soup F

I love, love, love Swiss chard, but I sometimes find myself with leftover stems or wilted greens. Here is a healthy golden-hued soup made to use up those good-for-you greens with the addition of one sweet potato, giving the soup luscious body.

3 Tbsp oil

1 onion, diced

2 cloves garlic, finely chopped

1 bunch Swiss chard (see substitutions)

1 carrot, diced

1 celery, diced

1 medium sweet potato, diced

¼ cup finely chopped fresh parsley stems

1 cup sliced mushrooms (optional)

Pinch of cayenne (optional)

1-inch knob fresh ginger, grated

1-inch knob fresh turmeric, grated or 2 tsp ground turmeric

4 cups Stone Soup (page 79) or Vegetable Stock (page 187)

½ bunch spinach, roughly chopped

¼ cup chopped fresh basil

Salt and pepper

USES UP Swiss chard, sweet potato, vegetables, stock

SERVES 4–6

TOTAL TIME 30 minutes

KEEPS FOR up to 3 days in the fridge or 6 months in the freezer

CAN SUBSTITUTE
- Swiss chard with other hardy or bitter greens

1. In a large saucepot, heat the oil over medium heat. Add the onion and garlic and cook until softened, about 3 minutes.

2. Meanwhile, prepare the Swiss chard. Separate the stems and chop them, and set aside. Coarsely chop the leaves and set aside.

3. Stir in the carrot, celery, sweet potato, parsley, Swiss chard stems, mushrooms, cayenne, ginger, and turmeric and continue to cook to let vegetables soften slightly, about 5 minutes.

4. Pour in the soup or stock, bring to a boil and then lower the heat to simmer, uncovered, until vegetables are tender, about 10 minutes. Add the remaining Swiss chard, spinach, and basil and season with salt and pepper. Let simmer until the greens are wilted.

5. With a hand immersion blender, food processor, or regular blender, blend to desired consistency.

Zero-Waste Tip Nutrient-dense and flavorful roots like ginger, turmeric, and galangal hold up incredibly well to freezing, so it is easy to always have some on hand. Wash the roots whole, dry, and freeze unpeeled in a freezer-safe container and grate off as you need using a box grater or Microplane (which saves time since finely chopping them can be time-consuming).

Marvelous Minestrone F P L

The soup that smells like lasagna. This is a classic combination of fresh vegetables and tomatoes in a flavorful broth. I grew up thinking it always had to have pasta and beans in it. Nope. It is, as it turns out, extremely adaptable. Don't get alarmed at the lengthy list of ingredients here. There are just so many possibilities! Green beans, cabbage, kale, Swiss chard (stems and/or leaves), corn, peas, and/or zucchini also go great in the base of this recipe.

Base

3 Tbsp olive oil

1 onion, diced

4 cloves garlic, finely chopped

2–3 carrots, peeled and diced (about ¾ cup)

2 stalks celery, chopped + tops/ leaves, diced and chopped

1 potato, diced (about 1 cup)

2 cups chopped fresh or canned tomatoes or tomato purée

1 Tbsp fresh or 1 tsp dried chopped thyme and/or oregano

½ tsp red pepper flakes (optional)

Salt and pepper

6 cups Parm Broth (page 191) or Vegetable (page 187), Poultry (page 188), or Meat (page 188) Stock

Optional Add-Ins

1¾ cups cooked or one 14 oz can beans, rinsed and drained (cannellini are good)

2 cups mixed vegetables (e.g., chopped green beans or zucchini)

1 cup cooked pasta or 4 oz dried pasta, cooked

Parm rinds

Optional Garnishes

Croutons (page 182)

Fresh basil, chopped

Parmesan cheese, grated

Nice-tasting extra-virgin olive oil or finishing oil

Crispy Veggie Skins (page 43)

USES UP cooked pasta, vegetables, Parmesan rinds, stock, tomatoes, beans

SERVES 6

TOTAL TIME 30 minutes

KEEPS FOR up to 4 days in the fridge or 6 months in the freezer

1. In a large saucepot over medium heat, add the olive oil. Sauté the onion until softened, about 3 minutes.

2. Add the garlic, carrots, celery, and potato and sauté for 5 minutes, adding more oil or a little water if the vegetables start to stick.

3. Stir in the tomatoes, herbs, and red pepper flakes and season with salt and pepper. Simmer for 3 to 5 minutes.

4. Pour in the broth and add the beans and mixed vegetables, if using. Bring back to a simmer and cook until the vegetables are tender-crisp, 10 to 15 minutes.

5. Stir in the cooked pasta and serve with any of the suggested garnishes.

Very Celery with(out) Chorizo Soup █F

Celery, you have never really gotten the admiration you deserve, and for this I am truly sorry. Most people probably don't even know where you came from. Your roots! That being said, I hadn't ever seen your root, celeriac, before my time in chef school. What I am really trying to say here is that even though we all buy you, it is usually only for a stalk or two. Your leaves go discarded and your roots go unnoticed. Celery, this one's for you . . . all of you.

8 oz dry-cured chorizo, cut into slices or cubes (optional)

3 Tbsp oil or butter

1 onion, diced

2 cloves garlic, finely chopped

1 head of celery, stalks chopped, leaves reserved for garnish

2 cups cubed celeriac (celery root), cut into ½-inch cubes (see substitutions)

Salt and pepper

3 cups Vegetable (page 187), Poultry (page 188), or Meat (page 188) Stock

1 Tbsp chopped fresh dill

USES UP celery, celery tops, and celery root (celeriac)

SERVES 6

TOTAL TIME 35 minutes

KEEPS FOR up to 4 days in the fridge or 6 months in the freezer

CAN SUBSTITUTE
• Celeriac root with cubed potatoes

1. If using chorizo, brown in a large saucepot over medium heat with the oil, about 5 minutes. Use a slotted spoon to transfer the chorizo to a bowl for later. Use the chorizo oil left in the saucepot for the next step.

2. Set a large saucepot over medium heat. If not using chorizo, add the oil. Sauté the onion, garlic, celery, and celeriac, stirring occasionally, until softened, 5 to 7 minutes. Season with salt and pepper.

3. Add the stock and simmer until all the vegetables are tender.

4. Carefully transfer the hot soup to a food processor or blender and blend until smooth. Transfer the soup back to the pot. Add the dill and chorizo (if using) and adjust seasoning to taste. Serve with chopped celery leaves.

Zero-Waste Tip The biggest food waste problem with celery is that it is mostly sold as a bunch, and sometimes it is hard to go through a whole bunch before it expires. It would be nice to have the option to buy a half bunch or single stalks . . . maybe someday. The good news is that you can revive limp celery by placing cut stems in cold water for a few minutes. Also, limp doesn't mean that it has lost its flavor, which means it is still a welcome addition to soups and stews.

Vegan Crackling `L` `S`

Vegan crackling is a great salad topper you can use in place of croutons (page 182). If you like to juice, then you may have heard of this method already. If not, this one is for you. You can use any combination of juice pulp that you like to make vegan crackling. However, if you're a big juicer and you don't want, say, a lot of lemon and ginger pulp in your crackers, juice these things first. Discard that pulp and then juice the items where you want to save the pulp for crackling.

2 cups juice pulp

¼ cup ground flax or chia seeds

¼ cup seeds

Good pinch of salt

Pepper

¼ cup or more water (depending how wet your pulp is) (see substitutions)

Optional Add-Ins

¼–½ cup grated hard cheese

1–2 tsp honey or maple syrup

Flavor Variation

Curry 1 tsp curry powder + 1 tsp ground turmeric + ½ tsp ground cumin + ½ tsp ground coriander

Italian 1 tsp garlic powder + 1 tsp onion powder + 1 tsp dried rosemary + 1 tsp dried oregano + 2 Tbsp grated Parmesan or nutritional yeast

Lemon Rosemary and Olive Oil 1 Tbsp lemon zest + 1 Tbsp chopped fresh rosemary + 2 Tbsp extra-virgin olive oil

1. Preheat the oven to 350°F and line a baking sheet. Or, if using a dehydrator, prepare the dehydrator according to the manufacturer's instructions.

2. Mix all the ingredients and any flavor variations, except water, in a bowl until combined.

3. Slowly stir in water to form a ball that is not too sticky. Press or roll the dough directly onto the baking sheet to form an even layer. If making crackers, score lines to make squares in the dough to break into crackers after baking.

4. Bake for 40 minutes or until cooked through. Or, dehydrate for 4 hours, check the crackling, and if you think it needs more time, peel off, turn over, and dehydrate for another hour or so.

5. Allow to cool and break into crackling or crackers.

USES UP vegetable pulp left over after juicing

MAKES about 24 crackers or 2 cups cracklings

TOTAL TIME 45 minutes on a stovetop or 4–6 hours at 118°F in a dehydrator

KEEPS FOR a short while—pulp is best used up ASAP for crackling, or store it in the fridge and use within a day. Crackling is best eaten ASAP.

CAN SUBSTITUTE
- Water with up to 3 Tbsp of tamari, soy sauce, or coconut aminos

Re-Growing Vegetable Scraps

Can I really re-grow my vegetables? Short answer, yes. With the right preparation, a little water, and some sunlight and love, turning scraps into a garden is easier than you think.

EASIEST VEGETABLES TO PANT AND RE-GROW
Green onion ends to re-grow green onion; lettuce root ends to re-grow lettuce leaves; beet, carrot and parsnip roots to grow greens only; celery stumps to grow celery leaves only

HOW? Stick a few toothpicks into the sides of the stumps, roots, or ends, and balance your scrap over a recycled vessel (like a jam jar or yogurt container) filled with enough water to reach and cover the base of the scrap. Place in an area that gets lots of sunlight—the warmer, the better. Once you see sprouts or shoots growing, transfer the plant to a plant pot, covered in potting soil, or directly into your garden.

OTHER SCRAPS YOU CAN RE-GROW
HERBS Trim the bottom off each herb stem below the leaves, then place the stem(s) in a vessel and fill with enough water to cover the bottom of them, like you would a flower. Once some teeny roots start to sprout down into the water, transplant into soil.

TOMATO SLICES Fill a pot with potting soil until it's almost full, add a few wrinkly tomato slices, and cover with a sprinkling of more soil. Place in a sunny area, water, and keep moist. It may take up to 2 weeks to start growing, so be patient. Eventually you will watch these teeny tiny seeds grow into tomato vines.

Plant–Based Proteins

I t was tough trying to find the right title for this chapter: Vegan, Vegetarian, Beans and Legumes? I settled on Plant-Based Proteins as a way to cover it all. Even though plant-based proteins can be swapped in for any other proteins in the recipes throughout this book, I still wanted a chapter to highlight my favorite recipes where they are the star. Besides, who doesn't have a pantry full of beans or legumes waiting to be eaten? Whether dried or canned, here are some tasty ways to use them up.

Terrific Tofu

Tofu is an extremely versatile plant-based protein that comes in a wide variety of textures and flavors. You can use it as the creamy ingredient in smoothies, dressings, or sauces; or scramble, chop, or crumble it, then cook it however you please. Anywhere you see "cooked protein" in this book, tofu can be your go-to. It tends to be a cheaper protein than meat, so rotating it into your weekly meals can help the planet and save food dollars. Tofu also comes in small, pre-portioned "blocks," so you do not need to overbuy, but packaging can be a dilemma when buying tofu. So far I have only come across three ways to address packaging with tofu and other vegan protein replacements: buy it in bulk to reduce the amount of packaging, then freeze; look for a zero-waste grocer or an Asian market that sells tofu in bins and take your own container with you (some say this is the best type of tofu to buy); or make your own from scratch.

BUYING TOFU

Generally, depending on the brand (and each brand will be a little different), the firmer the tofu, the less it will absorb flavors. You may also see "pressed" tofu for sale, which means it's pressed down to squeeze out the moisture and create a firmer texture that does not fall apart when cooked. Here are the main types of tofu from softest to firmest:

SILKEN A super silky thickened soy cream, with the texture of pudding. Typically eaten raw and perfect for smoothies, desserts, dressings, and sauces. You can also buy this fruit-flavored.

SOFT Great for absorbing flavors. A perfect addition to soups and stews. Also very versatile—can be eaten raw, and is great battered and deep-fried.

MEDIUM Ideal for baking or crumbling in scrambles. Can also be battered and stir fried.

FIRM TO EXTRA-FIRM Best for grilling, pan-frying and deep-frying. Buy them smoked and/or flavored with herbs and spices, or marinate to your liking (see my recipes on page 91).

PREPPING TOFU

DRAIN AND PAT Drain tofu to get rid of any excess moisture. For medium and firmer tofus, wrap the block in a clean tea towel for a few minutes to absorb excess moisture. If you have the time, you can press it down by placing a heavy item on top of it to drain the water while prepping the rest of your recipe. Then chop or slice and layout on a clean tea towel. If grilling, make sure to cut tofu into slices about 1½ inch thick instead of cubes to prevent them from falling through the grill. If cooking from frozen, thaw until all of the water has been released first, then drain well.

SEASON You can simply season tofu with a little salt and pepper before cooking or marinate it for a few hours in all sorts of flavors (such as my barbecue sauce (page 197), dill brine (page 132), or Spicy Chipotle Barbecue Strawberry marinade (page 91)). Tofu can be marinated for up to 4 days in the fridge, or kept frozen in the marinade for up to 3 months. Just thaw in the fridge before cooking.

COAT You can also turn tofu into crispy fried golden nuggets by tossing cubes of it in cornstarch before frying, or whipping them up in a tempura style batter to deep-fry.

COOKING TOFU

There are many ways to cook medium, firm, and extra-firm styles of tofu.

BAKE Preheat the oven to 400°F and lay the prepared cubes or slices on a lined baking tray. Bake for 30 minutes, flipping part way through, until browned.

PAN-FRY In a preheated pan over high heat, lightly coat the bottom of the pan with high smoke point oil and brown tofu on all sides, a few minutes per side.

GRILL Great for firmer tofu. Prepare the grill and get it up to a nice high heat (over 400°F) and grill until brown on all sides.

REPURPOSING TOFU

Leftover cooked tofu can be repurposed just like any other protein—try it in a taco, on a salad, or in a fried rice, or in the Grain Bowl (page 166), Easy Peasy Soup (page 96) or my Quinoa Surprise (page 169). See my Mapped-Out Meals on page 34 for more ideas.

Food 911 To buy the most ethically-produced and organic tofu, check out the Cornucopia Institute's Organic Soy Food Scorecard, where tofu is scored based on country of origin and farming practices: www.cornucopia.org/scorecard/soy.

Smashed Strawberry and Maple Barbecue Sauce (page 197)

Black-Eyed Peas with Kale and Dill (page 93)

Spicy Chipotle Barbecue Strawberry Tofu (see right)

Noodles with Spicy Peanut Sauce (page 170)

Tofu: *2 Ways* M F

If you are going to marinate tofu, you might as well marinate extra for future meals. With these two recipes, you can enjoy barbecue tofu steak or black bean tofu one night and then reuse the leftovers throughout the week (see page 34).

SPICY CHIPOTLE BARBECUE STRAWBERRY TOFU

2 blocks (about 1½ lb) extra-firm tofu

Marinade

4 cloves garlic, finely chopped

½ onion, grated, with its juice

3 Tbsp vinegar (rice or apple cider vinegar are good here)

2 tsp smoked paprika or 1 Tbsp paprika

2 Tbsp ground chipotle powder

½ cup soy or tamari sauce

½ cup mashed or puréed strawberries (see substitutions)

¼ cup honey

High smoke point oil, for grilling or searing

Optional Add-Ins

½ hot chili, finely chopped, or hot chili oil or sauce, to taste

Fresh hardy herbs

Splash of barbecuey booze like whisky or bourbon

BRILLIANT BLACK BEAN TOFU

2 blocks (about 1½ lb) extra-firm tofu

Marinade

¼ cup black bean sauce (see tip)

6 cloves garlic, finely chopped

2 Tbsp grated ginger

2 Tbsp crushed szechuan peppercorns

2 tsp celery seeds

Handful kaffir lime leaves, chopped or crushed

2 Tbsp oil

2 Tbsp soy sauce

1 Tbsp rice wine vinegar

1 Tbsp honey

Optional Garnishes

Chopped chives

Chopped cilantro

Chopped green onions

Chopped Thai basil

1. Lay each block of tofu on a clean tea towel and pat dry. Let it rest so the moisture is absorbed. Meanwhile, in a large bowl, mix the desired marinade ingredients together. You could also use a blender.

2. Cut the tofu into ½-inch steaks. Place them in a container and cover with the marinade. Seal. Marinate the tofu in the barbecue sauce in the refrigerator for at least 1 hour or up to 24 hours, and the black bean sauce for at least 4 hours or up to 4 days.

3. Once marinated, preheat a grill or cast-iron pan over high heat. Lightly oil the grill and then barbecue each side of the tofu, brushing excess marinade on the tofu while grilling, until browned, 3 to 5 minutes per side.

Zero-Waste Tip Black Bean Sauce, a salty briny paste, adds huge flavor to stir fries, sauces, stews, soups, or dips. A little goes a long way, but you can use it up in A Pot of Chili (page 141), Meatballs 101 (page 144), Beefy Black Lentil Stew (page 150), Fancy Fried Rice (page 165), or Simple Roasted Vegetables (page 40).

USES UP tofu

SERVES 6

TOTAL TIME 10 minutes (plus 1 hour to 4 days for marinating)

KEEPS FOR cooked tofu can be stored for up to 3 days in the fridge, and marinated tofu for up to 4 months in the freezer

CAN SUBSTITUTE
- Strawberries with 2 Tbsp strawberry jam or 4 Tbsp other mashed or puréed fruits like mango, cherries, pears, or blueberries

All About Legumes

Legumes are an invaluable, cheap plant-based protein, but cooking them can get a little confusing. Here is a handy chart and some helpful tips to keep your finger on the "pulse."

1. AVOID SALT Buy no-salt-added or low-sodium canned beans where possible. Rinse the beans and reserve the canned bean juice (aquafaba) as it has nutritional value and can be used as an egg white substitute (page 102), or to thicken stews and soups. If you are wary of BPA and BPS in cans, then buy dried beans with paper packaging or in bulk (just bring a reusable jar).

2. REMEMBER TO SOAK Some dried legumes require soaking in water to reduce cook time and deliver the best beany texture. You can soak them overnight or do a quick soak (see the table below). Even "old" mystery beans are still good! Just soak them overnight and note the older they are, the more likely they will need a good soaking.

3. UNDER PRESSURE? Pressure cookers can cook dried beans in an hour or less, depending on the bean. To produce intact cooked beans they will still need a presoak, but if you are not worried about split or mushy beans, skip it. Make sure to follow the manufacturer's instructions.

	Dried	Canned	Fresh	Freezer (from cooked)
Cost (may vary depending on your location)	About 10 cents per serving	About 40 cents per serving	Depends, but most are expensive	Depends, but less expensive than fresh
Nutrients	Most nutritious	Maintains most of the nutritional value	Most nutritious when eaten ASAP	Maintains most of the nutritional value
Sodium	None	Sodium added, not rinsed: 1,000 mg/cup; rinsed: 700 mg/cup No salt added: up to 15 mg per serving (check label)	None	None
Shelf life	Up to 2–3 years; after, they lose some moisture	1–4 years unopened, 5 days opened	Up to 1 week	1 year or more
Flavor	Best	Great	Best	Great
Soak time	Quick soak: boil for 1 minute then soak off the heat for 1–4 hours, strain Overnight soak: soak with 1 Tbsp salt per quart of water, strain Note: no soaking needed for black-eyed peas, lentils, and split peas	Not required	Not required	Not required
Cook time	45 minutes–1 hour Add aromatics e.g., half an onion, garlic cloves	Can eat straight from can, improved when cooked with aromatics e.g., herbs	Depends; cook time is up to 1 hour	Defrost time + recipe cook time
Zero-waste tip	Buy in bulk or in paper bags	Rinse and recycle cans	Recycle food scraps	Cook large batches and freeze for another use

Black–Eyed Peas with Kale and Dill F P

I make no mention of curry in this recipe title, but for me, it's the curry leaves that really are the star of this dish. They are not the same as curry powder, and, to my disappointment, not the same as the curry plant (which smells like curry) I had in my backyard either. Curry leaves are the herb that comes from a curry tree and they have a unique aromatic nutty flavor that makes any dish shine. They're not the easiest ingredient to find, but try looking at your local Indian grocer or ordering online—once you do find them, you will fall in love. Fresh leaves last up to two weeks in the fridge and they can be easily frozen (see page 58). If you find them dried, they will not be as strong, so add more than the recipe calls for. This is a great recipe for using those black-eyed peas you bought but never got around to using. As well the explosion of kale in your backyard, or any other bitter greens you have on hand.

1 cup dried or one 14 oz can black-eyed peas, rinsed and drained

3 Tbsp olive oil

2 shallots or ½ onion, finely chopped

3 cloves garlic, finely chopped

10 fresh or 15–20 dried curry leaves (see substitutions)

1 tsp ground cumin

1 tsp yellow mustard seeds

1 bunch Tuscan (or dinosaur) kale, finely sliced into ribbons (see substitutions)

2 tsp sweet chili powder

Salt and pepper

6 Tbsp plain yogurt (the more fat, the better!)

¼ cup finely chopped fresh dill

½ cup water or Vegetable (page 187), Poultry (page 188), or Meat (page 188) Stock

8½ oz Halloumi, cut into small cubes

1 cup diced bell pepper

Squeeze of fresh lime juice (optional)

Citrus wedges, for serving

1. If using dried black-eyed peas, soak them overnight with 1 tablespoon of salt to cut down your cooking time. Drain and rinse. In a large pot, bring the dried beans to a simmer in 8 to 10 cups water until tender, about 45 minutes to 1 hour. Drain and set aside.

2. Preheat a large skillet over medium heat. Add the oil and then the shallots, garlic, and curry leaves and sauté until softened. Stir in the cumin and mustard seeds and listen to hear the mustard seeds popping; this means they are toasted.

3. Stir in the kale, chili powder, salt, and pepper and continue to cook until wilted. Stir in the yogurt a bit at a time so it is absorbed. Stir in the chopped dill.

4. Slowly add the water and stir to create a sauce. Stir in the beans, Halloumi, and bell pepper to heat through. Stir in the lime juice, taste, and adjust the seasoning.

5. Serve with the citrus wedges.

USES UP black-eyed peas, kale, yogurt, bell pepper, citrus

SERVES 4 as a main, or 6–8 as a side

TOTAL TIME 20 minutes–50 minutes (+ 1–12 hours for soaking, if needed)

KEEPS FOR up to 3 days in the fridge.

CAN SUBSTITUTE
- Curry leaves with basil, lime zest, bay leaves (remove bay leaves before serving), or any combination
- Kale with hardy or other bitter greens

Garlicky Tahini Soup aka Tahinosoupa (page 97)

Apple Curry Dal (see right)

Chow Chow (page 199)

Chunky Squash Raita (page 68)

Apple Curry Dal F P

I thought dal was always a very specific version of stewed lentils until I started digging into more Indian curries. Dal is actually a term used for any legume but also refers to a multitude of splendidly spiced humble stews where legumes are simmered until mushy and served over or with cooked grains or bread, like roti. This is a simple vegan stew that delivers huge flavor, comforting smells, and full bellies using pantry staples and that one lost apple rolling around the bottom of your crisper.

2 Tbsp oil or butter

½ tsp cayenne pepper or chili powder

1 tsp ground cumin

1 tsp ground coriander

1 tsp ground turmeric

1 tsp garam masala

1 large onion, diced

2 cloves garlic, finely chopped

1 Tbsp finely chopped fresh ginger

1 large or 2 small apples (unpeeled), grated on the large holes of a box grater (see substitutions)

1½ cups dried red or black lentils, or a combination of both (see substitutions)

One 14 oz can coconut milk

2½ cups Vegetable (page 187), Poultry (page 188), or Meat (page 188) Stock (I love vegetable)

Salt and pepper

2 Tbsp fresh lemon or lime juice (optional)

Optional Add-Ins

1 bell pepper, diced

2 cups diced tomatoes

½–1 cup dried currants, raisins, or chopped dried apricots

Optional Garnishes

¼–½ cup seeds, nuts, or toasted coconut

6–8 dollops of plain yogurt

2–3 Tbsp of chopped cilantro, mint, or basil

1. In a large saucepot over medium-high heat, add the oil and then add the cayenne pepper, cumin, coriander, turmeric, and garam masala. Stir the spices until toasted and fragrant, about 1 minute.

2. Stir in the onion, garlic, and ginger and cook until softened, 3 to 5 minutes.

3. Add the apples and lentils and stir to coat in oil and spices. Stir in any optional add-ins.

4. Add the coconut milk and stock and bring to a boil. Reduce the heat to a simmer, stirring occasionally, until the mixture is thick and mushy, 20 to 25 minutes. Season with salt, pepper, and lemon juice. Serve with garnishes, if desired.

5. Serve and divide the garnishes among the serving bowls.

Food 911 Did you know 1 serving (½ cup cooked) of lentils contains 9 grams of protein and 8 grams of fiber?

USES UP apples, dried lentils, coconut milk, stock, spices

SERVES 6–8

COOK TIME 25–35 minutes

KEEPS FOR up to 3 days in the fridge or 6 months in the freezer

CAN SUBSTITUTE
- Apples with pears or Asian pears
- Dried lentils with dried pigeon peas, mung beans, or split black chickpeas (cooking time may vary)

Easy Peasy Soup F P L

A pot of pea soup simmering on the back of the stove after a big ham dinner is what I call home. But I put this soup in the plant-based section because a great pea soup is just as good without the ham. When making this soup vegan, I love to bulk it up with the addition of smoked tofu and some hardy greens to wilt through at the end.

3 Tbsp oil

1 large onion, chopped

2 carrots, chopped (about 1 cup)

2 stalks celery + tops, chopped (about 1 cup)

4 cloves garlic, finely chopped

1½ cups dried split peas, rinsed (see substitutions)

6 cups Vegetable (page 187), Poultry (page 188), or Meat (page 188) Stock

2 bay leaves

1 Tbsp fresh or 1 tsp dried thyme

Salt and pepper

Optional Add-Ins

8 oz smoked ham or smoked tofu, cubed or chopped

1 cup cooked mashed potatoes, mashed turnip, or mashed cauliflower

⅓ cup chopped parsley

2 good handfuls of chopped hardy greens

Vegan Version

1 Tbsp smoked paprika

Flavor Variation

For Indian-spiced pea soup, add a heaping Tbsp finely chopped fresh ginger, 1 tsp ground turmeric, and 2 tsp curry powder (or to taste) in step 1 with the garlic.

1. In a stockpot over medium heat, add the oil and onion and sauté until softened. Add the carrots, celery, and garlic and continue to sauté for an additional 5 minutes, being careful not to burn the garlic.

2. Stir in the split peas, stock, bay leaves, and thyme. Season with salt and pepper. Bring to a boil, reduce to a simmer, and let cook for about 20 minutes or until the split peas are tender. You can add some water or additional stock if you feel it's a little too thick.

3. Stir in the protein mashed potatoes (if using), and greens. Simmer until the greens are wilted. Stir in the chopped parsley, if using. Taste and season with more salt and pepper if needed.

4. If making the vegan version, stir in a heaping tablespoon of smoked paprika.

5. Remove the bay leaves and serve.

USES UP split peas, vegetables, cooked ham or tofu, stock

MAKES 6 servings

TOTAL TIME 35–45 minutes

KEEPS FOR up to 4 days in the fridge or 6 months in the freezer

CAN SUBSTITUTE
- Dried split peas with lentils, mung beans, or pigeon peas (may change cook time slightly)

Garlicky Tahini Soup aka Tahinosoupa F P L *Recipe pictured on page 94*

I had no idea you could make a soup with tahini paste until I was all torn up over throwing a much-expired jar of tahini away. I love tahini, but it tends to come in large vats that I just never seem to get through before their best before dates. So instead of complaining about the size of the jars, I just decided to look for more ways to use it, like in this garlicky, tomatoey, lemony soup.

2 Tbsp oil

4–6 cloves garlic, finely chopped

2 stalks celery, diced

1 carrot, diced

1 cup chopped fresh or canned tomatoes with their juices

4 cups Vegetable Stock (page 187)

½ cup tahini paste

Juice of 1 lemon, divided

Salt and pepper

1 Tbsp chopped fresh soft herbs (e.g., basil or thyme)

1 cup cooked grains or pasta (optional)

1–2 packed cups chopped hardy greens

USES UP tahini paste, vegetable stock, baby spinach, chard, or kale

SERVES 4–6

TOTAL TIME 20 minutes

KEEPS FOR up to 3 days in the fridge or 6 months in the freezer

1. In a saucepot over medium heat, add the oil and sauté the garlic until translucent, about 3 minutes.

2. Stir in the tomatoes, celery, and carrots and saute for about 3 minutes to soften. Add the vegetable stock and bring to a simmer. Cook for about 5 minutes.

3. In a medium-size bowl, mix the tahini with half of the lemon juice and then stir in 1 cup of the hot soup. Pour the tahini-soup mixture back into the saucepot and whisk well. Season with salt, pepper, and additional lemon juice to taste.

4. Stir in the chopped herbs and, if desired, cooked grains and greens and continue to cook until the greens are just wilted.

Armenian Lentil Soup   P   F

Oh, the many things we can do with lentils. I had such a hard time scaling back the lentil recipes for this book. This one, though, had to stay. There are a lot of ingredients listed here, but the method is simple. The ingredients are what makes this soup so special, so robust, and such a powerhouse of a meal. You've got to give this one a shot, and have it vegan or not!

2 cloves garlic, finely chopped

1 cup dried lentils, rinsed

4–5 cups Vegetable (page 187), Poultry (page 188), or Meat (page 188) Stock

½ cup chopped dried apricots

3 Tbsp olive oil

½ cup chopped onion

1 lb ground meat or crumbled tofu (optional)

½ tsp ground cinnamon

¼ tsp ground allspice

¼ tsp cayenne

1 Tbsp ground turmeric

1–2 tsp ground cumin

Salt and pepper

1–2 cups chopped cabbage (optional)

1 bell pepper, diced

3½ cups chopped fresh or canned tomatoes

4 cups chopped eggplant, cut into ½-inch cubes (about 1 medium-size eggplant)

1 Tbsp sugar (optional)

1 Tbsp vinegar

2 cups packed fresh or frozen hardy greens (optional)

Optional Garnishes

4 dollops of sour cream or yogurt

2 Tbsp chopped Moroccan Preserved Lemons (page 204)

Chopped chives, cilantro, and/or parsley

1. In a large saucepot, combine the garlic, lentils, stock, and apricots and bring to a boil. Reduce to a simmer and cook, covered, for 20 minutes.

2. In the meantime, preheat another saucepot over medium heat. Add the oil and the onion. Cook until the onion softens, about 3 minutes. If using ground meat or tofu, add it now and let brown slightly, about 5 minutes. Sir in the cinnamon, allspice, cayenne, turmeric, and cumin and continue to sauté another 2 minutes. Season with a pinch of salt and pepper.

3. If adding cabbage, add it now with the bell pepper, tomatoes, eggplant, sugar, and vinegar and bring to a simmer for 10 minutes.

4. Pour the vegetable mixture into the lentil mixture and let simmer for an additional 30 minutes. Taste and adjust the seasonings with salt, pepper, sugar, or cayenne. If adding greens, add them at the end to wilt and heat through.

5. Serve and divide the garnishes among the serving bowls.

Food 911 Legumes can foam a little bit when cooking. Not to worry. This will not impart any odd flavor to your dish.

USES UP lentils, eggplant, tomatoes, ground meat or tofu

SERVES 4

TOTAL TIME 1 hour

KEEPS FOR up to 3 days in the fridge or 6 months in the freezer

Zero-Waste Tips from Bob Blumer

You might know Bob Blumer as the creator and host of the Food Network's Surreal Gourmet *and* Glutton for Punishment. *He's also a cookbook author and an ambassador for Second Harvest in Toronto, and Love Food, Hate Waste, a national zero-waste initiative, and at last count, he holds eight Guinness World Records!*

Q. You have been in the food, TV, and media business for some time now. What have you seen change (or not change) when it comes to food waste and food waste awareness?

A. Ten years ago, it wasn't uncommon to see shoppers exiting the grocery store carrying several plastic bags—even doubling them up if the groceries were heavy. In retrospect, it's hard to fathom how no one realized that the 3 billion plastic bags a year we were using had to go somewhere. Of course, now we know they were draining resources and wreaking havoc on the ecosystem. Today, it's heartening to know that bringing reusable bags to the grocery store is second nature for most people.

Now it's time to do the same thing for kitchen waste. Until very recently, most consumers never stopped to think about the impact that wasted food has on the environment. And some people still haven't heard the news. But the sad truth is that more than one-third of all the food we produce is wasted somewhere along the pipeline. And consumers are the ones who waste the most.

Unlike so many other issues that affect us, but leave us feeling helpless because we can't do anything about them, food waste at home is 100% in our control. And the choices we make on our plates have a direct effect on the planet.

Q. You are a spokesperson for Love Food, Hate Waste Canada, which is a website and campaign provided by the National Zero Waste Council. I guess that means you know a thing or two about keeping a waste-free kitchen! Can you share how you approach shopping and cooking at home when it comes to waste-free living?

A. Food waste really is one of those problems where little changes can make a big difference. For example, if every household in North America rescued and repurposed that last ⅛ of an onion a week—you know, the one that's easier to toss out rather than wrap up—it would save more than 17 million onions a week. That's powerful math.

Q. What are some foods that make you cringe when you see them being thrown away?

A. Fennel fronds, beet tops, celery tops, etc. All of these can be used in pestos, soups, stews, and my personal favorite, frittatas (or as I like to call them Free•ttatas™).

Q. Can you share a tip you use to help prevent food waste?

A. If you need some extra incentive, imagine that there is a surveillance camera focused on you in the kitchen. It's a lot harder to be lazy and toss perfectly repurposable ingredients when you know your friends—and the world—are watching.

Q. You have had many culinary adventures around the world. How has this affected your views on food waste?

A. Watching how people in other cultures respect their food, and use every bit of it, is inspiring.

Q. What is the biggest piece of advice you can give for those who are starting their zero-waste journey?

A. Don't be hard on yourself. We are just now becoming aware of the magnitude and impact of the problem. But now that we are aware, it's time we educate ourselves.

Dips: 3 Ways F P

Dips are easy to buy but just as easy to make, and you can make it creamy or chunky and flavor it to your liking. Dips can also use up legumes, which nicely bind the other fresh or cooked ingredients together. I bet if you look in your pantry or fridge right now you can drum up a few things to whip a good dip together. A can of beans, some frozen peas, a few random veggies, and that wrinkled tomato are screaming for you to dive in. Here are three easy dip recipes to get your creative juices flowing.

MOJITO PEA HUMMUS

1½ cups (about 11 oz) fresh or frozen thawed peas (for a quick thaw, run under cool water)
¼ cup chopped fresh mint
¼ cup chopped fresh basil

Zest and juice of 1 lime
2 Tbsp extra-virgin olive oil
¼ tsp cayenne
Salt and pepper
Pinch of sugar (optional)

USES UP peas, mint, basil, citrus

MAKES a little over 1 cup

TOTAL TIME 5 minutes

KEEPS FOR up to 3 days in the fridge

1. In a food processor or blender, pulse all of the ingredients until the hummus reaches your desired consistency, super smooth or chunky. You can always add a splash of water or more olive oil to loosen it up. If it is too thin, add more peas.

2. Taste and adjust the seasoning. If it's too sweet, add more lime juice; if too sour, add a pinch of sugar.

TOASTED GARLIC ROSEMARY CANNELLINI DIP

⅓ cup olive oil
2 Tbsp finely chopped fresh rosemary
2 cloves garlic, finely chopped
One 14 oz can cannellini beans, drained and rinsed

1 Tbsp citrus zest
1–2 Tbsp citrus juice
Salt and pepper
⅓ cup crumbled goat cheese or feta cheese (optional)

USES UP beans, goat cheese, citrus

MAKES 1½ cups

TOTAL TIME 15 minutes

KEEPS FOR up to 3 days in the fridge

1. Place the oil in a small saucepot over medium-high heat. Once the oil is hot, add the rosemary and garlic to infuse. Cook until the garlic starts to turn golden brown, about 5 minutes. Do not let the garlic burn. Once the garlic is browned, transfer the infused oil to a bowl to cool slightly, about 5 minutes.

2. In a blender or food processor, pulse the beans with the infused oil, citrus zest and juice, salt, and pepper.

3. Stir in the goat cheese for added texture and taste. Adjust seasonings if necessary.

BEET IT BLACK BEAN SALSA

1 beet, peeled and grated (about 1 cup)

½ red onion, finely chopped (about ¼ cup)

2 cloves garlic, finely chopped

1 cup chopped fresh tomatoes or canned, drained and chopped tomatoes

Zest and juice of half a lime

One 14 oz can black beans, drained and rinsed

2 Tbsp chopped fresh cilantro, basil, parsley, and/or mint

1 jalapeño, ribs and seeds removed, finely diced

Salt and pepper

Optional Add-Ins

½ cup fresh or thawed frozen corn kernels

½ cup chopped bell peppers

½ cup chopped tomatillos

¼ cup diced mangoes or peaches

1 chopped avocado

USES UP beets, black beans, tomatoes

MAKES over 3 cups

TOTAL TIME 5 minutes

KEEPS FOR up to 3 days in the fridge. If it gets a little watery, drain off the liquid.

1. In a medium-size bowl, combine all of the ingredients. Toss to coat. Taste and adjust the seasoning.

ALL ABOUT DIPS

Dip and chips? Dip and veggies? The combinations are endless. Here are some of my favorites items to pair these dips with:

- Assortment of chopped vegetables (e.g., cucumbers, carrots, radishes, zucchini sticks, etc.) aka crudités
- Assortment of deli meat or dry cured meats (e.g., ham, salami, prosciutto, chorizo etc.) aka charcuterie
- I'm Feeling Crackers (page 181)
- Pizza Chips (page 180)
- Crispy Rice Crepes (page 172)

You can also spread these dips on sandwiches, in wraps, or add to your next tacos (page 136).

Aquafaba: 2 Ways P L

What is aquafaba? Aquafaba is the leftover water (aqua) in which legumes (faba) have been cooked. Aquafaba sure sounds better than bean water, doesn't it? You will start seeing this curious item listed on vegan restaurant menus more and more, as it is the ultimate vegan replacement for egg whites. Chickpea aquafaba (below) is most commonly used in place of egg whites for baking. It is clear with a yellow tinge (like eggs) and is less beany in flavor than, say, black bean liquid. Aquafaba can be used in, for example, the Chili Yogurt Cornbread (page 69), Pancakes (page 240), Dried Plum Brownies (page 222), or Raspberry Financiers (page 224). Whipped aquafaba is also great for items such as egg white foam in fancy cocktails. Just don't make the mistake of using it as a direct egg replacement. This does not make for scrambled eggs.

AQUAFABA

One 14 oz can chickpeas, undrained

1. Drain the can of chickpeas, setting aside the liquid and storing the chickpeas for another use (hummus, anyone?). Use 3 tablespoons of the liquid in place of 1 whole egg, or 2 tablespoons in place of 1 egg white.

WHIPPED AQUAFABA

About ¾ cup aquafaba (above)
1 tsp cream of tartar

1. Combine the aquafaba and cream of tartar. Using a handheld or stand mixer fitted with the whisk attachment, whip to the desired peak stage and incorporate into your chosen recipe.

Food 911 If you are using aquafaba from salted beans, decrease the amount of salt you add elsewhere in the recipe.

USES UP aquafaba

MAKES 1 egg or egg white replacement

TOTAL TIME 1 minute

KEEPS FOR Up to 3 days in the fridge or 2 months in the freezer. Ice cube trays are great for freezing liquids into smaller portions to defrost as needed. Just add 1 Tbsp aquafaba in each ice cube cell and thaw when needed.

USES UP aquafaba

MAKES about 1½ cups

TOTAL TIME 3–10 minutes (depending how firm you want your whip)

KEEPS FOR the day of— it's best to use up right away!

Zero–Waste Tip Leftover nut pulp is a bonus! For the frugal and adventurous, dehydrate the reserved pulp for 4 hours at 115°F in a dehydrator or about 2 hours at 200°F, or lowest setting, in a conventional oven. Cool, then transfer to a blender or food processer to grind into flour. You can also experiment when baking by adding it to your next pancake, muffin, or loaf.

Plant-Based Milks `F` `P`

If you've got a cup of nuts, seeds, oats, or coconut, you've got milk! Fresh and frothy homemade dairy-free milk alternatives are way easier than you think. And homemade nut and seed milks are easy, affordable, and all around waste-free. Plus, you get to personalize them. You want unsweetened vanilla cashew milk? Sure! Or, how about cinnamon hemp milk? You got it. What about an almond pumpkin pie–spiced milk sweetened with a little stevia? Yep, you're covered.

Any nut milk will benefit from the nuts being soaked overnight. However, note that softer nuts like cashews can be used with only an hour or two of soaking if you are pressed for time. Here are some general soak times to guide you:

Almonds: 12–48 hours

Brazil nuts: No soaking required

Cashews: 2–24 hours

Hazelnuts: 12–48 hours

Macadamias: 6–12 hours

Peanuts: 6 hours

Pecans: 4–6 hours

Pistachios: No soaking required

Pumpkin seeds: 6–12 hours

Alternative Milk Source

1 cup nuts or pumpkin seeds, soaked, rinsed, and drained (see note) OR

1 cup oats OR

1 cup hemp seeds OR

2 cups unsweetened flaked or shredded coconut OR

Any combination of the above

Base

4 cups cold water

Pinch sea salt

Flavor Variation

1 Tbsp Pure Vanilla Extract (page 212)

1 tsp ground cinnamon

½ tsp ground nutmeg

¼ tsp ground allspice

1 tsp ground ginger

¼ tsp ground cardamom

4 drops stevia, or to taste

Drizzle of maple syrup or honey or 2–4 pitted dates

¼ cup berries (for berry-flavored milk)

1. In a large jar or container, add the desired plant-based milk source and immerse in water. If needed, soak at room temperature or in the fridge for 8 to 12 hours or overnight (see introduction).

2. Drain and rinse the milk source well. Place in a blender with the cold water, salt, and any additional flavorings. Using the highest setting, blend until smooth, 1 to 3 minutes.

3. Strain the milk through a strainer lined with a double layer of cheesecloth or through a nut milk bag draped over a bowl. Twist the fabric from the top down to squeeze out as much milk as possible. Reserve the pulp for another use (see tip).

4. Pour into a clean glass jar or jug with lid, such as a recycled glass milk jug.

USES UP nuts, seeds, oats, unsweetened shredded or flaked coconut

MAKES 4 cups

TOTAL TIME 2 minutes (+ 0–24 hours, for soaking)

KEEPS FOR up to 1 week in the fridge

Fish and Seafood

I f there is one thing I struggle with, it's versatile recipes for using up leftover fish and shellfish. Every seafood recipe you read says "use the freshest possible." That's all fine and dandy, but rarely do I say, "tonight I will cook a whole fresh fish," as I negotiate finding something sustainable and reasonably priced on the way home from a 12-hour workday. I love seafood. I grew up near the ocean for goodness' sake, where I ate seafood almost every day. But let me tell you, even though there was an abundance of gloriously fresh fish a lot of the time, the fish we ate at home was often frozen. I distinctly remember a freezer full of halibut lasting us for what seemed like forever. These days, the prices are so high for fresh sustainable seafood that when I buy it, it's for something really special or it's on sale. One thing I needed while writing this book was recipes that use frozen sustainable seafood AND recipes that use up fresh- or cured-seafood and/or transform cooked leftovers.

The Whole Fish M F

It sounds intimidating to cook a whole fish. But cooking a whole fish is easier than cooking its parts, and it's truly a zero-waste meal: fish bones become fish stock (page 189), and leftover cooked fish can be used in many recipes, including Nan's Fish Cakes (page 117). Here are a few more incentives to get you hooked on the whole fish: 1) It's more flavorful. 2) You can guarantee your fish is fresher (by the clear eyes and bright-pink gills). 3) It looks cool. 4) A five-minute prep time. 5) You can buy a whole fish that is already cleaned, gutted, and scaled for cooking whole, and if not just ask a fishmonger as they will prep it for roasting or grilling whole and will probably tell you a bunch of fantastic tips on how to cook it.

Whole fish, cleaned and scaled
Olive oil or high smoke point oil if grilling
Salt and pepper
Lemon, lime, and/or orange slices

Optional Seasonings

Herby: dill, basil, oregano, lemongrass, lime leaves, mint, parsley, thyme, tarragon, sage, lemon verbena

Aromatic: celery tops, sliced fennel, garlic cloves, ginger slices, sliced onions, etc.

Spicy: cumin, coriander, curry leaves, curry powder, sumac, etc.

Briny: capers, fennel, olives, sundried tomatoes

1. Preheat the oven the oven to 375°F or grill to medium-high heat.

2. Rinse your fish and pat dry. Using a sharp knife, score the fish skin (not too deeply) 3 to 5 times vertically across the fish, about 1 inch apart. This helps the fish cook more evenly and helps flavors infuse deeper into the flesh.

3. Brush the oil inside the cavity and on the outside of the fish. Season inside and out with salt and pepper.

4. Stuff the cavity with the desired seasonings. If necessary, depending on the size and shape of your fish, you can secure fish closed with toothpicks or tie it up with cooking twine.

5. If baking, grease a baking dish and set aside. If you have additional seasonings you would like to use up, you can use them in the baking dish as a flavor bed for the fish.

6. Place the fish in the prepared dish or on the hot grill and roast or grill for 15 to 20 minutes (time will vary depending on size) or until the fish flakes easily with a fork and the internal temperature is 135°F. If grilling, flip halfway through the cooking time. For smaller whole fish, check after 15 minutes.

USES UP whole fish

SERVES depends on size of fish (allow 1 lb whole fish per person)

TOTAL TIME 20–25 minutes (depending on size)

KEEPS FOR up to 3 days in the fridge

Food 911 To avoid the fish skin sticking to your grill, make sure your grill is hot, clean, and oiled. Wait until one side is nicely browned before flipping the fish. Fish baskets are a great grilling tool since they keep the fish and its stuffed contents intact when flipping.

Rustic Coconut Fish Stew M F

Traveling in the Dominican Republic, I noticed that all of the grocers carry lots of frozen white fish. Fresh fish was less common, and I was told to pull over if I saw fresh fish being sold on the side of the road. The fish of choice there seems to be dorado, aka mahi-mahi, but any lean white fish, shrimp, or even chicken works, and this dish will soon transport you to the beautiful sunny beaches of the Dominican Republic. Typically made with fresh ingredients, this rich flavorful stewp (not quite stew, not quite soup), traditionally known as Pescado con Coco, is so versatile that you can add any frozen fish and seasonal veggies. Enjoy this on its own, with some toasted bread, or served over rice, rice and beans, quinoa, barley, potatoes of any kind, cooked plantains, rice noodles, or even mashed avocado.

¼ cup orange, lemon, or lime juice

1 Tbsp dried oregano

1 tsp ground coriander

1 tsp ground cumin

1 tsp paprika

4 cloves garlic, crushed

Salt and pepper

2 lb lean white fish, cut into large chunks (see substitutions)

2 Tbsp oil

1 large or 2 small onions, diced

2 cubanelle peppers (or any bell or field peppers), diced

1 cup chopped tomato, fresh or canned

2 cups chopped vegetables

One 14 oz can coconut milk

Optional Add-Ins

¼ cup chopped soft herbs

Citrus zest, to taste

Handful of chopped hardy greens

Handful of snap or snow peas, corn, or peas

Hot sauce or Hawaiian Chili Water (page 195), to taste

1. In a large bowl, mix the citrus juice with the oregano, coriander, cumin, paprika, garlic, and salt and pepper. Add the fish, mix to coat, and set aside. This can be done up to 1 hour ahead of time.

2. Preheat a large saucepot or Dutch oven over medium-high heat. Add the oil and sauté the onions for about 3 minutes until golden brown.

3. Add the peppers and tomato and continue to cook, about 3 minutes. Add the vegetables, and continue to sauté until the vegetables are slightly softened, about 5 minutes.

4. Stir in the coconut milk, add the coated fish, and mix. Bring to a boil, then reduce to a simmer. Continue to simmer until the fish and vegetables are cooked and the sauce is thickened, about 20 minutes.

5. Stir in any optional add-ins. Taste and adjust the seasoning with hot sauce, salt, pepper, or citrus zest.

USES UP white fish, vegetables

SERVES 6

TOTAL TIME 35 minutes

KEEPS FOR up to 3 days in the fridge or 3 months in the freezer

CAN SUBSTITUTE
- White fish with shrimp or chicken

Bouillabaisse M F L

Bouillabaisse sounds lavish, but it really is just a fish stew. It's the classic and tasty addition of saffron and fennel that makes it memorable. Traditionally it calls for a minimum of three kinds of seafood, including one shellfish. It's a great recipe if you have leftover cooked shellfish such as shrimp, lobster, crab, etc. Just go for whatever is seasonally available.

3 Tbsp oil

1 onion, diced

1 leek, white and light-green parts only, thinly sliced

3 cloves garlic, finely chopped

1 large or 2 small fennel bulbs, diced (save fronds for garnish)

2 cups chopped fresh or canned tomatoes

1 Tbsp chopped fresh tarragon (see substitutions)

1 bay leaf

Pinch saffron

1 cup diced potatoes (see substitutions)

Splash Ricard or Pernod (optional)

4–5 cups Fish Stock (page 189)

Salt and pepper

2½ lb combined fish and/or shellfish (if using shrimp, peel and devein)

Optional Garnishes

Fresh parsley, chopped

Handful of fresh fennel fronds

1. Preheat a stockpot over medium heat. Add the oil and sauté the onion and leek until translucent. Add the garlic and fennel and continue to cook until softened, 3 to 5 minutes.

2. Stir in the tomatoes, herbs, bay leaf, saffron, potatoes, and Ricard, if using. Bring to a simmer.

3. Add the stock and salt and pepper. Bring to a simmer until the potatoes are tender.

4. Add the fresh raw fish or shellfish or any already cooked seafood. Simmer until everything is just cooked through. Taste and adjust the seasoning. Garnish with the fennel fronds and, if desired, parsley.

Food 911 With leeks, why do you tend to see "white and light-green parts only"? The dark-green parts of leeks have a tough texture but are full of flavor. Add them to your next stock, chop them for a long braise, or use as an aromatic bed for roasted fish or chicken.

Leeks are sandy. They need to be washed well before using. Chop and place them in a large bowl of cold water or cut them in half lengthwise, keeping the root end intact, and rinse under cold water using your hands to get the grit out from between the layers.

Zero-Waste Tip Fennel bulbs have long stalks that are too tough to eat but extremely flavorful, just like the tough dark green parts of leeks, so save them for stocks. Fennel fronds double as herbs that taste as good as they look.

USES UP cooked or raw seafood and shellfish

SERVES 4

TOTAL TIME 50 minutes

KEEPS FOR up to 3 days in the fridge and 6 months in the freezer

CAN SUBSTITUTE
- Tarragon with other fresh herbs such as thyme or chives
- Potatoes with any other root vegetables

Maritime Seafood Chowder `F` `L`

Precious chunks of seafood bathing in a pool of creamy broth. There really is nothing quite like a hot, steaming bowl of chowder. Chowder is also a great way to use up leftover cooked seafood, so don't be afraid to halve this recipe to adapt it to the amount of leftovers you have.

6 oz (about 6 slices) bacon, chopped (see substitutions)

1 onion, finely chopped

2 cloves garlic, finely chopped

1 stalk celery, finely diced

1 carrot, finely diced (½ cup)

½ cup chopped green pepper (optional)

1 cup chopped leeks (white and light-green parts only) (optional)

½ cup finely chopped fennel (optional)

1 bay leaf

1 Tbsp finely chopped or puréed fresh or 1 tsp ground turmeric

¼ tsp ground or freshly grated nutmeg

¼ tsp cayenne

Splash white wine (optional)

2 cups diced potatoes

6 cups Fish Stock (page 189) (see substitutions)

2 Tbsp finely chopped parsley stems

Salt and pepper

2 cups milk (see substitutions)

1 cup light or heavy cream (see substitutions)

2 lb cubed or chopped fresh fish or cooked fish or shellfish (see substitutions)

Optional Add-Ins

1 Tbsp chopped tarragon

1 Tbsp thyme leaves

1 cup fresh or frozen peas and/or corn

Garnish

Fennel fronds (optional)

1. In a large saucepot over medium heat, brown the bacon until crisp, about 8 minutes. Transfer the bacon to a plate.

2. In the same saucepot with the bacon fat, over medium heat, sauté the onion, garlic, celery, and carrot and, if using, the pepper, leeks, and fennel until softened. Stir in the bay leaf, turmeric, nutmeg, and cayenne. Add the white wine, if using.

3. Add the potatoes, fish stock, parsley stems, and salt and pepper. Simmer until the potatoes are cooked through, about another 10 minutes.

4. Stir in the milk and cream, and bring to a simmer.

5. Add the seafood. If using raw seafood, simmer until cooked through. Add the optional add-ins. If using cooked or smoked seafood, cook until warmed through, about 3 minutes. Add the crispy bacon. Remove the bay leaf. Taste and adjust the seasoning.

6. Garnish with the fennel fronds, if desired.

Food 911 Corn cobs and/or silks simmered in a simple broth makes it subtly sweet and milky. So it makes sense to throw them into a corn, seafood chowder, or veggie soup. Just discard before serving.

USES UP cooked or raw fish or seafood

SERVES 6

TOTAL TIME 30 minutes

KEEPS FOR up to 3 days in the fridge or 3 months in the freezer

CAN SUBSTITUTE
- Bacon with 3 Tbsp oil or butter
- Some of the fish with smoked fish
- Milk + cream with coconut milk + broth
- Fish stock with Poultry (page 188) or Vegetable (page 187) Stock

Seafood Scramble F L

A pile of steamy scrambled eggs tossed with shrimp or smoked salmon is one great way to ease the pain of last night's festivities, and use up its leftovers at the same time. Add some thick toasted sourdough and sprouts, and you've got a stellar breakfast sandwich. Either way results in a happy belly ready to take on another day.

3 eggs
Salt and pepper
Oil
1 cup chopped cooked seafood or
    smoked fish
2 green onions, finely chopped
2 Tbsp chopped chives, dill, parsley,
    or basil (optional)

Optional Garnishes
Sprouts
Spinach or mixed lettuce greens
Toasted buttered bread, for serving

USES UP eggs, cooked seafood, smoked fish

SERVES 2

TOTAL TIME 10 minutes

KEEPS FOR the day of

1. In a bowl, beat the eggs with the salt and pepper until frothy.

2. Preheat a sauté pan over medium heat and add enough oil to coat the bottom of the pan.

3. Pour in the eggs and as they settle and cook around the edges, use a heatproof spatula to pull the set eggs into the middle of the pan, letting the uncooked eggs run to the outer edges of the pan. This makes the scrambled eggs fluffy.

4. Add the seafood, green onions, and herbs if using, and fold in until the eggs are cooked to your liking and seafood is warmed through.

5. Top with sprouts or spinach, if desired. Serve with toasted buttered bread.

Nan's Fish Cakes F L

Newfoundland cod cakes were and still are a staple growing up on the East Coast of Canada. Traditionally made with salt cod and crumbled saltine crackers, now they have advanced to fresh cooked fish and potatoes. I'm picky about my cod cakes though, for two very specific reasons. They often have: 1) WAY too much potato and not enough fish. 2) Not enough seasoning, making for bland fish cakes. These down-home favorites, on the other hand, are packed with fish seasoned to perfection—match made in heaven for leftover fish and potatoes.

2 cups (about ¾ lb) cooked mashed potatoes (see substitutions)

¼ cup finely chopped onions

¼ cup finely chopped celery tops (see substitutions)

2 Tbsp chopped fresh parsley and/or parsley stems

2 Tbsp chopped fresh dill (see substitutions)

1 tsp smoked paprika

⅛ tsp ground or freshly grated nutmeg

1 egg, beaten

2 good pinches of salt

Pinch pepper

1 lb cooked boneless skinless salmon, cod, trout (any white fish really), flaked (see substitutions)

¼ cup oil or butter

Optional Add-Ins

2 tsp ground sumac

Chili powder

Citrus zest

Favorite hot sauce

For Serving (Optional)

Chow Chow (page 199)

Best Tartar Sauce (page 197)

USES UP cooked fish, cooked potatoes, celery tops

MAKES twelve 2½-inch cakes

TOTAL TIME 30 minutes

KEEPS FOR up to 3 days in the fridge (cooked), or up to 3 days in the fridge or 3 months in the freezer (uncooked). Thaw in the fridge overnight before cooking.

CAN SUBSTITUTE
- Cooked fish with well-soaked salt cod, cooked 5 minutes in boiling water and drained well
- Potatoes with ½ cup dry breadcrumbs (page 182) or crushed crackers
- Dill with savory, thyme, sage, chives, oregano, or curry powder
- Celery tops with bell pepper

1. In a large mixing bowl, combine the mashed potatoes with the onions, celery tops, parsley, dill, paprika, nutmeg, and any optional add-ins.

2. Mix in the egg, salt, and pepper. Fold in the flaked fish.

3. Using your hands, portion out about ¼ cup of the mixture. Form it into a fish cake about 2 to 3 inches in diameter and 1 inch thick and place on the baking sheet. Repeat with the rest of the mixture. If you have the time, place in the fridge for 20 minutes to allow them to firm up and hold their shape better during frying.

4. Preheat a large cast-iron pan or sauté pan over medium heat. Add the oil and fry the cakes until well browned on both sides, 7 to 9 minutes total.

5. Make your meal a real East Coast one and serve the fish cakes with some Chow Chow (page 199) and the Best Tartar Sauce (page 197).

Neptune's Pasta `F` `P` `L`

Have canned tuna in the cupboard or leftover cooked seafood? Here's a recipe that is known for making use of a little bit of seafood you have on hand and stretching it a long way. Think of this as a seafood version of aglio e olio *(garlic and olive oil spaghetti) with the welcome addition of lemon and dill.*

3–4 Tbsp olive oil

½ cup finely chopped onions or shallots

2–3 cloves garlic, finely chopped

1 tsp hot chili pepper flakes (optional)

1 Tbsp lemon zest and lemon juice

1–2 cans of tuna (6 oz each), drained and flaked (see substitutions)

2½ cups cooked pasta or 4 oz dried pasta, cooked (see substitutions)

2 Tbsp chopped fresh dill

Salt and pepper

Optional Garnishes

Hot chili oil

Olive oil

Parmesan cheese, grated

1. In a large sauté pan over medium heat, add the oil and sauté the onions until softened, about 3 minutes. Add the garlic and continue to cook until softened, about 3 minutes. Lower the heat if the garlic starts to burn, but a little toasty is OK. Add the chili flakes, if using.

2. Stir in the lemon zest and juice and cook for 1 minute. Stir in the flaked tuna.

3. Stir the cooked pasta to coat in the Neptune's sauce, fold in fresh dill, season with salt and pepper to taste, and garnish as desired.

Zero-Waste Tip   How do you buy canned tuna that is safe for the planet? At the moment our best option is "pole and line" or "troll"-caught tuna. The terms "wild caught" and "dolphin safe" don't really mean much when it comes to sustainability. Also look for the MSC-certified label.

USES UP canned tuna, cooked seafood, pasta

SERVES 2

TOTAL TIME 30 minutes

KEEPS FOR up to 2 days in the fridge

CAN SUBSTITUTE
- Canned tuna with 1 to 2 cups raw or cooked seafood (if using raw seafood, sauté until cooked all the way through)
- Pasta with one 3-pound spaghetti squash, roasted and forked to resemble pasta, or zucchini noodles

Pizza Chips (page 180)

Roasted Garlic
Brandade
(see right)

Salt Cod Ceviche
(page 122)

Smoky Seafood
Spread (page 122)

Fish Dips: 3 Ways F L

If you are from Portugal, Spain, or Newfoundland, you know how valuable salt and smoked fish can be thanks to the rainbow of recipes that stem from it. Its lengthier shelf life and low cost are very appealing. Here are three recipes that use salt cod and smoked trout, and while ceviche is not something you really would think of making with salt cod, this old-school Portuguese recipe has made it new school. Enjoy with Pizza Chips (page 180) or see some other serving suggestions on page 101.

ROASTED GARLIC BRANDADE

1 garlic bulb

¼ cup olive oil (+ extra for drizzling)

1 lb salted cod, cut into chunks and soaked in fresh water for 18–24 hours (change water at least twice during this soak)

1 onion, peeled and halved

4 whole cloves

1 bay leaf

4 whole parsley sprigs

3 sprigs fresh thyme

½ lb potatoes, cubed, or 2 cups cooked potatoes, mashed (see substitutions)

½ cup heavy cream or half milk and half cream

¼ tsp ground or freshly grated nutmeg

Pinch cayenne

Salt and pepper

Optional Add-Ins

1 Tbsp chopped parsley and/or rosemary

Celery tops, chopped

Lemon zest

1. Preheat the oven to 425°F. Slice the pointy top off the garlic bulb to expose the cloves without cutting into them too deeply. Place the garlic on a small baking tray and drizzle with a little oil to coat. Season with salt and roast until golden brown, about 20 minutes.

2. Drain the cod and transfer to a saucepot. Pour in just enough water to cover. Take your onion and press the cloves into it. Add the clove-studded onion, bay leaf, parsley, and thyme to the saucepot. Bring the mixture to a boil, then lower to a simmer. Cook for 5 minutes or until cooked through. With a slotted spoon, remove the fish and set aside to cool. Once cool, pick out any remaining bones and skin.

3. Meanwhile, cook the potatoes in the same pot with the same water until soft. Drain and give them a quick mash.

4. Squeeze the inside of the garlic cloves to form the roasted garlic purée. With a hand mixer or stand mixer fitted with the paddle attachment, beat the potatoes with the roasted garlic purée and cod, adding enough cream to make a good mash. Add the nutmeg, cayenne, and a drizzle of olive oil and continue to beat until you have more of a purée. Season with salt and pepper and add the optional add-ins.

USES UP cooked potatoes, salt fish, garlic

SERVES 6–8 as an appetizer

TOTAL TIME 35 minutes (+ 18–24 hours soak time)

KEEPS FOR up to 3 days in the fridge

CAN SUBSTITUTE
- Mashed potato with mashed cauliflower or rutabaga

Food 911 Look for cod carrying the blue MSC label, which certifies that it is sustainable.

SALT COD CEVICHE *Recipe pictured on page 120*

8 oz salt cod

½ cup finely chopped shallots or red onion

2 cloves garlic, finely chopped

1 Tbsp chopped chili pepper (e.g., red finger chilies or jalapeños)

½ bell pepper, finely chopped

2–3 Tbsp olive oil

Juice of half a lemon or lime

Salt and pepper

2 Tbsp chopped parsley

1. Soak the salt cod in fresh water for 18–24 hours, changing water at least twice. Drain the cod and transfer to a large bowl, shred the cod with a knife and fork.

2. In another medium-size bowl, combine the shallots, garlic, chilies, bell pepper, olive oil, and lemon juice.

4. Pour the mixture over the cod and stir. Let the cod marinate in this mixture for at least 1 hour, covered in the fridge. Taste and adjust the seasoning with salt, pepper, more olive oil, or lemon or lime juice.

USES UP salt cod

SERVES 6 as an appetizer

TOTAL TIME 15 minutes (+ 18–24 hours + 1 hour to marinate)

KEEPS FOR the day of

SMOKY SEAFOOD SPREAD *Recipe pictured on page 120*

Spread

¼ cup plain Greek yogurt (see substitutions)

¼ cup whipped cream cheese spread

1 Tbsp lemon or lime juice

1 Tbsp Dijon mustard

¼ cup finely chopped celery tops (see substitutions)

½ shallot, finely chopped (see substitutions)

1 finely chopped chipotle in adobo

Pinch cayenne or splash hot sauce

4 oz skinned and deboned smoked fish

1 Tbsp chopped fresh dill or parsley

Salt and pepper

Optional Add-Ins

1 cup cooked or canned white beans

¼ cup chopped canned artichoke hearts

¼ cup chopped roasted red peppers

3 chopped sun-dried tomatoes

1 Tbsp chopped capers or pickles

1. In a bowl, combine the yogurt, cream cheese, lemon juice, and mustard until smooth. Mix in the celery, shallot, chipotle, and cayenne.

2. Using your hands or a fork, flake the smoked fish and fold it into the mixture with the chopped dill and any optional add-ins. Season with salt and pepper to taste.

Zero-Waste Tip My daughter and I just happen to love smoked fish, so it's something I buy regularly to have on hand as a high-protein snack. We have it as is, on toast, or sprinkled on a salad. You typically can find a few kinds from smoked herring to trout, flavored or simply plain smoked, in almost every major grocer (I gravitate toward plain smoked trout).

USES UP smoked fish, cream cheese, Greek yogurt, fresh dill

SERVES 4

MAKES about 1 cup

TOTAL TIME 5 minutes

KEEPS FOR up to 3 days in the fridge. Just drain a little water off the top of the yogurt and give it a good stir before serving.

CAN SUBSTITUTE
- Greek yogurt with sour cream
- Shallots with chives or onions
- Celery tops with bell pepper or fennel

Zero-Waste Tips from Jeremy Bonia

Sommelier and restaurateur Jeremy Bonia sat down with me for a quick chat after the loveliest pot-bellied brunch at the Merchant Tavern in St. John's, the little sister of the fine dining restaurant Raymonds. Bonia co-owns both restaurants with the other Jeremy, Jeremy Charles. The number one thing you must order there for brunch? Toutons (a kind of pancake) with molasses and butter.

Q. You're a sommelier—is there any such thing as wine waste, or leftover wine? And if so, how is it repurposed?
A. Nothing gets wasted here. Our restaurants are known for being local and seasonal, especially Raymonds, where we have a reputation built on using only Canadian ingredients. If we can't source it locally, for example, greens or more delicate lettuces in winter, it's just not on the menu. Any excess of wine is used for cooking, or we make house vinegars.

Q. What is one routine or practice you use to reduce food waste?
A. We bring in whole fish and animals or large cuts of meat and break them down. Newfoundland is the only province in Canada where you can legally serve wild game (except migratory birds). When our staff sees a whole moose leg coming in to butcher, they see the value of every part, and how it is used in the menu. Any trim from seafood goes in our seafood soup, any off cuts for charcuterie, and of course, bones go to stocks. This also helps with cost control.

Q. What one thing off the menu really speaks to the vibe of the Merchant Tavern but also to a zero-food waste mentality?
A. Our seafood soup and the lamb pasta. For dessert, the vinegar pie (for my take, see page 230).

Q. We need to talk about the toutons, one of my favorite things to eat, probably ever. My mom and I made bread regularly, and we always made these with any leftover bread dough. I love that you have them on the menu. Are they made from your leftover in-house bread dough?
A. At one point, yes, this was the idea. However, the demand for them has far surpassed any leftover dough we have, so now we have to make an extra batch just for the toutons.

Q. Can you share any tips or tricks about how local restaurants cope with the long winters, harsh climate, and the limited availability of fresh local seasonal ingredients in Newfoundland?
A. Well, we have a packed freezer full of local seasonal berries. We go more towards root veggies in winter, and we source from a geothermal greenhouse close by. Some kind of seafood is available all year round, but we have to rotate based on what's available when. When the ice comes in, we know it's going to be slim pickings. Some wild game, like partridge and rabbit, can be frozen whole, and we also freeze braised meat in sauces or stocks to keep their integrity. Also, this may not be for the everyday home cook, but you can actually age fish like you would beef. The oilier species can benefit from this technique.

Q. What is the number one challenge you have had becoming a sustainable restaurant?
A. I hate to say this, but sometimes it's just cheaper to toss things. Repurposing and reinventing takes time and effort. There was a time when, if we needed milk, we had to raise a cow. We have a strong initiative here, but it doesn't come without a cost. For example, we are raising our own pigs at a farm nearby, but raising animals is work and it costs money. We offset that with feeding our veggie scraps to our pigs.

Meat and Poultry

Growing up, my father would go on seasonal hunting and fishing trips. I remember walking in the woods and my dad pointing out traps or moose tracks, and seeing rabbits hanging in the basement. We were lucky enough to have a supply of local moose, duck, cod, and rabbit in our basement's deep freezer. His influence made me feel more connected to these food sources. Today, however, it's harder to see where our meat is coming from. If we continue to eat animals, we need to be smarter about how we are farming and consuming our protein sources. Let's source them responsibly and introduce better cooking practices, like using all parts of the animal and cooking it once, dining on it twice or better yet thrice. Note that plant-based protein sources can be used in place of meat proteins in most recipes in this chapter.

Two Roast Chickens   M

Nothing is quite as comforting as perfectly roasted chicken. But why roast one chicken when you can roast two? Eat one for your dinner and use the juicy leftovers from the other throughout the week. See Mapped-Out Meals on page 34 for more details. An added bonus with whole roast chicken, you can use up the nutrient-dense giblets and odd bits (liver, kidney, gizzard, etc.) left inside your poultry in other ways (turn to page 128 for ideas).

2 whole chickens
Salt and pepper
Olive oil
½ cup butter, softened
1 onion, cut in half

6 unpeeled cloves garlic
Fresh sprigs of herbs (see note)
1 lemon, cut in half
1 knob ginger, coarsely chopped
   (optional)

USES UP the whole chicken

MAKES 2 roast chickens

TOTAL TIME 1 hour, 10 minutes, depending on size of chicken

KEEPS FOR up to 4 days in the fridge or 6 months in the freezer, stored in an airtight container with stock, gravy, or pan juices to prevent it from drying out.

1. Season both chickens with salt and pepper inside and out. If you like, refrigerate in advance (see Tip). Let the chickens come to room temperature an hour before roasting.

2. Preheat the oven to 400°F and lightly grease a pot or pan big enough for both chickens with olive oil.

3. Using your hands, at either end of the chickens, gently loosen the skin over the chickens' breasts. Divide the butter into 4 portions and wedge each pad of butter (or compound butter—see Tip) under the skin of each breast. Divide the onion, garlic, herbs, lemon, and ginger into two, and place the mixture inside each cavity.

4. Roast the chickens breast side up for 20 minutes, then gently turn them upside down and roast for another 20 minutes. Then, yes, turn them breast side up again to finish, for another 20 minutes or until the internal temperature is 165°F.

5. Let rest for 15 minutes before carving.

Food 911 Place the seasoned uncooked chickens in a covered dish and refrigerate for up to two days for an even juicier chicken with extra crispy skin. I find it easiest to do it as soon as you bring the birds home. Compound butter is also a great addition. Just mix a few table-spoons of chopped mixed herbs like fresh parsley, sage, rosemary, or thyme with a pinch of salt, pepper, and slices of garlic with ½ cup softened butter and place under the skin of the chicken before roasting.

Zero-Waste Tip Take all of the leftover chicken bones, neck, and carcass and keep them for chicken stock. Squeeze the soft purée out of the whole cloves of garlic from inside the chicken and spread on a fresh baguette or serve alongside vegetables.

Bong Bong Chicken F L

The best way to rescue last night's leftovers is to send them to some far-off land where nobody will recognize them, in witness protection if you will. Here leftover roast chicken (but you could also use pork, duck or turkey) and cool crispy cucumber are smothered in a spicy Szechuan sauce that you can serve on top of simple greens or a sprout salad, nestle in lettuce cups, or roll up in corn tortillas or a batch of Crispy Rice Crepes (page 172).

Bong Bong Dressing
1 clove garlic, finely chopped
1 tsp finely chopped or puréed fresh
   ginger
2 Tbsp red wine or rice vinegar
2 Tbsp toasted sesame oil
1 Tbsp chili oil or paste
6 Tbsp soy or tamari sauce
2 tsp ground or crushed Szechuan
   peppercorns
2 tsp sugar

Bong Bong Chicken
4 cups (about 1 lb) pulled cooked or
   roasted chicken (see substitutions)
2–3 green onions, chopped
1 cucumber, cut lengthwise into 2-inch
   sticks

Optional Garnishes
¼ cup chopped cilantro, mint, or basil
¼ cup toasted sesame seeds
Handful of peanuts, cashews, or any
   other nuts or seeds
Handful of sprouts or microgreens
   e.g., pea shoots, alfalfa, bean, or
   broccoli sprouts

1. For the Dressing: In a small bowl, whisk all of the dressing ingredients together. Taste and adjust the seasoning if necessary. If it's not sweet enough, add more sugar. If it's not spicy enough, add more chili oil.

2. For the Chicken: Plate the salad by stacking pulled roast chicken and green onions on top of the cucumber sticks. Drizzle with the dressing and garnish to your liking.

USES UP cooked protein, cucumber

SERVES 4, makes ½ cup of dressing

TOTAL TIME 15 minutes

KEEPS FOR up to 3 days in the fridge

CAN SUBSTITUTE
• Chicken with turkey, duck, or pork

FOUR WAYS TO USE YOUR GIBLETS

Giblets are free nutrient-dense proteins filled with vitamins and minerals that you can find inside whole chickens (however, this is becoming less common), but you can also ask your butcher if they have some. If you do have them, don't let them go to waste!

1. Add them to your gravy: Simmer giblets in just enough water or stock to cover with 1 chopped carrot, 2 chopped celery stalks, 1 chopped onion, 1 Tbsp peppercorns, and 4 sprigs of fresh thyme for at least 30 minutes or up to 1 hour. Strain this liquid gold and add it to your pan juices and proceed with your time-honored family gravy recipe.

2. Toss them into your next stock or broth (see page 188).

3. If you like the taste of fried liver and organ meats, slice, season, fry up, and enjoy.

4. Hide them in your next stew or batch of burgers or meatballs. Purée them in a blender or food processor and stir them into the mixture for added nutrients.

Crispy Rice Crepes
(page 172)

Bong Bong Chicken (see left)

Curried Chicken and Grape Salad `F` `L`

So simple but oh so great. I have to say that there is something quite special about this chicken salad. Maybe it's the way the layers of curry, fresh turmeric, and ginger mingle with the bright bursts of grapes and fresh peas. And it's flexible enough that you could sub in a whole bunch of different vegetables and fruits, depending what you have on hand. I strongly recommend taking the extra minute or two to make a 1-Minute Mayo (page 196) for this. Stack this on crunchy toasted sourdough, tossed greens, or tortillas.

Curry Mayo

¼ cup finely chopped red onion

½ clove garlic, finely chopped

½ tsp grated fresh ginger

1 tsp curry powder

1 Tbsp grated fresh or 1 tsp ground turmeric

1 Tbsp lemon or lime juice

½ cup mayo or 1-Minute Mayo (page 196)

Salt and pepper

Pinch cayenne

Curry Chicken Salad

2 cups (about ½ lb) pulled or chopped cooked chicken (see substitutions)

3 Tbsp finely chopped pickles or pickled vegetables

¾ cup diced celery and/or celery tops

¼ cup diced bell pepper (see substitutions)

¼ cup fresh peas (see substitutions)

½ cup halved grapes (see substitutions)

Optional Add-Ins

1 cup chopped Roasted Vegetables (page 40)

¼ cup raisins or dried cranberries

Chopped Thai basil, basil, or cilantro, to taste

1. For the Curry Mayo: In a bowl, combine all of the ingredients. Taste and adjust seasoning.

2. For the Curry Chicken Salad: In a large bowl, toss all of the salad ingredients, including your desired add-ins, and then fold in half of the curry mayo. Mix gently. Add more mayo to your liking.

Zero-Waste Tip Reserve the rest of the curry mayo to have with sandwiches, French fries, or roasted potatoes. It keeps for 3 to 4 days in the fridge.

USES UP cooked chicken, grapes, vegetables

MAKES a little over 2 cups

TOTAL TIME 20 minutes

KEEPS FOR up to 3 days in the fridge

CAN SUBSTITUTE
- Chicken with turkey
- Bell pepper and peas with any other vegetable
- Grapes with sliced apples or pears, berries, cherry tomatoes, or cubed peaches or nectarines

Dill Pickle Chicken Tenders M F L

If you're chomping on that last pickle, don't even think about dumping that jarful of puckery pickle juice. Pickle juice is a perfect brining liquid, especially for lean meats like chicken, pork, and turkey that tend to dry out and are prone to overcooking. Brining keeps meat juicy and tender. In this recipe, you have a crunchy seedy coating encrusting tender juicy dill pickle–flavored chicken.

1–2 cups pickle juice or brine

4 boneless skinless chicken breasts, cut into tenders (see substitutions)

Salt and pepper

¼ cup black sesame seeds (see substitutions)

¼ cup hemp seeds (see substitutions)

¼ cup nutritional yeast or grated Parmesan

Favorite dipping sauce, for serving

USES UP pickle juice, chicken

SERVES 4

TOTAL TIME 15 minutes + 2 hour soak time

KEEPS FOR best eaten ASAP, but up to 3 days in the fridge

CAN SUBSTITUTE
- Chicken with two blocks of tofu
- Black sesame seeds and hemp hearts with white sesame seeds (not toasted), raw chopped nuts or seeds, quinoa, crushed dill pickle chips, Breadcrumbs (page 182), or Crispy Coatings (page 183)

1. Place the brine and chicken tenders in an airtight container or reusable bag with just enough pickle brine to cover. Marinate the chicken for up to 2 hours.

2. Preheat the oven to 350°F and grease a baking sheet or line with a silicone mat.

3. Drain the chicken and season both sides with salt and pepper.

4. In another medium-size bowl, mix the seeds with the nutritional yeast. Using your hands or with a fork, take each chicken tender and coat both sides with the seed mix then place on the prepared baking sheet. The wetness from the pickle juice will be enough to help the seed coating stick.

5. Bake for 15 minutes or until internal temperature reaches 165°F. Serve with your favorite dipping sauce, like creamy dill.

Zero–Waste Tip Pickle brine can add zesty flavor to other recipes, like the Quinoa Surprise (page 169). Try adding it to your next marinade, salad dressing, dip, sauce, or even martini!

Wild Blueberry and Ginger Pulled Chicken Tacos F L

These are my favorite tacos, and bonus: they make great use of leftover roast chicken (or pulled pork or braised beef), but the secret is really in the blueberries. I grew up picking wild blueberries—my favorite berry by far—but since you can only buy them fresh for about two weeks in August, I keep a bag of frozen ones on hand year-round. This is not your average taco filling, but I swear the spicy hit of fresh ginger pairs swimmingly with the wild blueberries.

Wild Blueberry and Ginger Barbecue Sauce

½ onion, diced

2 cloves garlic, finely chopped

¼ cup finely chopped or grated fresh ginger

¼ cup ketchup

¼ cup brown sugar

¼ cup honey

1¼ cups fresh or frozen wild blueberries (see substitutions)

Salt and pepper

Pulled Chicken Filling

3 Tbsp olive oil

1 red onion, thinly sliced

2–3 cloves garlic, minced

1 bell pepper, thinly sliced

2 Tbsp Mexican Spice Mix (page 140)

½ cup Poultry Stock (page 188)

2–3 cups pulled chicken from ½ Roast Chicken (page 127) (see substitutions)

Salt and pepper

Taco shells or tortillas, for serving

1. For the Wild Blueberry and Ginger Barbecue Sauce: In a medium-size saucepot, combine all of the barbecue sauce ingredients and bring to a simmer, stirring occasionally for 10 minutes or until sauce reduces by one-third, from roughly 2 cups to 1⅓ cups.

2. Let the sauce cool slightly. You can leave the sauce chunky or transfer it to a food processor or blender and blend until the sauce is fairly smooth. Set ½ cup of the sauce aside for the pulled chicken and store the rest for another use.

3. For the Pulled Chicken Filling: In a large saucepot over medium heat, add the oil, and sauté the onion and garlic until softened.

4. Stir in the peppers and spice mix and sauté until the peppers soften.

5. Add the broth and ½ cup of the reserved Wild Blueberry Barbecue Sauce and bring to a simmer.

6. Stir in the pulled chicken and bring to a simmer. Cook until the chicken is heated through, adding more barbecue sauce or broth if necessary. Taste and season with salt and pepper.

7. Serve in taco shells with any additional toppings.

USES UP cooked meat, wild blueberries

SERVES 4, makes a little over 1 cup of dressing

TOTAL TIME 40 minutes

KEEPS FOR up to 3 days in the fridge or 6 months in the freezer for the filling, and up to 1 week in the fridge or 6 months in the freezer for the sauce

CAN SUBSTITUTE
- Chicken with pulled pork or braised beef
- Wild blueberries for regular

Food 911 Just because fresh wild blueberries are only in season for a very short time doesn't mean you can't still enjoy them year round. Frozen wild blueberries retain their antioxidant and nutritional values for up to 1 year.

Taco Tuesdays

Any day can be taco day, but on a Tuesday, you may still have some leftovers from Sunday supper that need some care. There is no better way to show your food some hot and spicy love than to stuff it into a taco. This is not a recipe but more of a road map to taco heaven, with *picante* pit stops along the way.

FIRST STOP: THE TACO SHELL
No tortilla shells? Here are a few things that you can use instead! Wraps, any edible leaves large enough to hold your fillings (e.g., lettuce, kale, or Swiss chard), seaweed, pita, roti, or even place your toppings on top of a fried egg.

SECOND STOP: THE MAIN EVENT
- Barbecued or grilled tofu (page 91)
- Browned ground meat or meat alternative
- Chili (page 141) or stew
- Fried or roasted cauliflower
- Grilled fish, shrimp, seafood
- Grilled Halloumi cheese
- Pulled pork
- Pulled roast chicken

THIRD STOP: PICK YOUR PRODUCE
- Avocado
- Barbecued corn kernels
- Charred eggplant
- Chopped grilled portobellos
- Crispy Brussels sprouts
- Grilled pineapple
- Roasted cauliflower
- Roasted sweet potato
- Sautéed mushrooms

FOURTH STOP: OFF THE BEATEN TRACK GARNISHES
- Any kind of pickle
- Crispy fried onions
- Crumbly cheeses like feta
- Kimchi, sauerkraut, and/or any other fermented vegetables
- Popcorn
- Rice and beans
- Roasted shredded coconut
- Sliced chilies

FIFTH STOP: SAUCE IT
- Beet It Back Bean Salsa (page 101)
- Favorite salad dressing
- Guacamole
- Hawaiian Chili Water (page 195)
- Pesto
- Salsas and dips
- Spicy aioli
- Yogurt/kefir

Spicy Vietnamese Cabbage and Duck Coleslaw M F L

There is no reason why coleslaw can't be a main dish with the simple addition of some protein. Don't have duck, don't worry. This recipe is adaptable to any cooked protein you have on hand. Here is a great example of how an ordinary coleslaw can spark into a spicy sumptuous, salad. Also, check out my Custom Coleslaw (page 49) recipe if you really want to get crazy with it.

Vietnamese-Style Dressing

1 clove garlic, finely chopped

1 Thai chili, seeds and ribs removed, finely chopped

Zest and juice of 1 lime

2 Tbsp finely chopped onions or shallots

2 Tbsp rice wine vinegar

2 Tbsp fish sauce

1 Tbsp toasted sesame oil

1 Tbsp honey or maple syrup (optional)

Salt and pepper

Coleslaw

2–3 cups shredded cabbage

1 cup shredded carrot

2 or more cups cooked sliced duck breast or shredded duck meat (see substitutions)

½ cucumber, diced

3 green onions, finely chopped

¼ cup chopped fresh mint (see substitutions)

¼ cup chopped nuts or seeds

USES UP cooked meat, vegetables

SERVES 4, makes about ½ cup of dressing

TOTAL TIME 15 minutes

KEEPS FOR up to 2 days in the fridge

CAN SUBSTITUTE
- Cooked duck with cooked chicken, pork, or vegan protein
- Mint with basil, Thai basil, or cilantro

1. For the Vietnamese-Style Dressing: In a small bowl, combine all of the ingredients. Adjust the seasoning to taste depending how sweet, salty, or sour you like it.

2. For the Coleslaw: In a large salad bowl, toss the cabbage with the carrot, duck, cucumber, green onions, and mint.

3. Pour the dressing over top and toss. Sprinkle with the chopped nuts or seeds and season with salt and pepper.

Ham It Up

Here are my top tips for cooking the perfect ham, along with ideas for those yummy leftovers.

WHAT AND HOW MUCH TO BUY When it comes to ham, you want about ¾ lb per person bone-in or ½ lb per person boneless. Bone-in ham has more flavor, and you can save the bone for a delicious stock (page 188), soup, or stew. Cooked ham will lasts for up to 4 days in the fridge and makes amazing leftovers, so yes, in this case, you may want to think about buying more than you need.

HOW TO PREPARE Cover the bottom of a roasting pan with about ½ cup of liquid to prevent your ham from drying out (the specific amount will depend on the size of your ham and your roasting pan). This liquid can be as simple as water or fruit juice, or you could use beer, wine, stock or any combination of the above. Each imparts a slightly different flavor, but adding the liquid is key.

HOW TO COOK Most often the ham sold in grocery stores is already cooked and/or smoked (be sure to ask your butcher if it doesn't say so on the package). So all you are really doing when "cooking" it is bringing it up to temperature and adding additional flavor. Low and slow is key: Bake at 300°F to keep your ham juicy. Make sure you position the ham, flat side down, in the roasting pan with liquid, and then cover the ham as tightly as you can with a lid or foil to retain as much moisture as you can.

HOW TO GLAZE Making your own glaze from scratch is easier than you think. All you need is a little something sweet, a little something spicy, and a little something tangy. Sweeter glazes, if left in your oven for too long, may end up burning, so set a timer to remind yourself to glaze the ham during the last 30 minutes of its cook time.

IS IT DONE YET? Rule of thumb when cooking ham is 15 minutes per pound. If you have a digital thermometer, it should read 130-140°F near the bone or in middle of ham. Make sure to let your ham rest 20 minutes before carving. Use this resting time to get your other sides and fixings finished up and plated.

EXTRA, EXTRA! Cooked ham is one of the easiest and tastiest leftovers to transform, whether it's pan-fried for breakfast, or served in a sandwich for lunch. Try it in the following recipes in this book: Ham and Cheese Hand Pies (page 174), Brussels Fried Hash (page 55), Croquettes (page 56), Easy Peasy Soup (page 96), Freestyle Paella (page 164), Callaloo (page 153), or Crispy Fried Pasta with Spicy Chorizo (page 159), or simply serve it with some delicious condiments like Chow Chow (page 199).

Perfect Roast Ham M F

Every holiday season growing up, we looked forward to my Dad's cooked ham. He would order it in advance and it came in a large metal can, so I grew up thinking ham was rectangle shaped! My mom would freeze leftovers for future soups and stews, and the rest we would enjoy in the following days. I have learned a lot about cooking ham since then; like how ham is typically round and comes with a bone!

Ham

1 (8–10lb) cooked bone-in ham (preferably smoked)

½ or more liquid (water, stock, or juice)

Optional Add-Ons

Pineapple rings, pitted cherries, or orange or mandarin slices

Whole cloves

Glaze

½ cup pineapple juice

½ cup melted butter or oil

1 cup maple syrup

2 Tbsp mustard (Dijon is my pick)

2 cloves sliced garlic

2 Tbsp chopped hardy herbs (I like to use thyme)

¼ tsp ground cinnamon

¼ tsp ground cloves

Optional Add-Ins

2–3 Tbsp jam

2 Tbsp Hawaiian Chili Water (page 195)

2 Tbsp barbecue sauce (page 197)

1 Tbsp chopped hot peppers, or to taste

1 Tbsp fresh chopped ginger

1 Tbsp mustard seeds

1 chopped chipotle in adobo

2 tsp smoked paprika

Handful of fresh or frozen chopped berries

1. Preheat the oven to 300°F.

2. Prep ham by placing it cut-side down in a roasting pan. With a sharp knife, score any fat cap with a diamond pattern and top with any of the optional add-ons: stud every few inches of the ham with cloves, or add the fruit skewered on toothpicks.

3. Pour enough liquid into the bottom of roasting pan to coat it. Cover the ham tightly with a lid or foil.

4. Bake until the internal temperature reaches 130°F to 140°F, about 15 minutes per pound (2 to 2 hours and 30 minutes in total). Carefully check the bottom of the pan a few times during cooking and add more juice as needed to keep the pan wet.

4. Meanwhile, in a small saucepot, bring all glaze ingredients to a boil and allow to thicken slightly, about 3 minutes. About 30 minutes before the ham is done, remove it from the oven and brush some of the glaze over the sides and top of ham. Return to the oven and continue to bake, uncovered, so the glaze can caramelize, glazing again if needed. Once cooked through, allow the ham to rest on a platter or board for 20 minutes.

6. If you have some glaze leftover, add any liquid remaining in the roasting pan to the saucepot of glaze. Bring to boil, then lower the heat and reduce until thickened to make additional sauce.

7. Carve the ham and serve with sauce poured over the top.

USES UP Ham, fruit juice

SERVES 8-10 (or less people plus leftovers!)

TOTAL TIME about 15 minutes per pound

KEEPS FOR up to 4 days in the fridge

CAN SUBSTITUTE
- Pineapple juice with any other juice, pop, beer, cider, stock, water, or any combination of the above
- Maple Syrup with sugar, brown sugar, agave, or honey

Mexican Spiced Pork Tenderloins M F

This recipe is simple: just meat and a spice mix. It's pork tenderloin, so it's lean and budget-friendly with no bones or fat to deal with. It cooks quickly, and I get no complaints when I ring the dinner bell. Yes, I bought a very loud annoying dinner bell at an antique store a few years ago and since nobody can stand hearing it, they all come running. You don't have to cook two tenderloins, but one sometimes is not enough for four people, and two gives you the perfect amount for leftovers for another day, perfect in tacos (page 136) or salads (see page 46). The Mexican spice mix is my all-purpose salt-free spice mix I use in soups, stews, roasted veggies, and even in a salad dressing.

No-Salt-Added Mexi-Spice Mix
4 Tbsp sweet chili powder
1 tsp chili flakes
¼ tsp cayenne
2 tsp ground cumin
1 tsp ground coriander

1 tsp garlic powder
1 tsp onion powder
1 tsp paprika
2 tsp smoked paprika
1 tsp dried oregano

Pork Tenderloins
2 pork tenderloins (1–1¼ lb each)
(see substitutions)
Salt

1. For the Mexi-Spice Mix: In a small bowl, mix all of the spices together.

2. For the Pork Tenderloins: Preheat the oven to 400°F and grease a baking sheet or line with a silicone mat.

3. Season the pork tenderloins with salt on all sides. Then season on all sides with 2 to 3 tablespoons of the Mexi-Spice Mix per pound of pork tenderloin. I like to season this liberally to create an almost crust-like seasoning.

4. Place the tenderloins on the prepared baking sheet and roast in the oven for about 20 minutes, rotating halfway through the cook time, or until the internal temperature is 145°F.

5. Let the pork rest for 5 minutes before slicing.

Food 911 You can also marinate the pork in the spice mix overnight for more of a Mexican-flavored infusion.

Zero-Waste Tip Pork tenderloins can be sliced into thick small steaks called medallions (also called a "poor man's steak"). Tenderloins are among the cheaper cuts of incredibly lean protein and are easy to prepare.

USES UP whole pork tenderloin, spices

SERVES 6, makes about ½ cup of spice mix

TOTAL TIME 30 minutes

KEEPS FOR up to 3–4 days in the fridge for the pork. The Mexican spice mix can be stored up to 6 months at room temperature.

CAN SUBSTITUTE
• Pork with chicken

A Pot of Chili M F P

As soon as I feel a chill in the air, I start craving a hearty chili. I like mine spicy, with bacon and smoked paprika, but most importantly, I like it packed with vegetables—so throw whatever you have in there (including leftover cooked proteins). Since chili is typically better the next day and freezes so well, none of it will get wasted. Freeze it in portioned containers for lunch on-the-go or a lazy weeknight dinner. Besides piling it on top of nachos, try repurposing it in other dishes, like the Packed Peppers (page 70).

About 8 oz bacon, diced

1 lb ground meat (see substitutions)

1 large onion, finely diced

2 cloves garlic, chopped

2–3 carrots, diced

2 stalks celery, diced

2 bay leaves

1 Tbsp ground cumin

1 Tbsp chili powder

1 Tbsp dried oregano

2 tsp smoked paprika

1 tsp cinnamon

½ can (about 2¼ oz) tomato paste

½–1 chipotle in adobo sauce, finely diced (optional)

2 Tbsp cocoa powder (optional)

One 14 oz can black beans, rinsed and drained or about 2 cups cooked drained black beans

3 cups Vegetable (page 187), Poultry (page 188), or Meat (page 188) Stock, divided

1 bell pepper, diced

1 cup mixed vegetables and/or vegetable stems (optional)

Salt and pepper

Optional Garnishes

1–2 tsp store-bought black bean sauce

Chives or green onions, chopped

Cilantro, chopped

Cheese, grated

Lime wedges

Sour cream, plain yogurt, or kefir

1. Line a plate with paper towel. In a Dutch oven or large saucepot, fry the bacon over medium heat until crispy. Use a slotted spoon to transfer to a plate.

2. Line another plate with a paper towel. In the same pot, brown the ground beef in the bacon fat over medium-high heat. Transfer to another plate.

3. In the same pot, sauté the onion until translucent, about 3 minutes. Stir in the garlic, carrots, and celery. Sauté for another 3 to 5 minutes until slightly softened.

4. Stir in the bay leaves, cumin, chili powder, oregano, paprika, and cinnamon and toast for 1 minute. Stir in the tomato paste and cook for 2 to 3 minutes. Stir in the chipotle and cocoa powder, if using.

5. Add the beans. Return the beef to the pot and pour in enough stock to just cover the chili. Bring to a low simmer.

6. Add the chopped pepper, mixed vegetables (if using), season with salt and pepper to taste, and simmer the chili, covered, for 15 to 20 minutes or until the vegetables are tender.

7. Stir in the bacon, taste, and adjust seasoning if necessary. Garnish as desired.

USES UP veggies, cooked or ground meat, bacon, black beans

SERVES 6

TOTAL TIME 50 minutes

KEEPS FOR up to 4 days in the fridge or up to 6 months in the freezer

CAN SUBSTITUTE
- Ground meat with cubed meat, such as cubed pork or beef, and add in step 2, or stir in leftover cooked pulled pork, chicken, or other cooked proteins in step 5

Zero-Waste Tip Leftover bacon fat? Save it in the fridge or freezer and use it to replace oil for your next pot of chili.

Veggie and Cheese–Stuffed Meatloaf M F

I never had meatloaf growing up, and the first time I had it, I was unimpressed. Not anymore! This recipe is an upgrade from the traditional. The sticky ketchup coating is replaced with salty, crunchy prosciutto, and the center is filled with layers of spinach, tender veggies, and gooey melted cheese. It really is otherworldly. And it's a great way to use up leftover cooked vegetables, and the deli meats in your meat drawer.

½ cups Breadcrumbs (page 182)

¼ cup grated fresh Parmesan cheese or nutritional yeast (+ extra for sprinkling)

½ onion, grated

1 egg, beaten

1–2 Tbsp chopped fresh or 2 tsp dried hardy herbs (mix and match)

½ tsp salt

Pinch pepper

1 lb ground meat

1 bunch spinach (see substitutions)

8 slices prosciutto (see substitutions)

1 cup grated semi-soft cheese, divided

4 cooked (blanched) carrots, sliced in half lengthwise and cut to fit length of loaf pan (see substitutions)

Olive oil, for drizzling

1. Preheat the oven to 400°F.

2. In a large bowl, stir together the breadcrumbs, Parmesan cheese, onion, egg, herbs, salt, and pepper. Add the ground meat and mix with a fork or by hand until combined. Cover well and set aside in your fridge. Can be made the day before.

3. In a pot of salted boiling water, blanch the spinach until wilted. Drain the spinach and set aside to cool. Squeeze out all of the excess water.

4. With your hands, line a loaf pan with the slices of prosciutto, leaving some overhang to wrap around the top when filled.

5. Fill the pan one-third of the way with the meat mixture. Then add a layer of grated cheese followed by the spinach and carrots. Finish with the remaining meat mixture. Pat down to form a loaf.

6. Wrap any overhanging prosciutto over top, sprinkle with Parmesan, and drizzle with olive oil.

7. Bake for 30 to 40 minutes, or until the internal temperature reaches 165°F. Let rest a few minutes before slicing.

Food 911 How about some mini meatloaves? Just use 1 slice of prosciutto per mini pan or small ramekin. Then cook them for half the time. They are great on the go.

Zero-Waste Tip Water that is left behind from steaming or blanching veggies can be used in stocks (page 187), as a base for soups (page 79), or even in smoothies.

USES UP vegetables, ground meat, cheese, breadcrumbs

MAKES 1 meatloaf or 4–6 mini meatloaves

TOTAL TIME 45 minutes

KEEPS FOR up to 4 days in the fridge or 4 months in the freezer

CAN SUBSTITUTE
- Spinach with baby spinach, or thawed frozen spinach, squeezed of excess water
- Prosciutto with thinly sliced deli ham, bresaola, or speck
- Carrots with any cooked vegetables that are not mushy, such as broccoli, cauliflower, parsnips, turnips, or green beans

Meatballs 101 F L

Everyone should know how to make meatballs, or polpette in Italian. It's an easy recipe using inexpensive ingredients, spiced to your desire, that is comforting to eat. Make a big batch one day and save some for something completely different the next. Eat them plain, served in a soup, simmered in a sauce, or stuffed in a sandwich. They are also a great catchall for little bits and pieces you may have hanging around the kitchen: nuts, seeds, pickles, grated cheese, leftover stuffing or cooked grains or veggies etc. all go great in meatballs.

Base

1 egg, beaten

¼ cup Breadcrumbs (page 182) or ½ piece bread, broken into pieces and moistened in milk, cream, or water

½ onion, grated

2–3 cloves garlic, finely chopped

3–6 Tbsp chopped fresh or 3–6 tsp dried herbs

1 tsp salt

½ tsp pepper

Optional Add-Ins

½ cup grated semi-soft cheese

½ cup grated Parmesan or nutritional yeast

¼ cup chopped nuts or seeds

2 Tbsp chopped pickles

1 Tbsp mustard or Dijon mustard

1–2 tsp chili powder or splash chili sauce

1–2 tsp smoked paprika

1–2 tsp store-bought black bean sauce Splash Worcestershire sauce

2 lb ground meat

1. Preheat the oven to 400°F.

2. In a large bowl, combine all of the base ingredients and desired optional add-ins except the ground meat. Stir to mix well.

3. Add the meat and, using your hands, mix until thoroughly combined, about 3 minutes. Portion the mixture into 2-inch meatballs or slightly flattened mini sliders. Set aside on a baking sheet.

4. Preheat an ovenproof heavy-bottomed skillet or large cast-iron pan over high heat. Add just enough oil to lightly coat the bottom of the pan. Cook the meatballs on all sides until browned, about 6 minutes. Avoid overcrowding the pan, cooking in batches if necessary. Add more oil if necessary.

5. Transfer the pan to the oven. If you don't have an ovenproof skillet, transfer the meatballs to a lined baking sheet. Bake for 10 to 15 minutes or until the internal temperature is 165°F.

Food 911 Try these with a Marinara Sauce (page 77) or instead of baking them in the oven, simmer the browned balls in your favorite tomato sauce, covered, for 45 minutes.

USES UP binders e.g., breadcrumbs, stale bread, or crackers; ground meat

MAKES 12–15 meatballs

TOTAL TIME 20–25 minutes

KEEPS FOR 3–4 days in the fridge or up to 4 months in the freezer (even better stored in a sauce)

Zero–Waste Tip Think beyond the breadcrumb. There are so many foods we can use as a binder, such as ground up unsalted crackers, plain cereal, rolled oats, or tortilla chips (see more breadcrumbs suggestions on page 182). Mix in cooked grains like quinoa (page 146), leftover stuffing, or cooked mashed veggies. Or, mix in panko, grated coconut, coconut flour, or stale bread soaked in a little cream, wine, or stock.

Quinoa Meatballs
(page 146)

Quinoa Meatballs M F L *Recipe pictured on page 145*

*Leftover quinoa easily replaces traditional breadcrumbs in these gluten-free meatballs.
If you love your meatballs slowly simmered in a sauce, try my Tomato Sauce recipe on
page 77. Alternatively, I like to add a few of these gems on top of a pile of greens for
a post-workout meal. I use turkey in this recipe, but it will work just as well with any
ground meat, or even a combination.*

¾ cup cooked quinoa

½ onion, grated

1 egg, lightly beaten

1 Tbsp Dijon mustard

⅓ cup grated Parmesan
   (see substitutions)

1 Tbsp fresh or 1 tsp dried oregano

1 tsp dried savory

1 tsp garlic powder

1 Tbsp fresh thyme

1 tsp chili powder or chili flakes
   (optional)

1 lb ground turkey (see substitutions)

1 tsp salt

Pepper

1–2 Tbsp oil, divided

USES UP quinoa, ground meat

MAKES about 18 meatballs

TOTAL TIME 35 minutes

KEEPS FOR up to 4 days in the fridge or up to 4 months in the freezer (even better stored in a sauce)

CAN SUBSTITUTE
- Turkey with any ground meat
- Parmesan with any grated or shredded cheese, or nutritional yeast

1. Preheat the oven to 400°F.

2. In a large bowl, stir together the cooled cooked quinoa, onion, egg, mustard, Parmesan, oregano, savory, garlic powder, thyme, and chili powder until combined. Add the ground turkey, salt, and pepper, and mix together until combined.

3. Portion the meat into meatballs, about ⅛ cup in size, or flatten them into sliders. Set them aside on a baking sheet.

4. Preheat an ovenproof heavy-bottomed skillet or large cast-iron pan over high heat. Add 1 tablespoon of oil. In batches, cook the meatballs on all sides until browned, about 6 minutes. Avoid overcrowding the pan. Add more oil if necessary.

5. Transfer the pan to the oven. If you don't have an ovenproof skillet, transfer the meatballs to a lined baking sheet. Bake for 10 to 12 minutes or until their internal temperature is 165°F.

Red Thai–Style Curry Flank Steak   F

If you're feeling adventurous and have a bell pepper and a few chilies in the fridge, why not make your own almost-instant curry paste? This Thai-style red curry paste encompasses all the spicy and fragrant flavors you could want, while the addition of strawberry preserves helps to balance out the heat. Bonus: It uses up the whole lemons and limes that may be wrinkling in your fruit basket.

This recipe makes about 1½ cups of curry paste, and is a great marinade for raw protein. Here I use it with flank steak, but you can use the extra on tofu, chicken breasts, beef, or shrimp. You only need ½ cup of paste per 1 pound of protein. It also makes a flavorful addition to recipes like my Easy Peasy Soup (page 96), sauces like my Creamy Cauliflower Mac and Cheese (page 66), or to add a kick to vinaigrettes (page 46). It can also be used in any recipe that calls for red curry paste.

Curry Paste:

½ tsp ground coriander

1 tsp ground cumin

1 red bell pepper

2–4 medium red hot chilies

1 stalk lemongrass, root and tip
    trimmed, then chopped

1–2 Tbsp roughly chopped ginger

3 cloves garlic

1 Tbsp fresh or 1 tsp ground turmeric

Zest and juice of 1 lemon (see
    substitutions)

Zest and juice of 1 lime (see
    substitutions)

½ cup diced onions, shallots or
    green onions

2–3 Tbsp neutral-flavored oil, + extra
    for frying

3 Tbsp strawberry preserves or low
    sugar jam (see substitutions)

Salt and pepper

½–2 lb flank steak

1. Place all of the curry paste ingredients in food process or blender, and blend until smooth.

2. Coat the flank steak with 1 cup of the curry paste and place in an airtight container. Marinate in the fridge for a minimum of 2 hours or up to 2 days.

3. Preheat the oven to 400°F. In the meantime, bring the flank steak to room temperature.

4. When ready to cook, preheat a large ovenproof sauté pan or cast iron pan over medium-high heat. Add the oil. Sear the flank steak on one side, about 3 to 5 minutes or until nicely browned. Turn over and sear for an additional few minutes, brushing any excess paste on the meat.

5. Transfer to the oven and let cook for an additional 12 to 15 minutes, or until the internal temperature is 130°F for medium-rare or 140 to 145°F for medium-well. Let rest for 5 minutes before slicing flank steak against the grain into ½ to 1 inch strips. Serve with your favorite sides.

USES UP Flank steak, bell pepper, chilies, spices, lemon and lime

MAKES 1½ cups of paste; serves 4–6

TOTAL TIME 25 minutes, + 2 hours to 2 days of marinating

KEEPS FOR paste keeps for up to 10 days in the fridge or 3 months in the freezer; marinated raw protein keeps for up to 3 months in the freezer in an airtight container (thaw in fridge before cooking)

CAN SUBSTITUTE
- Strawberry preserves with another flavor
- Flank steak with chicken breasts, pork tenderloin

Pot Roast (see right)

Greek Chickpea
Salad (page 47)

Pipian Verde aka
Mexican Pumpkin Seed Stew
(page 63)

Pot Roast ⬛M ⬛F

The thought of a pot roast slowly bubbling away and filling my home with wonderful smells makes me excited for robustly flavored meaty leftovers.

1 pot roast (about 2½ lb) e.g., bone-in pork loin or boneless beef chuck, top blade, cross rib, bottom blade, or boneless brisket

Salt and pepper

6 oz bacon or other cured meat that renders fat, chopped

2 Tbsp olive oil

1 large onion or 1 cup (or more) shallots, roughly chopped (see substitutions)

6–12 garlic cloves, sliced (depends on how much you love garlic)

2 stalks celery + leaves, coarsely chopped

1 cup red wine or the juice of 1 orange

2 cups braising liquid e.g., Vegetable (page 187), Poultry (page 188), or Meat (page 188) stock or stock mixed with tomato sauce

2–3 Tbsp chopped fresh or 2–3 tsp dried oregano and/or thyme

2–3 bay leaves

3–4 cups root vegetables, cut into 2-inch chunks (see substitutions)

2 tsp dried fennel or anise seeds (optional)

A few Tbsp chopped fresh rosemary or Herbes de Provence

1. Preheat the oven to 325°F. Prep the pot roast by seasoning with salt and pepper on all sides.

2. In a large Dutch oven over medium heat, sauté the bacon until crispy. Remove using a slotted spoon, and set aside, reserving the bacon fat in the pot.

3. In the same pot over high heat, use the leftover bacon fat to brown the pot roast on all sides, 7 to 10 minutes. Lift the roast out of the pot and transfer to a plate.

4. In the same pot over medium heat, add the olive oil, then sauté the onion, garlic, and celery for about 3 minutes or until slightly softened. Add the wine, braising liquid, herbs, and bay leaves.

5. Add the roast and bacon and bring to a simmer. Then transfer to the oven and cook for about 2½ hours or until the internal temperature is 145°F for medium rare or 160°F for well done.

6. Add the root vegetables during the last 30 minutes of cooking time so the vegetables are tender-crisp and not mushy. Remove the bay leaves before serving.

Food 911 Slow cookers and Instant Pots are amazing for pot roasts. Just remember to: brown the roast on all sides first in some oil; place the roast in the cooker, with vegetables surrounding it, and pour liquid overtop; cook low and slow for 8 to 10 hours.

Zero-Waste Tip Save the roasted bones, gravy, or pan juices in the freezer to add flavor to a stew (page 150), chili (page 141), or soup (page 63).

USES UP beef, pork

SERVES 6–8, ½ lb per person or ¾ lb per person with leftovers

TOTAL TIME 2 hours, 40 minutes

KEEPS FOR meat and veggies can be stored up to 3–4 days in the fridge or up to 4 months in the freezer (best stored with a sauce, gravy, pan juices, or stock)

CAN SUBSTITUTE
- Onion with pearl onions or peeled cipollini onions
- Root vegetables with any other vegetables such as broccoli and cauliflower, taking into account that they cook more quickly

Beefy Black Lentil Stew `F` `P` `L`

Prime cuts of red meat, like prime rib, are expensive . . . so I can't bear to discard any pan drippings, bones, or leftover meat. The last time I cooked a small prime rib roast, I decided to braise lentils the next day in the robust leftovers I saved. This can be made just as easily with leftover gravy, braising liquids from a pot roast, or a simple broth. The beefiness of this dish pairs perfectly with seared broccolini, or serve it over some leftover mashed potatoes. Make sure to cut the carrots larger than the other vegetables so that they retain their shape and texture while everything else goes all stewy.

2–3 Tbsp oil

1 onion, diced

2 cloves garlic, finely chopped

2 stalks celery, diced

1 carrot, cut into ½-inch chunks

1 large tomato, chopped

¾ cup dried black or green lentils, rinsed well

2 (or more) leftover roasted beef rib bones

3 cups water + 1 cup leftover beef jus or gravy or 4 cups low-sodium beef stock (see substitutions)

1 bay leaf

1 Tbsp fresh or 1 tsp dried thyme

Salt and pepper

2 cups cubed or pulled cooked beef

1–2 tsp store-bought black bean sauce (optional)

1. In a large heavy-bottomed saucepot or Dutch oven over medium heat, add the oil and sauté the onion and garlic until softened, about 3 minutes.

2. Add the celery, carrot, tomato, and lentils and stir to coat the vegetables. Add the beef bones.

3. Pour in the water and beef jus mixture and add the bay leaf, thyme, salt, and pepper. Bring to a simmer and cook until the lentils are tender, about 30 minutes.

4. Add the cooked beef and simmer to heat through. Add the store-bought black bean sauce, if using. Taste and adjust the seasoning, and remove the bay leaf before serving.

USES UP beef, beef bones, beef jus, gravy, lentils

SERVES 6

TOTAL TIME 1 hour

KEEPS FOR up to 3 days in the fridge or up to 4 months in the freezer

CAN SUBSTITUTE
- Beef jus or pan drippings with 4 cups Vegetable (page 187), Poultry (page 188), or Meat (page 188) Stock + 1 Tbsp juniper berries + 3 tsp mixture of dried rosemary, thyme, and sage

Sour Cream and
Chive Potato Biscuits
(page 59)

Zero-Waste Tips from Todd Perrin

Todd Perrin has been a chef for over 25 years. A graduate of PEI's Culinary Institute of Canada (aka Holland College), he was operating a bed and breakfast prior to opening Mallard in St. John's Newfoundland, six years ago. His appearance on Top Chef Canada *sparked a fire and got him back into the restaurant business.*

Q. Let's talk about *Top Chef.* Did you win?

A. (chuckling) I didn't even come close, but I seemed to be entertaining enough! The impact of that got me back into thinking of the vision I always had, and what I wanted to see here in a restaurant. It was time.

Q. Since opening the restaurant in Quidi Vidi Village, you have opened the picturesque Inn by Mallard Cottage across the street, the new Waterwest Kitchen, and now a butcher shop. How has this been strategic to the businesses when it comes to waste-free living?

A. We run them as separate businesses that feed off each other. For example, Mallard restaurant is a customer of the Waterwest butcher shop, and the bakery makes bread and pastries for the Inn. On top of that, the staff get the chance to rotate and learn other aspects of the businesses.

Q. What is the most strategic thing you do in your kitchens to minimize food waste?

A. We fully use every aspect of the ingredients coming in, and we are in very close proximity to the ingredients we use. Our farmers are just up the street, not hours away. Since we operate this way, it's not even like we have to educate our staff. I cannot ever remember saying to anyone, "Don't waste that." However, if I were to nail it down to one thing, it would be the way we break down and change our menu. Our menu changes all the time to make sure everything is being rotated and used up.

Q. One of my favorite things I have eaten here at Mallard over the years are your cod napes. I am always amazed to see more challenging food items on the menu that I would have never seen when I was growing up here in Newfoundland. How has the response been?

A. People are used to some of the items, like fish cheeks and tongues, since they grew up eating them. But yes, things like sweetbreads and pickled tongues have been more of a learning curve.

Q. What is the number one challenge you run into when it comes to limiting the amount of food waste coming back on customers' plates?

A. Balancing the expectations of our customers about the volume of food we serve has always been the hardest thing to determine, forecast, and educate on. Customers have gone from expecting a huge slab of meat on their plate to proper portion sizes, and that is due to us changing our menu, plating, etc. so that food doesn't get tossed after they pay their bill. But balancing those expectations is for sure our biggest challenge.

Q. How has running these businesses affected how you shop and eat when you are not working?

A. All I eat at home are hummus, carrots, apples, and cheese. If I have a day off, I still love to spend it cooking for friends, but, I always buy what I need day of. I am not a big fan of a packed fridge or freezer. A freezer, to me, is where things go to die. I just don't understand the idea of a packed fridge or buying things in bulk because they may be cheaper. That bag of fruit isn't so cheap if you end up throwing half of it away.

Q. What's one item from the Water West Kitchen that really speaks to a zero-waste kitchen?

A. Head cheese. We are fully nose to arse (tail), so all the off bits are used up in our head cheese.

Callaloo M F

Callaloo is the name for the large green leaves of the taro root. Depending on where you live, they may be difficult to find. Don't let that stop you. This stewp (stew/soup), also known as a pepper pot, can be adapted to any hardy green and uses cheap cuts of meat in a spicy coconut broth. The stewed meat is sometimes seen served on top of the stewp, and the stewp is sometimes purée into a thick sauce. Serve over cooked grains, cauliflower rice, or even zucchini noodles.

8 oz smoked ham hock

4 cups Vegetable (page 187), Poultry (page 188), or Meat (page 188) Stock

2–3 Tbsp olive oil

1 lb stewing meat, diced into 1-inch cubes

1 onion, diced

3 cloves garlic, finely chopped

2 stalks celery + tops, chopped

1 carrot, diced

2 cups (½ lb) diced potatoes (see substitutions)

1 cup chopped okra, fresh or frozen (optional) (see substitutions)

3 fresh thyme sprigs or 2 tsp dried

1 hot chili pepper, finely chopped (Scotch bonnet is good here)

4 cups chopped hardy greens (see substitutions)

Salt and pepper

1 cup coconut milk

Zest and juice of 1 lime

Optional Garnishes

Chives

Green onions, chopped

Lime wedges

1. Place the ham hock and stewing meat in a pot with just enough stock to cover (about 2 cups). Bring the stock to a boil, reduce the heat, and simmer, covered, for about 1 hour or until the meat is tender. Set aside.

2. In a large saucepot over medium heat, add the oil and sauté the onion and garlic until tender, 3 to 5 minutes. Stir in the celery, carrot, potatoes, okra if using, thyme, and chili pepper. Season lightly with salt and pepper. Sauté, adding more oil if needed, for an additional 5 minutes.

3. Transfer the smoked ham hock, meat, and remaining stock to the pot, along with the chopped hardy greens. Bring to a simmer for about 15 minutes until all the vegetables are tender.

4. Stir in the coconut milk, taste, and adjust the seasoning with salt, pepper, and lime juice. You can remove the thyme sprigs.

5. Remove the ham hock and the meat and set aside. If you want the soup smooth, purée, otherwise keep it chunky. If you like, adjust the consistency by adding some or all of the stock that the ham and meat were braising in. Shred the meat and pull it into chunks, or keep it whole and serve the soup over the meat and sides of choice.

6. Taste, adjust the seasoning, and garnish.

Food 911 Leftover canned coconut milk can last in an airtight container for 7 to 10 days in the fridge or 6 months in the freezer.

USES UP hardy greens, stock, meat, coconut milk

SERVES 4–6

TOTAL TIME 1 hour, 25 minutes

KEEPS FOR up to 3 days in the fridge or 4 months in the freezer

CAN SUBSTITUTE
- Hardy greens with fresh or frozen spinach, but add it with the coconut milk at the end to wilt through
- Okra with chopped green or yellow plantains
- Potatoes with other root veggies (mix and match)

Pantry-Inspired Staples

Wheat, flour, rice, pasta, millet, and so forth; these are some of the world's most popular food pantry staples. Even so, that large bag of farro you bought for one recipe can get overlooked, and forgotten leftover quinoa can sit in the back of your fridge and become a science experiment. And let's not forget about that loaf of bread going stale. The techniques in this chapter will leave no crumb unturned and no bite lost, so you can rework leftovers and use up groceries in simple and delicious ways!

Pasta Night

Whether you are craving pasta or have leftover cooked pasta to use up, think beyond bottled sauce. You can get as creative as you'd like with pasta and take the opportunity to use up what's on-hand. Follow the fridge first rule. One onion? Sure! A wrinkly tomato? Yes, add that. A few garlic cloves? Some leftover grilled broccoli? Oh, look, some cured chorizo! Yes, yes, and yes! Whether you feel like something creamy or saucy—or just pasta and vegetables simply tossed with olive oil and garlic—pasta night is a sure-fire way to reduce food waste. Here's a roadmap to creating your pasta du jour. And turn to page 159 for my fried leftover pasta recipe.

FIRST STOP: PICK YOUR PASTA
Dried or fresh pasta
Gnocchi (page 65)
Leftover cooked pasta
Plant-based noodles (e.g., konjac, black bean, or chickpea)
Zucchini noodles

SECOND STOP: PICK YOUR FIXINGS
Aromatics (e.g. onions, garlic, and leeks)
Cured meats, e.g., bacon or chorizo
Deli meats (e.g., ham, salami, prosciutto)
Raw and/or frozen thawed vegetables
Raw fish, meat, seafood, or plant-based protein
Smoked or cured fish or seafood

THIRD STOP: MAKE IT SAUCY
Butter
Cheese sauce
Creamy Cauliflower Sauce (page 66)
Heavy cream and/or white wine
Marinara (page 77)
Olive oil and garlic and/or herbs
Pesto (page 74)
Simple Tomato Sauce (page 77)

Ragù (page 78)
Store-bought sauce (tomato, rose, cream)

FOURTH STOP: EVEN MORE ADD-INS
Bacon bits
Canned artichokes
Capers
Chili peppers
Cooked eggs, any way
Cooked fish, meat, seafood, or plant-based protein
Marinated or pickled vegetables
Moroccan Preserved Lemons (page 204), chopped
Olives
Roasted garlic
Sundried tomatoes

FIFTH STEP: GARNISH IT UP
Breadcrumbs (page 182) or Croutons (page 183)
Cheese, shredded, grated or chopped
Crispy fried onions
Fresh herbs, chopped
Green onions, sliced
Nuts and/or seeds

Crispy Fried Pasta with Spicy Chorizo F L

Tomato sauced or not, this is one of the easiest and most delicious ways to serve pre-cooked pasta. All you need is a hot pan and some additional inspiration from your fridge, and you have an afternoon snack, side, or meal on your table in minutes. Since this recipe is more of a technique, I have only used the amount of ingredients for two people. Scale up or down for the amount of pasta hanging around.

2 Tbsp extra-virgin olive oil, divided
½–1 cup chopped cured spicy chorizo (see substitutions)
1 clove garlic, finely chopped
1 cup chopped raw or cooked vegetables
2 cups (or more) leftover pasta, with or without sauce

Optional Add-Ins
½ cup Tomato Sauce (page 77)
2 Tbsp pesto (page 74)
Parmesan, grated, or nutritional yeast

USES UP leftover pasta, cooked vegetables, chorizo, or cooked meats

SERVES about 2, depending on how much pasta you have left over

TOTAL TIME 15 minutes

KEEPS FOR the day of is best but can be reheated the next day

CAN SUBSTITUTE
- Chorizo with cooked ham, crispy bacon, or other cooked protein

1. Preheat a large cast-iron or sauté pan over medium-high heat. Add 1 tablespoon of the oil and the chorizo. Let the chorizo render and brown slightly, about 5 minutes.

2. Stir in the garlic and cook until softened. Add the vegetables and sauté until cooked to your liking.

3. Stir in the pasta, increasing the heat to high if necessary, and cook until golden-brown and crispy. Add any optional add-ins to your liking.

The Great Risotto F P L

Not enough rice to make for your guests or family? Have a mishmash of assorted grains—some rice here, some farro there—hanging out in the back of your pantry? Here's the answer—a great risotto recipe you make with rice, farro, barley, or whatever grains you have!

4 cups Vegetable (page 187), Poultry (page 188), or Meat (page 188) Stock

2 Tbsp olive oil

1 onion or 2 shallots, finely chopped

2 cloves garlic, finely chopped

½ cup white wine

1–2 Tbsp chopped fresh or 1–2 tsp dried herbs, e.g., thyme, sage, or parsley stems

1 cup mixed grains, rinsed

1 Parmesan rind (optional)

Salt and pepper

½ cup chopped celery leaves and tops

1 cup cooked vegetables (see substitutions)

Grated Parmesan cheese, to taste

USES UP grains, vegetables, stock, Parmesan rinds

SERVES 4

TOTAL TIME 20 minutes

KEEPS FOR up to 5 days in the fridge. Risotto will get dry in the fridge, so when reheating on the stovetop, stir in a splash of water, stock, wine, or even a dab of butter.

CAN SUBSTITUTE
- Vegetables with uncooked finely chopped hardy greens or spinach, just add at the end of the cooking time and cook until wilted through

1. In a medium-size saucepot, bring the stock to a simmer and then set aside on a back burner to keep warm.

2. In a medium-size saucepot over medium heat, add the oil and sauté the onion and garlic until translucent, being careful not to burn the garlic, about 3 minutes.

3. Add the white wine and allow it to reduce until almost dry, about 2 minutes.

4. Stir in the herbs, grains, Parmesan rind, if using, and the salt and pepper. Let the oil coat the grains. Sauté for about 2 minutes.

5. Ladle in 1 cup of the hot stock and let simmer and reduce until the bottom of the pot is no longer very wet, stirring occasionally.

6. Ladle in more stock and continue to cook, stirring occasionally so the grains do not stick to the bottom. As the liquid at the bottom is absorbed, keep adding more until the grains are tender, about 15 minutes. Add the celery and cooked veggies. Remove the Parmesan rind. Taste and adjust the seasoning with salt and pepper.

7. Sprinkle with the grated cheese and serve immediately.

Food 911 Turn risotto into cheesy baked risotto balls. Preheat the oven to 350°F and line a baking sheet. Place the leftover risotto in a bowl, add some grated cheese, and roll into golf-ball-size balls. Dip each ball in beaten egg, roll in Breadcrumbs (page 182), and bake until golden-brown, about 20 minutes.

Jamabalaya
(see right)

Chili Yogurt Cornbread
(page 69)

Jambalaya

I was running out of ways to use up an abundance of leftover turkey one Christmas, and I wanted something that didn't remind me, or my family, of turkey dinner again. This Louisiana-style rice stew, similar in preparation to another one-pot wonder, paella, takes leftover turkey on a Cajun vacation with smoky, sweet, and spicy in its forecast. Oh, and you can also make this recipe with leftover cooked rice.

1 onion, chopped
1 stalk celery, chopped
1 green pepper, chopped
1 jalapeño (optional)
2 Tbsp oil
1 clove garlic
2 bay leaves
2 Tbsp fresh or 2 tsp dried oregano
1 Tbsp fresh or 1 tsp dried thyme
2 tsp Cajun or Creole seasoning

Dash hot sauce or pinch cayenne
1¼ cups chopped smoked sausage (about 6 oz), e.g., smoked meat sausage, andouille, chorizo, or even spicy pepperettes
1 cup uncooked long-grain rice or 2–3 cups cooked long-grain rice
One 14 oz can tomato sauce or Basic Tomato Sauce (page 77)
1 cup Poultry Stock (page 188)

Salt and pepper
1 lb cooked turkey, cubed (see substitutions)
1 lb peeled cooked or frozen raw shrimp, thawed (optional)
Green onions or chives, chopped, for garnish (optional)

1. In a large skillet or Dutch oven over medium heat, add the oil and sauté the onion, celery, pepper, jalapeño, and garlic until softened.

2. Stir in the bay leaves, oregano, thyme, Cajun seasoning, hot sauce, and sausage and cook for 2 minutes.

3. If using uncooked rice, stir in the rice to coat and cook for 2 minutes. Add the tomato sauce, stock, and salt and bring to a simmer. Cover and simmer for 25 minutes or until the rice is cooked through, adding more stock if needed.

4. Stir in the cooked turkey and shrimp, if using. If using cooked rice, add it to the skillet and bring to a simmer for an additional few minutes. If using raw shrimp, it should take no longer than 5 minutes for them to cook through.

5. Taste and adjust the seasoning with salt, pepper, and hot sauce. Serve in a large bowl and garnish with the green onions, as desired.

USES UP cooked turkey, rice, cured sausages, poultry stock

SERVES 6

TOTAL TIME 35 minutes

KEEPS FOR up to 2 days in the fridge or 4 months in the freezer

CAN SUBSTITUTE
• Turkey with cooked poultry, chopped

Zero-Waste Tip When emptying canned and bottled sauces, swirl a little water into the remains to get all the yummy stuff stuck to the sides. Then wash and reuse glass food jars and lids for storing your food for later—they make free storage! Make sure to rinse and recycle any metal cans, or start upcycling (hello arts and crafts!).

Freestyle Paella `F` `P` `L`

A one-pan wonder, paella is one of the most flavorful ways to use up a whack of leftover proteins and veggies. This recipe is my go-to for when I'm craving something a little more exotic than your basic stir-fry. It's also a recipe I make when I really want to impress my guests, because all you need is a little Spanish flair to really step things up. The best paellas are made with rich-flavored stock. I personally love to make this with leftover gravy or braising liquid topped up with homemade stock.

4 cups Vegetable (page 187), Poultry (page 188), or Meat (page 188) Stock (see substitutions)
1 pinch saffron
7 oz cured chorizo (mild or hot), cubed (see substitutions)
2 Tbsp olive oil
1 onion, diced
4 cloves garlic, finely chopped
1 large tomato, grated or finely chopped

1 bell or field pepper, diced
2 tsp smoked paprika
2 bay leaves
½ cup wine (optional)
2 cups short-grain rice
2 cups cubed cooked protein
½ cup fresh or frozen peas and/or corn, thawed
Up to 1 cup cooked vegetables
Salt and pepper

Optional Add-Ins
1 cup canned or frozen artichoke hearts, thawed
Handful chopped mushrooms

Optional Garnishes
Handful of chopped green onions
Handful of chopped parsley
Lemon wedges

1. Heat the stock in a large saucepot over medium heat so it is hot when starting to cook paella. Mix the saffron with 1 cup of the hot stock, then set aside to steep.

2. In a large cast-iron pan or skillet, brown the chorizo in olive oil and set aside on a plate. In the same skillet, sauté the onion and garlic in the chorizo-flavored oil, adding more oil if necessary, until softened.

3. Stir in the tomato, pepper, smoked paprika, and bay leaves, and sauté for a few minutes longer. Stir in the wine and rice and let simmer for an additional few minutes.

4. Ladle in ½ cup of the stock, and stir until absorbed. Then spread the rice out in an even layer over the bottom of the pan and ladle in an additional 1 cup of the stock. Do not stir the rice. Let the rice absorb the liquid over medium heat, tasting the rice along the way to check doneness. The total cooking time is about 25 minutes.

5. Halfway through the rice cooking time, nestle in the cooked protein and reserved chorizo. Pour the steeped saffron broth over top.

6. When the rice is almost fully cooked, add the peas and vegetables, and heat through. Add a little water or more stock if needed. Season to taste with salt and pepper. Once cooked, cover with foil and allow to rest for 5 minutes before serving. Garnish as desired.

USES UP cooked proteins, rice, vegetables

SERVES 6

TOTAL TIME 30 minutes

KEEPS FOR up to 3 days in the fridge

CAN SUBSTITUTE
- Chorizo with ham, cured or fresh sausage, kielbasa, pancetta, or bacon
- Stock with gravy or pan juices mixed with water

Fancy Fried Rice F P L

I always cook more rice than I need just so I can make fried rice with my leftovers. Fried rice begs to be made with day-old . . . or three-day-old . . . rice to get the perfect crispy texture, and it loves odd bits of already-cooked protein and produce.

Here are a few tricks for making a magnificent fried rice: 1) Go easy on the soy sauce. 2) A scrambled egg or two is a cheap and perfect fluffy protein boost to any fried rice. 3) Don't be afraid of the heat. Keep it hot and moving. If the pan is not hot enough, the rice will stick to the bottom in a clumpy mess (still tasty, though). 4) Don't overcrowd the pan with too much rice. When you overwhelm a hot pan with too many ingredients, the temperature plummets, which leads to a clumpy, stuck-on mess. Fry in batches if needed. 5) When your fried rice is done, remove from the heat, and fold in fresh green elements like chopped herbs or chives to keep them fresh.

2 eggs, well beaten

Salt and pepper

2–3 Tbsp high smoke point oil for frying, divided

½ cup finely diced onion

2–3 cloves garlic, finely chopped

1 cup diced vegetables

2 cups cold leftover cooked rice, up to 3 days old

2 tsp light soy sauce

2 Tbsp toasted sesame oil (see substitutions)

½ cup frozen peas and/or corn

1 cup (or more) chopped cooked protein

2–3 green onions, finely chopped (see substitutions)

Optional Add-Ins

½ cup chopped kimchi

½ cup diced pineapple

Finely chopped hot chili pepper

Hot sauce or Hawaiian Chili Water (page 195)

1 Tbsp store-bought black bean sauce

1. In a bowl, combine the beaten eggs with a pinch of salt and pepper to season.

2. Preheat a large nonstick skillet or wok over medium heat. Add 1 tablespoon of the oil and scramble the eggs until just cooked through and fluffy. Transfer to a plate and break up any larger pieces.

3. In the same pan, over medium-high heat, add a little more oil and cook the onion until softened. Add the garlic and cook for another minute, then add your vegetables and cook until just softened, 3 to 5 minutes. You still want a little crunch. Transfer to the plate with the scrambled eggs.

4. Using your hands or a fork, break up any clumps that may have formed in the rice while it was sitting in the fridge.

5. In the same pan over high heat, add a little more oil, enough to lightly coat the bottom of the pan. Fry the rice, in batches if necessary, stirring occasionally, until golden-brown.

6. Reduce the heat and fold in the eggs, sautéed veggies, soy sauce, and toasted sesame oil. Fold in the frozen peas, cooked protein, green onions, and any additional add-ins to taste and cook through. Taste and adjust the seasoning.

USES UP rice, vegetables, eggs, cooked protein

SERVES 4 as a main or 6 as a side

TOTAL TIME 25 minutes

KEEPS FOR up to 2 days in the fridge

CAN SUBSTITUTE
* Toasted sesame oil with 1–2 Tbsp curry powder, added with the soy sauce
* Green onions with parsley, cilantro, mint, basil, or chives

Grain Bowl with Shrimp, and Lemon Dill Buttermilk Dressing `F` `P` `L`

There's nothing like a cold rice, pasta or grain bowl that showcases seasonal produce tossed in a bright perky dressing. Take that idea and raise the bar by adding shrimp and a lemon dill buttermilk dressing. I buy buttermilk for our weekend pancake breakfast, so buttermilk dressings are in regular rotation as a way to use it up. Great for parties, fundraisers, and potlucks.

Lemon Dill Buttermilk Dressing

1 finely chopped shallot (about 1 Tbsp)
½ clove garlic, finely chopped
2 Tbsp Dijon mustard
2 Tbsp lemon juice
1 Tbsp extra-virgin olive oil
1 cup buttermilk
¼ cup chopped fresh dill
Salt and pepper

Bowl

1 bunch asparagus, stalks trimmed, cut into ½-inch pieces
2 cups cooked grains or rice or ¾ cup uncooked grains or rice, cooked according to package instructions (see substitutions)
1 cup fresh or frozen thawed peas
½ cup thinly sliced or chopped radishes
1 lb cooked shrimp, cooled (see substitutions)
Grated hard cheese, for garnish

USES UP cooked grains or pasta, cooked shrimp, buttermilk

SERVES 4, makes about 1 cup of dressing (there will be extra dressing)

TOTAL TIME 20 minutes

KEEPS FOR bowl can be stored up to 3 days in the fridge. Dressing up to 4 days in the fridge.

CAN SUBSTITUTE
- Grains with 8–10 oz cooked pasta, like farfalle or penne, or cooked riced cauliflower
- Shrimp with other cooked proteins

1. For the Lemon Dill Buttermilk Dressing: Add all of the dressing ingredients to a jar with a lid and shake until combined.

2. Taste and adjust seasoning if necessary. Set aside.

3. For the Bowl: In a pot of boiling salted water, blanch the asparagus for 1 minute. Drain and then run under very cold water or plunge into an ice bath to cool. Drain well.

4. In a large bowl, toss the grains with the asparagus, peas, radishes, shrimp, and half of the dressing. Taste, and add more dressing if desired.

5. Sprinkle the cheese overtop.

Zero-Waste Tip Save your shrimp shells in the freezer for stock. Also, eat your radish greens. Younger, smaller radishes have tender greens that are great raw in salads; the larger greens have a rougher texture and are better cooked.

Fattoush Salad F P

Here's a twist on a classic summertime salad, the Fattoush! Fattoush is a Lebanese-styled bread salad, which uses pita or flatbreads as a base for larger chopped vegetables, tossed with a herby seasoning. It is a classic recipe to use-up stale pita leftover in your pantry. The vegetable combination listed here is what is traditionally used in a Fattoush, but you can use whatever crunchy vegetables you already have on-hand. Sumac and good-quality olive oil go a long way in this versatile salad.

Pita

2 pita breads (day old or stale pre-ferred) (see substitutions)

1-2 Tbsp olive oil

½ tsp ground sumac

Salt and pepper

1 heart Romaine lettuce, chopped (see substitutions)

Vegetables (see substitutions)

½ cucumber, chopped

2 large tomatoes, chopped

1 bell pepper, chopped

3 green onions, chopped

5 radishes, chopped

½ cup chopped fresh parsley, leaves and stems

½ cup chopped fresh mint leaves

½ cup pomegranate seeds (optional)

Sumac-Lime Vinaigrette

Juice of ½ a lime, or to taste

⅓ cup olive oil

Salt and pepper

1 tsp ground sumac

1 clove garlic, puréed or finely chopped

¼ tsp cinnamon and/or allspice

1 tsp pomegranate molasses, or to taste (optional)

1. For the Pita: Using a knife, slice each pita through middle of the bread length-wise, separating them into four rounds. Cut the rounds into triangles, or for a more rustic topping, tear them into pieces.

2. To Fry the Pita: Line a plate with paper towel. In a large pan over medium heat, heat about 1 tablespoon of oil. Fry the pita, in batches if necessary, for a few min-utes, tossing frequently, until browned. Season with salt, pepper, and sumac. Place the pita chips on the plate to drain any excess oil.

Or, to Bake the Pita: Preheat the oven to 350°F degrees. Line a baking sheet. Place the pita pieces on the prepared sheet and toss with enough oil to lightly coat them, and season with salt, pepper, and sumac. Bake for about 5 minutes, or until very crisp but not browned.

3. For the Salad: In a large salad bowl, toss the lettuce, cucumber, tomatoes, bell pepper, green onions, and radishes with the chopped parsley and mint, and the pomegranate seeds.

4. For the Vinaigrette: In a small bowl, whisk together all of the vinaigrette ingredi-ents, taste and adjust the seasoning if necessary.

5. To Serve: Dress the salad with the vinaigrette and toss lightly. Top with the pita chips, and sprinkle with more sumac to taste.

USES UP Pita, veggies, herbs

SERVES 4, as a main

TOTAL TIME 30 minutes

KEEPS FOR the day of (for tossed salad), but salad and dressing can be stored separately for up to 3 days

CAN SUBSTITUTE
- Pita with flatbread
- Romaine with another salad green of your choice
- Vegetables with other chopped raw, crunchy vegetables

Quinoa Surprise $\boxed{\text{F}}$ $\boxed{\text{P}}$ $\boxed{\text{L}}$

Here is my go-to grain salad recipe when I have leftover chicken and a bunch of random vegetables kicking around. It is never the same twice, hence the "surprise," and it can be served warm or cold—perfect for lunchboxes. You can omit the chicken altogether or add more to use it up. The addition of finely chopped pickles and brine is a great way to add flavor and crunch. Don't be shy about experimenting with the options below.

3 cups chopped raw or blanched
    vegetables

2 Tbsp sesame oil

4 Tbsp extra-virgin olive oil or
    avocado oil

2 dill pickles, finely chopped

1 Tbsp dill pickle juice

1–2 Tbsp freshly squeezed lemon juice,
    white wine, or apple cider vinegar

2 Tbsp finely chopped onions or shallots

Salt and pepper

1 cup cubed cooked chicken (see
    substitutions)

2 cups cooked quinoa or ¾ cup
    uncooked quinoa cooked accord-
    ing to the package instructions

Optional Add-Ins

½–1 cup chopped canned artichoke
    hearts

2–3 green onions, chopped

3 Tbsp chopped sauerkraut or kimchi

2 Tbsp chopped fresh dill, basil,
    parsley, and/or chives

Sun-dried tomatoes, chopped

Garnish

¼–½ cup raw seeds or chopped nuts
    (optional)

USES UP quinoa, pickle
brine, vegetables,
chicken

MAKES 4–6 servings

TOTAL TIME 20 minutes

KEEPS FOR up to 3 days
in the fridge

CAN SUBSTITUTE
• Chicken with any
  cooked protein

1. If using harder vegetables, like carrots or broccoli, blanch in boiling salted water for 2 minutes. Drain and run cold water over the vegetables to stop the cooking process.

2. In a large bowl, stir together the sesame oil, olive oil, pickles, pickle juice, lemon juice, onions, and salt and pepper.

3. Fold in the vegetables, chopped chicken, and quinoa, and if desired any of the optional add-ins. Taste and adjust the seasoning with salt, pepper, and lemon juice.

4. Garnish with the seeds, if desired.

Noodles with Spicy Peanut Sauce F L *Recipe pictured on page 90*

This is a simple spicy noodle and green bean recipe that everybody will love. This peanut sauce has the perfect combination of salty, spicy, and not-too-sweet flavors. I strongly suggest doubling the peanut sauce recipe so you can have it another night, maybe as a dip for Wrap It Up Fresh Spring Rolls (see right). If you love this peanut sauce as much as I do, try it as an ingredient in future soups, stews, or marinades.

Peanut Sauce:
Zest and juice of half a lime
2½ Tbsp soy or tamari sauce
1 Tbsp tahini paste
1 Tbsp unsalted peanut butter
1 Tbsp toasted sesame oil
½ Tbsp finely chopped garlic
½ Tbsp finely chopped ginger
1 tsp chili oil or paste
Sugar (optional)

Noodles
2 handfuls of trimmed green beans or cooked (blanched) green beans (see substitutions)
8 oz uncooked thin egg noodles or about 4 cups cooked thin egg noodles

Optional Add-In
1–2 cup cooked tofu, cubed

Optional Garnishes
Lime wedges
¼ cup toasted nuts or seeds
¼ cup crispy soybeans
2–3 Tbsp chopped fresh mint, cilantro, basil, or Thai basil
1 Tbsp Hawaiian Chili Water (page 195)
1 thinly sliced chili pepper

1. For the Peanut Sauce: Place all of the peanut sauce ingredients in a blender and mix well, or whisk them in a bowl.

2. Taste and adjust seasoning if needed with more lime juice, chili oil, or sugar.

3. For the Noodles: If the green beans are uncooked, simmer them in boiling salted water for 2 minutes—you don't want them mushy. Drain and set aside.

4. If the noodles are not cooked, cook according to the package instructions and drain and return to the pot. If the noodles are leftover and cold, transfer them to a saucepot over medium heat with 1 to 2 tablespoons of water and heat until noodles are loosened and the water is absorbed.

5. Add the peanut sauce to the noodles and stir until incorporated. Fold in the green beans and cooked proteins (if using) to warm through.

6. If desired, garnish with something crispy, something fresh, and maybe something spicy.

USES UP egg noodles, green beans, peanut butter

SERVES 2 as a main or 4 as a side, makes ½ cup of peanut sauce

TOTAL TIME 30 minutes

KEEPS FOR up to 2 days in the fridge

CAN SUBSTITUTE
• Green beans with chopped broccoli

Wrap It Up Fresh Spring Rolls `F` `L` `P`

If you have any leftover protein and a few vegetables kicking around, within minutes you can rice-paper-wrap yourself a meal. These easy-to-use, paper-thin, woven-looking rice paper wrappers make any food bundled inside quite charming. Healthy, kid-friendly, and gluten- and peanut-free, they are perfect solution for a guilt-free school lunch, quick weeknight dinner, or party tray. For a vegetarian option, just add more veggies, thin strips of your favorite firm tofu or tempeh, or even leftover scrambled or hard-boiled eggs.

Dipping Sauce
3 Tbsp rice wine vinegar
2 tsp toasted sesame oil
2 Tbsp tamari or soy sauce
1 tsp maple syrup or honey
1 green onion, finely chopped

½ clove garlic, finely chopped
1 tsp favorite hot sauce (optional)

Filling
2 cups cooked rice vermicelli noodles
   or other leftover thin noodles
Oil, for coating (optional)

Eight 8½-inch-diameter rice paper
   wrappers (see tip)
2 cups cooked protein (see tip)
2 cups thinly sliced vegetables (see tip)
⅓ cup fresh basil, cilantro or mint
   leaves

1. For the Dipping Sauce: In a small bowl, whisk together all of the ingredients.

2. For the Filling: Place the noodles in a large bowl. Drizzle a little oil or some of the dipping sauce over the cooked noodles and toss to prevent them from sticking together.

3. Fill a medium sauté pan with 1 inch of water and heat on the stovetop until very warm. You want it hot enough to soften the rice wrappers but not so hot you can't put your fingers in it.

4. Dampen a clean tea towel and place it on the counter. With your fingers, submerge a wrapper in the hot water and rotate until the wrapper softens, about 3 seconds.

5. Gently lay the wrapper flat on the damp tea towel and start placing your fillings in a row across the center, leaving 2 inches along the top and bottom and 1 inch on each side. Try not to overstuff with noodles; be sure to leave room for more of the "good" stuff, like all the veggie strips. Add a few basil or cilantro leaves.

6. Roll from the bottom up, tucking in the edges halfway through. The aim is to make a nice tight roll. Repeat with the remaining rolls.

Food 911 Rice paper wrappers can be found in the Asian food aisle of any grocer, but for more varieties of shapes, sizes, and brands, go to a Vietnamese or Chinese market. The best ones are those made with only rice or a combination of rice and tapioca starch.

For the cooked protein, try 10 oz thinly sliced chicken or turkey, or about 16 peeled cooked shrimp, some scrambled eggs, or slices of tofu or tempeh. For the vegetables, I like ½ bell pepper, ¼ cucumber, 1 carrot and ½ mango, peeled (as needed) and thinly sliced.

USES UP cooked protein, noodles, vegetables

MAKES 8 rolls, serves 3-4 as a main

TOTAL TIME 20 minutes

KEEPS FOR The moment—these are best eaten the same day. If not eaten right away, store in an airtight container with a damp clean tea towel overtop to prevent them from drying out. These can be made up to 8 hours ahead of time.

Crispy Rice Crepes F P *Recipe pictured on page 129*

Happen to have some leftover curry or stew and looking for a new way to serve it? Love sandwiches but tired of bread and bagels? Or what about taking a break from the traditional fruit-filled crepe? These Vietnamese-style crepes will have you coming back, again and again, and you will want to stuff everything into them. Try layering them with Bong Bong Chicken (page 128) or fill them with some leftover meat, salsa, and condiments like a taco.

1 cup rice flour
2 Tbsp tapioca flour
1 tsp salt
1 tsp ground curry powder
   (see substitutions)

¾ cup coconut milk
1½ cups water
Neutral-flavored oil, for frying

USES UP leftover stews, curries, chicken salads, protein, cooked veggies, taco fillings, fruit compote

MAKES 5–6 crepes

TOTAL TIME 25–40 minutes

KEEPS FOR up to 1 day, cool completely and store at room temperature in an airtight container or wrapped tightly.

CAN SUBSTITUTE
• Curry powder with 1 tsp ground turmeric

1. In a medium-size mixing bowl, whisk together the rice flour, tapioca flour, salt, and curry powder.

2. Whisk in the coconut milk and water to make very loose crepe batter. Adjust the consistency with more water if too thick to pour, or more rice flour if it's too watery.

3. Heat a medium-size nonstick sauté pan over medium heat. Add enough oil to lightly coat the bottom of the pan. Once the oil is hot, ladle ⅓ cup of the batter into the pan and give it a little swirl to coat the bottom. Cook 2 to 3 minutes per side, until the edges are crispy. Repeat with the remaining batter.

4. Use them warm or cool. Just like traditional crepes, these can be stuffed or layered.

Savory Pies: 3 Ways F L P

They say "pies are defined by their crusts." Here are three recipes—a pot pie, a hand pie, and a galette—that make use of these crusts. They use phyllo, puff pastry, and even grated root vegetables to hug a variety of fillings. Pies are a great way to use up leftover cooked poultry (page 127), meat (page 149) and fish (page 109), or roasted vegetables (page 41) and greens. Don't be limited by the recipes below; you can get super creative with what you put in crust!

SUNDAY'S ROSTI POT PIE

2 Tbsp oil or butter

1 onion, diced

2 cloves garlic, minced

⅓ cup flour

4 cups Vegetable (page 187), Poultry (page 188), or Meat (page 188) Stock, leftover gravy, or pan juices (see substitutions)

2 Tbsp chopped fresh or 2 tsp dried hardy herbs

2 or more cups cooked protein

3 cups diced cooked vegetables

1 cup fresh or frozen peas or corn, thawed

Salt and pepper

2 parsnips, grated (about 1½ cups) (see substitutions)

USES UP cooked protein, cooked vegetables, parsnips, leftover gravy or pan juices

SERVES 6

TOTAL TIME 50 minutes

KEEPS FOR up to 3 days in the fridge

CAN SUBSTITUTE
- 1 cup stock with 1 cup milk or cream
- Rosti crust with 1 pie crust or puff pastry crust, thawed according to package instructions

1. Preheat the oven to 400°F and grease a baking dish or pie plate.

2. Preheat a large sauté pan over medium heat. Add the oil and let heat through. Add the onion and garlic and cook until softened, about 3 minutes. Mix in the flour and cook for an additional 3 minutes.

3. Slowly whisk in the stock to avoid any lumps. Add the herbs and bring to a simmer until slightly thickened.

4. Add the protein, vegetables, peas, and cook until warmed and cooked through. Season with salt and pepper. Pour the mixture into the baking dish.

5. Season the grated parsnips with a little salt and pepper. Top the pie with parsnips and then drizzle a little olive oil over the top. Bake about 40 minutes or until the parsnip crust is golden brown and the inside is bubbling.

HAM AND CHEESE HAND PIES

1 cup chopped ham (see substitutions)

2 cups grated semi-soft cheese

Pinch pepper

Chopped herbs e.g., basil, oregano, or thyme (optional)

1 package puff pastry, thawed according to package instructions

2 Tbsp jam (optional)

1 egg, beaten

USES UP cooked ham, grated cheese, puff pastry

TOTAL TIME 10 minutes

MAKES 8 hand pies

KEEPS FOR the day of, or store for up to 2 days in the fridge then place in a warmed 350°F oven for a few minutes to heat through

CAN SUBSTITUTE
- Ham with other deli meat or finely chopped cooked protein
- Puff pastry with The Only Pie Dough You Need (page 226)

1. Preheat the oven to 425° F. Line a baking sheet.

2. In a medium-size bowl, toss together the ham, cheese, pepper, and any herbs if adding.

3. On a clean, floured surface, roll out the puff pastry, if necessary, to make a 14-by-14-inch square. Using a pizza cutter or knife, cut the pastry into 4 even squares and then divide each by half, for a total of 8.

4. If using jam, brush the jam lightly on one side of each hand pie, then layer on the ham and cheese, leaving a margin around the edge for crimping. Brush the edges with the beaten egg. Place the other half of the dough on top. With the back of a fork, crimp the edges closed.

5. Place the hand pies on the prepared baking sheet, brush tops with more egg wash, and bake for 10 minutes or until the puff pastry is golden.

Food 911 These instructions make rectangular hand pies, but by all means make them any shape or size you want. Baking time may vary depending on sizing.

CURRIED FETA AND HARDY GREENS GALETTE

1–2 Tbsp melted coconut oil or olive oil, divided

1 bunch fresh or frozen Swiss chard

1 bunch fresh or frozen kale

2 onions finely diced (about 2 cups)

1 clove garlic, finely diced

½ cup diced celery or fennel bulb

¼ tsp ground or freshly grated nutmeg

2 tsp curry powder

1 tsp garam masala

Salt and pepper

2 eggs

½ cup coconut milk or heavy cream

½ cup chopped seeds or nuts

½ lb feta, broken or chopped into small pieces (see substitutions)

2 Tbsp chopped fresh or 2 tsp dried herbs e.g., parsley, thyme, chives, Thai basil, or basil

10 sheets phyllo, thawed according to package instructions

USES UP phyllo, feta cheese, hardy greens

SERVES 6–8

TOTAL TIME 1 hour– 1 hour, 10 minutes

KEEPS FOR up to 3–4 days in the fridge

CAN SUBSTITUTE
- Feta with Halloumi, ricotta, queso fresco, or goat cheese
- Phyllo with The Only Pie Dough You Need (page 226)

1. Preheat the oven to 350°F. Brush a pie plate with some melted coconut oil. Meanwhile, bring a large pot of salted water to a boil.

Continued . . .

Sunday's Rosti Pot Pie (page 173)

Ham and Cheese Hand Pies
(see left)

Curried Feta and
Hardy Greens Galette (see left)

2. If using fresh chard and kale, make sure they are washed well since some types of greens can be very sandy. Separate the stems from leaves. Finely chop the stems and set aside.

3. Add the chard and kale leaves to the pot and boil until wilted, about 2 minutes. Drain in a colander and run under cold water in the sink to cool. Using your hands, give the greens a good squeeze, releasing excess moisture. Finely chop and set aside in a large bowl.

4. In a medium sauté pan over medium heat, add 1 tablespoon of the coconut oil and sauté the onion until translucent, about 3 minutes. Add the garlic, celery, reserved chard and kale stems, nutmeg, curry powder, garam masala, salt, and pepper. Sauté until softened, about 5 minutes.

5. In the meantime, in a small bowl, whisk the eggs with the coconut milk.

6. Mix the sautéed veggies with the spinach and chard, along with the seeds, feta, and herbs. Taste and adjust the seasoning if necessary. Let cool slightly, then stir in the coconut milk and egg mixture.

7. While the mixture cools, gently brush each phyllo sheet with melted coconut oil. Then layer in the pie plate, crisscrossing sheets on top of one another. Phyllo sheets dry out quickly, so keep the stack of remaining sheets covered with a slightly damp cloth while you work. Be sure to leave overhang to wrap around the filling after.

8. Add the filling to the phyllo crust and fold the overhanging phyllo over, leaving it ruffled in appearance. Brush the outer layer of phyllo lightly with melted butter or oil.

9. Bake for 35 to 40 minutes, or until the top is golden. Let rest 10 minutes before serving.

Zero-Waste Tip Most pre-made crusts come with packaging—though more and more you can buy them at your local bakery without—and there are some items, like pastry dough and phyllo that are extremely prone to drying out. Leftover sheets are best wrapped, as airtight as possible . . . and the only way to store them is in plastic wrap. To try to avoid this, I've been reusing a food-safe plastic bag solely for pastry dough instead. Since there are new zero-waste innovations coming out every day, I hope there is a better solution soon.

Zero-Waste Tips from Nick Liu

Nick Liu is Executive Chef/Partner at the critically acclaimed DaiLo and Little DaiLo in Toronto. His specialty? Bold Asian flavors prepared with traditional French techniques. With experience at Michelin-starred restaurants and an appearance on Iron Chef Canada, *he is an expert on New Asian Cuisine.*

Q. What makes you cringe when it comes to food waste in your restaurants?

A. We get really creative in using up items you wouldn't normally use up because of the respect we have for our products or for the animal. Nothing gets thrown away that can be used. We pay a lot of money for our products, so when menu items get sent back or come back not eaten, that makes us feel bad.

Q. What is your biggest everyday hurdle in reducing food waste in your restaurants?

A. One of the biggest struggles we have is the perception of value. Since we are considered an Asian restaurant, people may expect cheaper or larger portions. Adjusting portions and price points while still delivering the best products is a struggle.

Q. When it comes to take-out and food delivery, do you think we will start to see any reduction of packaging wastes in the near future?

A. I certainly hope so. I see it happening. In our Little DaiLo at Assembly Hall we were one of the first to stop using takeaway containers and buy melamine plates. Soon, all the other restaurants in the hall followed suit. At our events, all our serving vessels are edible, so all you need is a napkin.

Q. What's a dish you make at home that reduces food waste?

A. (*Laughs*) Noodles. I have quite a selection of all my favorite noodles, which I love to use with leftovers or food that needs to be used up. For example, I had some takeout fried chicken in my fridge the other day. I made a batch of noodles, put them in a bowl, and arranged some fried chicken overtop on one side. Then I added some leftover tapenade, and arranged chopped lettuce that needed using up and veggies on the other side.

Q. What dish would you say in the restaurant makes it a zero-waste kitchen?

A. The trout. We use the whole trout. It comes in whole, not gutted, so we can use the trout eggs, and use the liver for trout liver mousse. We cut trout "ribs" for a crispy snack upstairs at Lo Pan, and one of our bestselling and longest-lasting items on the menu is our Whole Fried Giggie Trout. The 90 Day Dry Aged Rib Eye is a good one, too. It comes into the restaurant with bones on and we break it down ourselves. The fat cap gets trimmed and we render it down to baste. Under the fat cap are these muscles that we use for carpaccio. Bones are used for braises or stocks. Any little bits of meat cleaned off the bones get saved up for special menu items or for fillings for dumplings.

Pizza Dough F P L

Pizza all starts with the dough. Thankfully, it freezes extremely well, so I make this in batches, and thaw in the fridge the night before. Using '00' flour is best (see tip on page 65), but you can use all-purpose, gluten-free, or any combination of your favorite flours. Have extra dough? Use it to make Pizza Chips (see page 180).

Dough

1½ tsp active dry yeast

1¼ cups warm water

3½ cups 00 flour, all-purpose flour, or flour of choice, plus extra for dusting

½ Tbsp salt

½ cup olive oil

Flavor Variations

Fresh Herb and Garlic 2 Tbsp chopped fresh herbs + 2 tsp garlic powder

Turmeric Spice 1 Tbsp ground turmeric + 1 Tbsp garam masala

Smoked Spice 2 tsp smoked paprika + 2 tsp sweet paprika + 2 tsp smoked chipotle powder

Toppings

Sauce, cheese, toppings and finishings of your choice (see Pizza Night, opposite)

1. In a medium bowl, mix yeast with warm water and set aside for until foamy, about 10 minutes.

2. In a large bowl, mix flour with salt and add any flavor variations. Make a well in the center of the flour mix.

3. Stir in the oil into the yeast mixture. Add the wet ingredients into the well.

4. With one hand, start incorporating flour into the wet ingredients, turning bowl with the other hand as you go, about 3 minutes.

5. Once the dough looks ragged and almost all of the flour is incorporated, transfer to a clean work surface and continue to knead until the dough is smooth, about 5 to 7 minutes.

6. Transfer the dough into an oiled bowl, and turn it lightly to coat with oil. Cover with a damp tea towel and set aside at room temperature for about 1 hour and 30 minutes or until it doubles in size.

7. Flour a baking sheet. Divide the dough into four rounds, punch down with your fist and roll into four nice balls. Transfer to the prepared baking sheet, cover with plastic wrap (see page 176) and let proof again in the fridge for 4 to 8 hours or overnight. If freezing, wrap in airtight freezer-safe packaging, just thaw in the fridge overnight.

9. Let the dough relax and come to room temperature before rolling. In the meantime, preheat the oven to 450 to 500°F. If you have a pizza stone, preheat this in the oven as well.

10. Using a rolling pin, roll out each dough ball to about ½-inch thick. Transfer to the prepared baking sheet and add your desired sauce, cheese and toppings. Transfer onto the hot pizza stone or bake on the sheet for about 8 minutes or until crust is browned and cheese is bubbling.

USES UP flour, herbs, spices, cheese, sauce

MAKES about 4 thin crust one-person pizzas

TOTAL TIME about 25 minutes, plus 8-10 hours proofing

KEEPS FOR up to 2 weeks in the fridge, wrapped well so it doesn't dry out or 6 months in the freezer, wrapped in airtight freezer safe packaging; thaw in the fridge overnight before baking. Once baked, pizza keeps up to 3 days in the fridge.

Pizza Night

Every few weeks we have a homemade pizza night and I love to clean out my fridge and pantry of all their pizza-friendly condiments, sauces, overripe produce, left-overs and greens (marinated vegetables, knobs of different cheeses, cooked proteins, you name it, I'll throw it on!). Whether you buy pizza dough or make it from scratch, here are my ideas for a waste-free pizza night. Just brush on your desired sauce, top with cheese, and pick your choice of produce, proteins and finishers. Note: some fresh finishers like basil or arugula are better to add after cooking.

FIRST STOP: MAKE IT SAUCY
The Red: One of my Tomato Sauce: 3 Ways (page 77) or store-bought
The White: Creamy Cauliflower Sauce (page 66) or store-bought alfredo
The Pesto: Put it in a Pesto (page 74) or store-bought
The Mix: A little pesto mixed with one of the white or red sauces above

SECOND STOP: PICK YOUR CHEESE
Any melty cheese (vegan or not) of your choice, such as mozzarella, cheddar, provolone, or any combination of

THIRD STOP: PRODUCE TOPPINGS
Canned (e.g. artichokes, pineapple chunks)
Cooked, roasted, or grilled (e.g. hardy greens, potatoes, spinach, squash)
Raw (e.g. corn, bell peppers, figs, hardy greens/stems, mango, mushrooms/stems, onions, peaches, pears, plums, tart apples, tomatoes)

FOURTH STOP: PICK A PROTEIN
Deli meats (e.g. smoked ham)
Leftover cooked proteins (e.g. roast chicken, lamb meatballs, ham, scrambled eggs)
Tofu, grilled or marinated (page 91)
Tuna, canned
Shrimp, cooked
Smoked fish

FIFTH STOP: FINAL FINISHINGS
Capers, olives or pickled vegetables
Chili flakes
Citrus zest
Cheese, crumbled (e.g. blue, goat, or buffalo mozzarella) or grated (e.g. Parmesan)
Fresh bitter greens (e.g. arugula) or herbs, chopped (e.g. basil, cilantro)
Nuts (e.g. pine, pistachios, walnuts)
Oil or vinegar, drizzled (e.g. balsamic vinegar, chili or sesame oil)
Sea salt
Sundried tomatoes

Pizza Chips L *Recipe pictured on page 120*

Just like with pizza (page 178), you can really let your imagination run wild with these chips. Great for any party and easy enough for an appetizer paired with dip, to serve as a side with soup (such as on page 97), or break them up to add crunch to a salad (page 46). A fun thing to do with any amount large or small of leftover pizza dough.

3 Tbsp oil (+ extra for greasing)
9 oz pizza dough (page 178), rested
    and at room temperature
Flour, for dusting
Salt and pepper

Optional Seasonings
3 Tbsp chopped fresh or 3 tsp dried
    herbs (e.g., oregano or thyme)
1–2 tsp smoked paprika
1 tsp ground turmeric
Citrus zest, to taste
Parmesan, grated, to taste
Pinch chili flakes or cayenne

For Serving (Optional):
Mojito Pea Hummus (page 100)
Toasted Garlic Rosemary Cannelini
    Dip (100)
Beet It Black Bean Salsa (page 101)
Roasted Garlic Brandade (page 121)
Salt Cod Ceviche (page 122)
Smoky Seafood Spread (page 122)

1. Preheat the oven to 350°F. Line or grease 1 large or 2 small baking sheets.

2. Divide the dough into 2 portions, making it more manageable to roll out, and dust rolling surface with flour to prevent sticking. Roll out the dough as thinly as possible so that when you lift it, you can see your hands through it.

3. In a small bowl, mix the salt and pepper and any optional seasonings with the oil.

4. Place each blanket of dough on a baking sheet, brush with the seasoned oil, and evenly sprinkle with additional Parmesan, zest, and spices.

5. Bake for 15 minutes, depending on thickness, or until golden brown. Let cool and break into chips.

USES UP pizza dough

MAKES about 40 chips, depending on size

TOTAL TIME 25 minutes

KEEPS FOR up to 3–5 days in the pantry

Food 911 Dough, just like all of us, is easier to handle when rested. The glutens relax, making it less like an elastic band when rolling it out. So if you are making pizza dough from scratch, let it rest, covered, for at least 20 minutes before rolling it out.

I'm Feeling Crackers P

Growing up, there was always a bag of Purity Hardtack in the cupboard. Purity Hardtack, also known as a ships biscuit, is used by fisherman for survival at sea. The absence of any fat in the ingredients is what gave it its long shelf life. I wish I had known back then that crackers are actually so easy to make and you can flavor them any way you'd like from citrus zest to grated hard cheese, chopped dried fruit to nutritional yeast!

1½ cups flour (or mix of flours)
1 tsp salt
1 tsp sugar
2 Tbsp olive oil
½ cup water (see substitutes)
Pepper (optional)

Optional Add-Ins
2–3 Tbsp freshly chopped or 2–3 tsp
    dried hardy herbs
Handful of seeds or chopped nuts
1 Tbsp citrus zest
Sprinkle of finely chopped dried fruit
Grated hard cheese or nutritional
    yeast, to taste

Optional Add-Ons
Sea salt

1. Preheat the oven to 450°F and lightly dust a baking sheet with flour.

2. In a large bowl, combine the flour with the salt and sugar, and any optional add-ins. In a small bowl, combine olive oil and water and stir into flour mixture to form a shaggy dough. Transfer to floured surface and knead to form a ball of dough. If too sticky add more flour, if too dry add more water.

3. Wrap the dough with a tea towel and let it rest for 30 minutes.

4. On a floured surface, roll the dough to ¼-inch thick. If garnishing with sea salt, brush the rolled-out dough lightly with water, and lightly sprinkle salt overtop. Cut the crackers into the desired shape and size.

5. Place the crackers on the prepared baking sheet, prick each one with a fork, and bake until lightly browned and cooked through, 12 to 15 minutes.

6. Let cool completely on cooling rack or baking sheet before storing.

Zero-Waste Tip If your crackers get a little stale, re-crisp them in a preheated 350°F oven for a few minutes.

USES UP flour, seeds, nuts

MAKES about 50 crackers

TOTAL TIME 30 minutes (+ 30 minutes resting time)

KEEPS FOR up to 1 week in an airtight container in the pantry

CAN SUBSTITUTE
• Water with leftover blanched or steamed vegetable water

Breadcrumbs and Croutons L P

Even with four people living in our home, we very rarely go through a whole loaf of bread before it starts going stale. I love bakeries that bake smaller loaves and demi-baguettes, but can I not buy half a loaf of sliced sandwich bread? I rarely buy full packages of bread, buns, or bagels anymore, and when I do buy a loaf of sandwich bread, I freeze half of it as soon as I get home. It seems like a no-brainer, but when was the last time you actually made your own breadcrumbs, croutons, crusts, or crispy coatings? There is no easier way to use up days-old bread, and believe me, the homemade version will have flavor and texture that you just don't get with store-bought.

There are two types of breadcrumbs: dry and fresh. Both can be made with day old or stale bread, both are easily frozen and can be used from frozen (no need to defrost), and both can be used as a breading for baking or frying. The main difference is that fresh breadcrumbs are used as a binder for recipes like meatloaf and meatballs whereas dry breadcrumbs are used to add a crunchy texture or topping to dishes like casseroles and baked pasta dishes.

There are also so many alternatives to the traditional breadcrumb (see Crispy Coatings, opposite), no matter how you want to use it—like in Croquettes (page 56), Stem Au Gratin (page 45), Dill Pickle Chicken Tenders (page 132), Veggie and Cheese-Stuffed Meatloaf (page 143), Meatballs 101 (page 144), Nan's Fish Cakes (page 117), or try rolling The Great Risotto (page 160) in breadcrumbs to turn it into balls. And see salads breakdown on page 46 for all the ways you can build a salad with croutons on top.

BREADCRUMBS: 2 WAYS

Fresh Breadcrumbs: Very fresh bread can be too moist to crumble, so one- or two-day old bread works best. Roughly chop and then pulse in a food processor or blender to desired texture.

Dry Breadcrumbs: Stale bread works best. Preheat the oven to 300°F and bake the slices for about 10 minutes or until dry. Cool and roughly chop. In a food processor or blender, pulse to desired texture. Or use a rolling pin (or something similar) to smash dry bread in a reusable bag to desired texture.

USES UP fresh or stale bread

MAKES as much as you have

TOTAL TIME 1–10 minutes

KEEPS FOR up to 1 month, stored in a sealed container in the fridge (fresh), 2 weeks in the pantry, 2 months in the fridge, or 6 months in the freezer (dry)

CROUTONS

1 loaf of bread, sliced or torn into
  desired shapes/sizes
Oil
Salt and pepper

Optional Add-Ins
¼–½ cup grated hard cheese
2 Tbsp chopped fresh or 2–3 tsp dried
  herbs
Dried spices

USES UP bread

MAKES about 5 cups,
depending on bread size

TOTAL TIME about
10 minutes

KEEPS FOR up to 1 week
in the pantry

1. Preheat the oven to 350°F and line a baking sheet.

2. Lightly coat the bread chunks with oil and season to your liking with salt, pepper, and optional add-ins.

3. Bake until golden brown, about 8 minutes. Cool, then store.

CRISPY COATINGS FOUND IN UNUSUAL PLACES
Want to make fried chicken, fried onions, or anything with a crispy
coating but are out of breadcrumbs? Want a gluten-free option?
Try these substitutions instead:

Cereal, crushed

Chia seeds, whole or ground

Coconut flour or shredded coconut

Cornstarch, seasoned with salt, pepper,
spices, and/or herbs

Crackers, ground or crushed

Croutons, crushed

Nutritional yeast

Nuts or seeds, chopped or ground

Oats, whole or ground

Panko

Parmesan or pecorino cheese, grated

Pork rinds, ground or crushed

Potato or corn chips, crushed

Potato flour

Pretzels, chopped or ground

Stocks and Condiments

There's no better way to use up every last bit of produce and protein than by repurposing them as a stock. In this chapter you'll find recipes for stocks and broths, and a whole host of other staples that will save you money and most definitely save you waste. For example, how many half-empty tetra packs, bottles, and jars have you got rattling around in that fridge door? Oh, and when was the last time you looked at their best before dates? All of your house staples—stocks, condiments, pickled ingredients, and even vanilla extract—are so easy to make at home, and not only are your homemade versions free of additives, you can make many of them, such as the 1-Minute Mayo (page 196) or Quick Pickle (page 193), with ingredients you probably already have. You can also flavor everything to just your liking. Just be sure to label your jars!

Stock: 4 Ways F L S

Stocks and broths are one of the best ways to use up trimmings from food prep throughout the week, from unwanted cuts of protein to mushroom trimmings and onion skins. Carrot ends, celery stumps, chicken bones, and tough leek greens can all get put to use when making stock. I collect these trimmings and store them in the freezer, so they are ready to go when it's stock time.

There are a few golden rules to making a great stock. 1) Always use cold water. 2) Simmer, don't boil. 3) Don't add salt. 4) Skim the stock. No matter the contents of my stock, I skim off any foam that rises to the top. Ridding the stock of impurities makes for a clearer stock and prolongs its shelf life.

When making a stock, I typically do not measure things out. Everyone has a different size stockpot, so I like to think in ratios instead: 10 parts water to 5 parts bones and/or meat to 1 part veggies and aromatics. Most stocks use a mirepoix, a fancy word for a vegetable aromatic flavor base, which typically has a ratio of two parts onion to one part celery to one part carrot. In a stock, it is important to even out the flavors of the mirepoix and weighing your ingredients is a good way to achieve this, but is by no means a must. However, the amounts in the recipes below are suggestions only, so if you have, say, one more celery stalk that needs to be used up, add it!

USES UP vegetables, poultry, meat and fish bones, herbs

MAKES 8 cups

TOTAL TIME Vegetable: 40 minutes–1 hour, 10 minutes; Poultry: 3–4 hours on a stovetop or 8–24 hours in a slow cooker; Meat: 6–8 hours on a stovetop or 18–36 hours in a slow cooker; Fish: 50 minutes

KEEPS FOR up to 4 days in the fridge or 6 months in the freezer

VEGETABLE STOCK

Mirepoix
2 Tbsp oil or butter
1 cup (125 g) chopped onions
1 cup (125 g) chopped carrots
1 cup (125 g) chopped celery stalk
A few garlic cloves, smashed
8 cups water

Optional Add-Ins
1–2 leeks or dark-green tops
1–2 cups chopped tomatoes
1 cup mushrooms
½ cup chopped fennel bulb
½ cup chopped parsnip

Seasoning
2 bay leaves
½ Tbsp peppercorns
Small bunch parsley stems
Thyme sprigs

Optional Seasoning (Add to Taste)
Knob of ginger
Oregano sprigs

1. In a large stockpot over medium heat, add the oil and sauté the onion, carrots, and celery until just softened, 5 to 8 minutes.

2. Add the water, seasonings, and any optional add-ins or seasonings you are using, and bring to a simmer. Simmer for 30 minutes or up to 1 hour for a deeper flavor.

3. Skim off any foamy impurities that may appear on the surface. Cool, strain, and use as a base for soups, stews, or braising.

POULTRY STOCK

Mirepoix

2 Tbsp oil or butter

1–2 cups (250 g) roughly chopped
    onion

1 cup (125 g) chopped carrots

1 cup (125 g) chopped celery stalk

3 lb chicken bones from cooked,
    roasted, or uncooked chicken
    (whole carcass can be used)

8 cups water

¼ cup vinegar or white wine

Optional Add-Ins

See Vegetable Stock (above), plus:

½ cup chopped celeriac

A few garlic cloves

Seasoning

See Vegetable Stock (above)

Optional Seasoning

2–3 lime leaves

2–3 stalks lemongrass

Knob of ginger

Hardy or soft herb sprigs (no mint)

1. In a large stockpot over medium heat, add the oil and sauté the onion, carrots, and celery until just softened, 5 to 8 minutes. Transfer to a slow cooker if using.

2. Add the bones, water, vinegar, optional add-ins, and seasonings (including optional seasonings) to the stockpot or slow cooker.

3. For stovetop cooking, bring to a simmer. Simmer for 3 to 4 hours and skim off any foamy impurities that may appear on the surface. For the slow cooker, cook on a low setting for at least 8 hours or up to 24 hours.

4. Cool, strain, and use as a base for soups, stews, or braising.

MEAT STOCK

Mirepoix

2 Tbsp oil or butter

1 cup (125 g) chopped onion

½ cup (70 g) chopped carrots

½ cup (70 g) chopped celery

3 lb bones from cooked or roasted
    meat (knuckles, shank, marrow,
    neck bones)

8 cups water

¼ cup vinegar or wine

Optional Add-Ins

See Poultry Stock (above)

Seasoning

See Poultry Stock (above)

Optional Seasoning

A few whole cloves

Hardy or soft herb sprigs (no mint)

1. In a large stockpot over medium heat, add the oil and sauté the onion, carrots, and celery until just softened, 5 to 8 minutes. Transfer to a slow cooker if using.

2. Add the bones, water, vinegar, optional add-ins, and seasonings (including optional seasonings) to the stockpot or slow cooker. For stovetop cooking, bring to a simmer. Simmer for 6 to 8 hours and skim off any foamy impurities that may appear on the surface. For the slow cooker, cook on a low setting for at least 18 hours or up to 36 hours.

3. Cool, strain, and use as a base for soups, stews, or braising.

Food 911 Bones with a lot of cartilage, connective tissue, and collagen add gelatin when cooking, which adds richness and body to your stock.

FISH STOCK

1 Tbsp butter or oil	**Optional Add-Ins**	**Seasoning**
½ cup (70 g) diced onions	1 shallot, chopped	2 bay leaves
½ cup (70 g) finely diced celery	1 leek, chopped	½ Tbsp peppercorns
3 lb rinsed raw fish bones from lean	½ cup chopped fennel	
fish (e.g., sole, halibut, cod) or	½ cup chopped mushrooms	**Optional Seasoning**
2 lb raw shrimp shells	A few garlic cloves, smashed	1–2 stalks lemongrass
8 cups water		Knob of ginger
½ cup white wine		Tarragon sprigs
		Thyme sprigs

1. In a large stockpot over medium heat, add the oil and sauté the onions and celery until just softened, 5 to 8 minutes.

2. Add the fish bones, water, wine, optional add-ins, seasoning, and optional seasoning and bring to a simmer. Simmer for 45 minutes, and skim off any foamy impurities that may appear on the surface.

3. Cool, strain, and use as a base for soups, stews, or braising.

Food 911 Fish stock isn't as common in the home kitchen, as most people tend to buy prepared deboned and shell-free seafood. But I think the real culprit is it sounds fancy or complicated. It's not. All it takes is a few fish bones, some flavorful odds and ends, and 45 minutes—and voilà! You can have a fabulous fish stock that goes great in many soups and sauces.

Parm Broth F S

I freely admit that I did not know this broth existed until I was working on this book. Using leftover cheese rinds as a base for a broth that then can be used for cooking beans and making simple soups, sauces, or risotto? Amazing. You can use your rinds from Parmesan or any other hard cheese you like to curate your own signature rind broth. The ratio is a simple eight parts water to one part rind. See how this broth is used in Marvelous Minestrone (page 81).

8 cups water
1 lb Parmesan rinds, rinsed and
    trimmed of any unwanted spots
1 bay leaf
½ onion
12 black peppercorns
Small bunch parsley stems

Optional Add-Ins
A few smashed garlic cloves
Aromatics e.g., celery stalks, leek,
    a carrot, or some fennel
Sage leaves or sprigs of thyme or
    oregano

USES UP Parmesan rinds, hard cheese rinds

MAKES 6 cups

TOTAL TIME 1–2 hours

KEEPS FOR up to 1 week in the fridge or 6 months in the freezer

1. Place all of the ingredients, including the optional add-ins, in a stockpot and bring to boil. Reduce to a simmer and cook for up to 2 hours. After 1 hour, taste, and if it is to your liking, it's done. If not, simmer up to 1 hour longer, tasting along the way.

2. Strain and let cool, then store.

Food 911 One pound of cheese rinds sounds like a lot, but they add up fast, especially since they can last in your freezer for years. Start stashing them there for your next batch of broth or to add flavor to your next soup, sauce, or stew. Since Parmesan rinds have become such a hot flavor commodity, you can buy them at the cheese section of your local deli or grocer (some give them away for free!). Just ask at the deli where you can find them.

All–Purpose Brine Spice Mix P

Brining gives you some wiggle room when cooking proteins that are prone to drying out, like turkey, pork, and chicken. It locks in moisture, tenderizes the meat, and adds flavor. It's also a great way to use up dried herbs and spices that you have had hanging about for too long. I like to make a big batch of the dry mix and store it in my pantry until needed. Just add water.

1 Tbsp black peppercorns
2 Tbsp sugar
¼ cup kosher salt or 2 Tbsp table salt
3 bay leaves
1 Tbsp dried thyme
½ tsp dehydrated garlic

Optional Add-Ins
Shallots, onions, or garlic, chopped
Fresh soft or hardy herbs, to taste
Dried spices or herbs

4 cups water (see substitutions)

1. In a bowl, combine the spice mix ingredients.

2. In a large saucepot, combine the water, spice mix, and optional add-ins and bring to a boil.

3. Let cool and use to brine protein in a suitable container for the suggested time, usually 1 hour per pound of meat. Turkey can be brined for up to 24 hours depending on size.

Food 911   Look at the shape and size of the protein you want to brine and place it in a suitable container. Then you can eyeball how many cups of brine you will need to submerge it.

USES UP dried spices, dried herbs, fresh herbs

MAKES spice mix for 4 cups of brine

TOTAL TIME 5 minutes

KEEPS FOR 1 year (dry spice mix only) in pantry; add water and optional add-ins as needed

CAN SUBSTITUTE
• Portion of water with beer, wine, or juice

The Quick Pickle F S

The Quick Pickle or the Quickle! I thought this name was the perfect fit for pickling at home. The brine in this recipe adapts to anything, from grapes to broccoli stems, squash to cherries, or any combination. Personally I fiddle with the amount of sugar, adding less when making a pickle with naturally sweeter fruits or veggies, like watermelon rinds.

1 cup white vinegar

1 cup water

¼ cup sugar

1 Tbsp kosher salt

½ Tbsp black peppercorns

½ Tbsp mustard seeds

4 cups peeled, sliced, or chopped veggies and/or fruits

Optional Add-Ins

½ onion, chopped

A few slices of fresh ginger or garlic

A few star anise pods

Chili pepper slices or pinch red chili flakes

Fresh sprigs of dill weed or thyme

1 tsp coriander seed or fennel seed

¼ tsp ground allspice

Pickling spice

USES UP vegetables, fruits, vinegar, herbs, and spices

MAKES two 2-cup canning jars

TOTAL TIME 10 minutes

KEEPS FOR up to 3 weeks in the fridge (be sure to label and date)

1. Bring the vinegar, water, sugar, salt, peppercorns, mustard seeds, and optional add-ins to a boil in a medium pot over high heat. Reduce the heat to a medium-low and simmer for 10 minutes.

2. While the brine is simmering, divide the veggies and fruits you are pickling among heatproof resealable jars.

3. Pour the hot brining liquid overtop. Let cool to room temperature, cover, and place in the fridge until chilled.

Zero-Waste Tip If you have a bunch of pickle jars in your fridge that are almost empty, eat up those pickles tonight and combine the brines for some quick pickles. Just bring this instabrine to a boil and pour it over chopped veggies.

Hawaiian Chili Water F P

In Hawaii, they make a hot chili water that is used not only as a condiment but also as a multipurpose flavoring ingredient while cooking, and sometimes as a little something to slowly sip. I was amazed when I stumbled upon it on my last trip there. Homemade hot sauce used to be my go-to recipe, until I made my very own Hawaiian chili water. You make a bottle of this once and it is a little spicy gift that keeps on giving. As it is used up, you can replenish the water and vinegar for up to 6 months. I know we are all not fortunate enough to have Hawaiian chili peppers close by, but this recipe is great with whatever hot chilies you have on hand. Add a few drops to spice up Tomato Sauce (page 77), Fancy Fried Rice (page 165), Marvelous Minestrone (page 81), or Black-Eyed Peas with Kale and Dill (page 93), to name a few.

3 cloves garlic, finely chopped

1½ tsp sea salt

¼ cup mild-flavored vinegar like rice
   or white vinegar

1 cup water

4–5 hot chili peppers, chopped (I like
   habaneros)

Optional Add-Ins

1 tsp soy, tamari, or Worcestershire
   sauce

Ginger, sliced

Splash of juice like pineapple or
   mango

1. In a small saucepot bring all of the ingredients, including any optional add-ins, to a boil, then lower the heat and simmer for 1 minute.

2. Let cool and transfer to a sealed jar. Let the flavors mingle in the fridge for 3 days before using.

Zero–Waste Tip Have an abundance of chili peppers? Make your own chili pepper flakes. Dehydrate halved chili peppers (stems removed), seeds and all, for 3 to 4 hours on the highest setting of the dehydrator or for up to 12 hours on the lowest setting (the lower setting preserves the nutrients). Or place the peppers cut side up on a lined baking sheet and bake at 200°F until dried, about 6 hours. Turn the oven off and let the peppers continue to dry until cool. Process in a blender or food processor until you have what looks like store-bought red pepper flakes.

USES UP hot chili peppers

MAKES about 1 cup

TOTAL TIME 6 minutes

KEEPS FOR as you use up the pepper water, top it up with more water and vinegar to keep it going for up to 6 months (be sure to label and date)

1–Minute Mayo F

You got one egg? Then you've got yourself a cup of homemade mayo that you can spread on everything. Homemade mayo tastes so much better than store-bought, and it really does only take a minute to make. We all buy the store-bought mayo-like dressings because of their shelf life, but the last thing I need is more condiments to add to my collection. We don't go through a lot of mayonnaise in our house, so I use this recipe when needed. Reminder, mayonnaise is also a base for, like, 50,000 other sauces and dips, like in my Turmeric Aioli (page 72).

1 egg
2 tsp white wine vinegar or fresh
    lemon juice
1 tsp Dijon mustard
½ tsp salt
Pepper
1 cup neutral-flavored oil

Flavor Variation

Chipotle 1 canned chipotle in adobo sauce, finely chopped + 1–2 tsp sweet chili powder

Herby 1 Tbsp finely chopped herbs, e.g., tarragon, chives, cilantro, or basil

Lemon Garlic 1 clove finely chopped garlic and 1 Tbsp lemon zest

Spicy A few dashes of your favorite hot sauce or 1–2 tsp prepared horse-radish or wasabi

USES UP eggs, neutral-flavored oil

MAKES a little over 1 cup

TOTAL TIME 3 minutes

KEEPS FOR up to 1 week in the fridge

1. Place the egg, vinegar, mustard, salt, and pepper in a food processor or blender. Pulse a few times to combine.

2. While the blender or food processor is running, slowly add the oil in a steady stream and count to 30 seconds, or until the oil is completely emulsified and you have a thick, creamy mayo. Taste and adjust the seasoning if necessary.

Zero–Waste Tip Eggs can last up to 1 month past their best before date. The age-old crack and smell test is probably your best bet when it comes to knowing for sure. If you are making hard-boiled eggs, you can do the sink or swim test: place the whole egg in water, and if it floats, it's not fresh anymore.

Best Tartar Sauce ⬛F ⬛P

What recipe ever calls for a whole jar of capers? There is always a half jar kicking around my fridge. Use them up in this quick tartar sauce that goes with any seafood or fish sandwich.

1 Tbsp capers, rinsed and finely
    chopped
2 Tbsp relish or chopped pickles
½ clove garlic, finely chopped

½ cup mayo or 1-Minute Mayo
    (page 196)
Salt and pepper
2 Tbsp chopped chives (optional)

1. Mix all of the ingredients together in a bowl until incorporated. Transfer the sauce to a sealed container.

USES UP capers, mayonnaise

MAKES ¾ cup

TOTAL TIME 5 minutes

KEEPS FOR up to 1 week in the fridge

Smashed Strawberry and Maple Barbecue Sauce ⬛F *Recipe pictured on page 90*

I started making my own barbecue sauces years ago, since I find store-bought ones too sweet. Swapping out the sugar used in store-bought versions for fruit give this sauce a subtle sweetness while adding fruity flavor profiles, and making the most of summer produce.

1 Tbsp olive oil
½ sweet onion, finely chopped (such
    as Vidalia)
1 clove garlic, minced
1 cup roughly chopped fresh or frozen
    strawberries (see substitutions)

1 chipotle in adobo sauce, finely
    chopped, or 1 tsp chipotle powder
2 Tbsp maple syrup
½ cup tomato purée (see substitutions)
2 Tbsp Dijon mustard or 2 tsp mustard
    powder
Salt and pepper

1. In a medium saucepot over medium heat, add the oil and sauté the onion with the garlic until softened, about 3 minutes.

2. Stir in the strawberries, chipotle, maple syrup, tomato purée, mustard, salt, and pepper and simmer, stirring occasionally, until the strawberries soften and the sauce thickens, 5 minutes.

3. Smash the strawberries with a fork or potato masher, then taste and adjust seasoning with salt, pepper, or more maple syrup.

USES UP berries, tomato purée

MAKES about 1 cup

TOTAL TIME 15 minutes

KEEPS FOR up to 1 week in the fridge or 3 months in the freezer

CAN SUBSTITUTE
• Strawberries with berries or other fruit such as peaches, mango, or papaya
• Tomato purée with chopped canned or fresh tomatoes or ketchup (reduce the maple syrup to 2 Tbsp)

Banana Peel Chutney F S

Did you know it can take up to two years for a banana peel to decompose? Eating the peels of the foods we eat reduces our foodprint and can also be better for our bodies, especially in the case of bananas. They have fiber (both soluble and insoluble), potassium, magnesium, B_6, B_{12}, vitamin A, lutein, and antioxidants. And they go great in this chutney, which tastes like a mixture between ratatouille and baba ghanoush. Believe me, nobody will be able to guess that this chutney was made out of banana peels. In fact, I placed a bet recently at a dinner party, and nobody could guess!

Peels (stems removed) from 2 bananas, diced

2 Tbsp oil

1 tsp mustard seeds

½ cup diced red onion

1 clove garlic, finely chopped

½-inch knob ginger, finely chopped or grated

½ cup diced bell peppers

½ chili pepper, finely chopped

One 1-inch-square piece tamarind paste, seeds removed

Salt and pepper

½ cup orange juice (see substitutions)

¼ tsp cinnamon

¼ tsp ground allspice

Optional Add-Ins

1 tsp coriander

1 tsp ground turmeric

½ tsp cardamom

1. In a pot, simmer the peels in boiling salted water for 5 minutes. Drain well and set aside.

2. In a small saucepot over medium heat, add the oil and mustard seeds and sauté until the seeds are popping, 2 to 3 minutes.

3. Stir in the onion, garlic, ginger, peppers, chili, tamarind paste, salt, pepper, and any other optional add-ins. Sauté for a few more minutes until everything is softened.

4. Add the orange juice, cinnamon, allspice, and banana peels and simmer for about 5 minutes or until everything is thickened and saucy. Taste and adjust the seasoning.

5. Keep chunky or blend in a food processor or blender for a smoother consistency.

USES UP banana peels

MAKES about 1 cup

TOTAL TIME 15 minutes

KEEPS FOR up to 2–3 days in the fridge

CAN SUBSTITUTE
- Orange juice with pineapple or mango juice

Zero–Waste Tip   Next time you make a post-workout smoothie, try tossing the whole banana in there, peel (stem removed) and all. The other yummy stuff cancels out any bitter flavor.

Chow Chow F S *Recipe pictured on page 94*

Chow Chow, a chunky relish-like condiment, was created as a way to use up end-of-season produce from the garden. It has roots not only in Atlantic Canada but also in the South and the Caribbean, where it is a favorite. This is a great starter recipe that you can alter to your taste and to what needs using up. East Coasters don't usually use cornstarch, but I added it to this recipe since it cuts down the cooking time significantly. Great served with sausages, pork, or ham, or used as any condiment. Note: it is best to try to cut all your vegetables the same size.

Vegetables
2 bell peppers, chopped (see substitutions)
1 cup chopped cauliflower florets and/or stems (see substitutions)
1 onion or 2 shallots, chopped (see substitutions)
1 carrot, chopped (see substitutions)
1 Tbsp salt

Chow Chow
10 cloves
8 pimento (cherry) peppers, chopped (optional)
1 Tbsp salt
2 Tbsp ground turmeric
1 tsp dry mustard or 1 Tbsp yellow mustard seeds
3 Tbsp sugar
2½ cups white vinegar
2 Tbsp cornstarch

Flavor Variation
Spicy 1 fresh chili pepper, chopped or ½ tsp chili flakes
Cinnamon Spice 1 tsp cinnamon + ¼ tsp ground allspice + 1 Tbsp fresh ginger or 1 tsp ground ginger
Garlic and Celery Replace a portion of vegetables with chopped celery + 1 tsp celery seed + a few garlic cloves, chopped

1. For the Vegetables: In a large bowl, brine the vegetables by covering them with water and adding the salt. Let sit at least 8 hours or overnight. Drain.

2. For the Chow Chow: In a heavy-bottomed saucepot, add the drained vegetables, the chow chow ingredients, and any optional additions. Bring to a boil, stirring occasionally to prevent lumps, then lower to simmer until the mixture thickens to a relish-like texture, about 20 minutes. The mixture will continue to thicken it cools.

3. Remove from the heat and store in a sterile airtight jar. Label and date.

USES UP vegetables, garlic

MAKES about 4 cups

TOTAL TIME 20 minutes (+8–12 hours for brining)

KEEPS FOR up to 1 month in the fridge

CAN SUBSTITUTE
• Vegetables with about 5 cups (mix and match) green tomatoes, cucumber, cabbage, zucchini, and/or squash

Zero–Waste Tips from Jason Cox

Chef Jason Cox has been at the helm of Toronto's award-winning Opus Restaurant for nearly two decades, playing with the boundaries of classic cuisines like French, Mediterranean, and Asian. We connected about his strategies for reducing food waste at the restaurant.

Q. What's the most efficient way to teach your staff about food waste?

A. I find the fastest way to learn is through your mistakes. You burned the almonds? Almonds are expensive, and now they have to be composted instead of eaten. You'll be more mindful the next time.

Our staff also learn by doing, and by following our processes. A restaurant kitchen is different than a home kitchen. We have stocks going and brines we make where we can use up citrus peels, bits of herbs, and peels of veggies. We also have more fridge and freezer space, and equipment like dehydrators that help preserve food longer. And restaurant kitchens label and date everything.

Q. What about limiting food waste when it comes to your clientele?

A. Most people we serve here are interested in the protein. That's what I tell my staff. They are ordering this dish because they want the steak, not the side or garnish. This gives us freedom to be more creative with the garnishes and sides—and being creative also means making use of, say, leftover citrus peels to make a trendy citrus ash.

Q. One thing I always struggle with is sending food back, especially in a restaurant I frequent and where I can tell something is off. How does it feel when plates come back with food still on them?

A. My heart sinks. Deflated. That said, it is always better to say something than not. If your server doesn't ask if everything is okay when you haven't touched your dish, then they are not doing their job. And if you feel uncomfortable doing that right then and there, send a quick note or message to the restaurant the next day.

We do have to remind ourselves about the realities of our clientele. Some people just order things because they can, even though they know they won't finish it all. There is a balance between not getting too broken up over it and having good communication with your staff and clientele.

Q. What tips can you share for home cooks who want to reduce their food waste?

A. Learn from your mistakes, label things, and take the time to store food properly. Know your clientele (in this case, your family) and what they like. Be honest about what they are not eating on their plates and what you are throwing away. Then, get creative and find ways to use it up. I have a bad habit of buying things I think my family will eat, because it's what I want them to eat. I bought a new cereal to go with the almond coconut milk, and then I got upset because it had gone bad. Change is good, but everyone has to be on board.

Shallot Marmalade S

Chef Jason Cox's versatile recipe takes full advantage of shallot scraps, and captures their marvelous quality to gain sweetness as cooked. The result is a sweet and savory condiment that elevates any sandwich, burger, roast-meat dinner, or charcuterie board.

3 cups roughly chopped shallots or
    onions
½ cup sugar
2 cups white wine vinegar
    (see substitutions)
Salt and pepper to taste

Optional Add-Ins
2 chopped garlic cloves
1 Tbsp chopped capers
1 tsp cinnamon
1 tsp dried thyme
1 tsp paprika

½ tsp chili flakes
½ tsp ground nutmeg
¼ tsp ground cloves

1. Place everything in a heavy-bottomed saucepot. Bring to a boil and then lower the heat and simmer until jammy, stirring occasionally, about 1½ hours. The marmalade will thicken as it cools.

2. For a less chunky consistency, pureé using a blender or food processor.

3. Label with the date and refrigerate.

Food 911 What can you do when your saucepot is not up to par? You see the term "heavy bottomed" used to describe pots in recipes, and this is because they distribute heat better and prevent scorching. Place any sub-par saucepot on top of an upside down cast-iron frying pan as a flame tamer.

(Recipe contributed by Jason Cox)

USES UP shallots, onions

MAKES about 1¼ cups

TOTAL TIME about
1 hour, 30 minutes

KEEPS FOR up to
3 months in the fridge

CAN SUBSTITUTE
- White wine vinegar with red wine vinegar, leftover white wine, or any combinations of vinegars (e.g., apple cider and white wine)

Slow Cooker Apple Butter F S

Having a few jars of this healthy, no-added-sugar silky-sweet buttery fruit spread has been a lifesaver. Plus it's a great way to use up the apples we picked every fall. No butter, peeling, or stirring involved. Using a slow cooker means you can sit back and relax while this is stewing. Eat it with a spoon, spread it on toast or pancakes (page 240), or pair it with something savory.

4 lb apples (about 12), quartered, with stems, cores, and seeds removed (use a combination of sweet and tart apples like Granny Smith with Honeycrisp) (see substitutions)

¼ cup water
½ cinnamon stick
½ vanilla bean, cut in half and sliced lengthwise
Pinch salt

Optional Add-Ins
2 star anise pods
1 tsp ground ginger
½ tsp ground nutmeg
½ tsp ground cardamom
¼ tsp ground cloves
Lemon juice or orange juice

1. Add the apples, water, cinnamon, vanilla bean, and salt to your slow cooker. Set the slow cooker to high and cook for 5 hours, stirring and mashing the fruit halfway through the cooking time.

2. Open the lid of the slow cooker and cook for an additional 45 minutes to 1 hour until the mixture darkens and most of the liquid evaporates. It should look nice and saucy. Check and stir occasionally.

3. Let cool slightly, remove the vanilla pod (save and wash for another use), cinnamon stick, and star anise (if using). Transfer to a food processor or blender. Blend until you have a buttery silky-smooth purée, emulsifying all those skins. Taste and adjust the seasoning with lemon juice if you like.

4. If your apple butter is watery after puréeing, put it back in the slow cooker with the lid open for an extra 15 to 20 minutes (or in a saucepot over medium-low heat), stirring occasionally until thick. Transfer to clean jars, seal, label, date, and refrigerate.

USES UP apples, apple peels

MAKES 3 or 4 canning jars (2 cups each)

TOTAL TIME 10 minutes (+ 5–6 hours in a slow cooker)

KEEPS FOR several weeks in the fridge, or at least 1 year in the pantry if sealed using the hot-water bath method (see below)

CAN SUBSTITUTE
- Apples with pears, apricots, or quince

Food 911 To sterilize your jars, boil in a boiling-water canner for 10 minutes or run them through the hot cycle in a dishwasher. Heat the new lids in a pot of warm water, setting aside the jar bands. Keep the jars and lids warm until ready to use. Ladle your preserves with appropriate headspace (see www.bernardin.ca). Wipe the rim with a damp clean cloth, place the warm lids on the jars, and screw the jar bands on until you just meet resistance. Carefully submerge the jars in the boiling-water canner and process for the appropriate amount of time (see www.bernardin.ca). Transfer jars to a clean tea towel and do not disturb for 24 hours. Place any unsealed jars (top of the lid pops when pressed) in the fridge and use within the week. Note that canning jars and bands/rings can be reused, but the lids need to be new.

Moroccan Preserved Lemons F

The thinly sliced skin of a preserved lemon is a delightful addition to any dish. They are quite flavorful and add a saltiness and brightness to tagines and stews. You can add preserved chopped lemons to a salad (page 46), soup (page 98), or roast a few slices with vegetables (page 41), add to stir fries, mix them into a relish, or even stir it into some butter with some herbs. Here is my go-to recipe for an overstock of lemons, and it's also a great foodie gift idea. Most methods have you cut one side of the lemon off and discard it, then quarter what is remaining. This method ensures that no lemon skin is lost.

About 5 organic lemons
5 Tbsp kosher salt, divided

1. Slice the lemons in half crosswise and juice them, leaving some of the pulp behind. Reserve the juice, and place lemon halves in a medium-size bowl.

2. Rub 3 tablespoons of the salt all over the inside and outside of the lemon halves.

3. Add 1 tablespoon of salt to the bottom of the jar. Squish the lemons (use some muscle) with the salt in the jar, and top with the remaining 1 tablespoon of salt.

4. Pour the reserved lemon juice into the jar, leaving a ½-inch headspace. Seal the jar and place it in a bowl (to catch any possible overflow) and let sit at room temperature for 7 days, then transfer to the fridge.

5. When using, rinse the lemon half and scoop out and discard any pulp. Slice and dice and use as desired. Preserved lemons get better with time, after about 3 weeks.

USES UP lemons

MAKES Two 2-cup canning jars

TOTAL TIME 5 minutes

KEEPS FOR up to 6 months in the fridge

Sweeter Stuff

I jump at any excuse to bake, so I am always pondering ways to bake up food items that are past their prime. From dented zucchinis and overripe fruits to leftover egg whites and grains, there is always a little something hanging about that you can transform into a sweet little pick-me-up. Baked goods tend to bear freezing well, which is another way I convince myself to bake. It can always be frozen for later, and I am always glad I have a little something sweet hidden in the freezer for those last-minute dinner parties or pop-ins.

Papaya Pops with Coconut, Avocado, and Lime F

Bought a whole papaya because it was on sale but didn't use it all up and now it's a little too ripe for your liking? Have half an avocado lying around? Here is a healthy take on some frozen ice pops that might be worthy of an Instagram photo.

Papaya Layer
2 cups chopped papaya
⅓ cup orange juice
1 Tbsp liquid sweetener (see tip)

Coconut Lime Layer
1 cup coconut milk
½ avocado
Juice and zest of half a lime

2 Tbsp liquid sweetener (see tip)
1 tsp Pure Vanilla Extract (page 212)
Pinch sea salt

1. For the Papaya Layer: In a blender or food processor, blend the ingredients until smooth and place in a container that will pour easily.

2. Pour 1 to 2 tablespoons of the blended papaya into each popsicle mold, enough to coat the bottom. Place in the freezer for 15 minutes to allow it to firm up a bit.

3. For the Coconut Lime Layer: In a blender or food processor, blend the ingredients until smooth and pour 1 to 2 tablespoons on top of the papaya layer. Freeze for another 15 minutes.

4. Repeat, alternating the papaya and coconut layers, until you have 4 layers and the popsicle molds are almost full (liquid expands when frozen).

5. Set a timer for 20 to 30 minutes to partially freeze the pops and then insert your sticks. Freeze the popsicles until completely frozen, at least 4 hours.

6. To serve, run the mold under hot water for a few seconds for easy release.

USES UP papaya, avocado, lime, coconut milk

MAKES about 6 popsicles

TOTAL TIME 5 minutes (+ 4 hours freezing time)

KEEPS FOR up to 6 months (popsicles may start to develop ice crystals over time)

Food 911 Always use a liquid sweetener like honey, maple syrup, agave syrup, or a homemade simple sugar syrup (1 part sugar to 1 part water, brought to a boil until the sugar dissolves) in popsicles. When using stevia drops or other sugar-free alternatives, use the amounts suggested on the package.

Zero–Waste Tip Eat your papaya seeds. They are edible and incredibly nutrition-boosting, (I love them with yogurt). Or turn them into papaya seed pepper. Just bake in the oven at 250°F for 2 hours or dry in the dehydrator overnight, and then grind with a mortar and pestle or in a small spice grinder to desired coarseness.

Popsicles: 3 Ways

Put it in a popsicle! No matter how many times I tell myself that I don't need those berries for sale on the side of that country road, I just can't help pulling over. I almost feel that if I don't buy all of them right now, I may never get to taste them again. Well, at least until next summer. Popsicles are one of many ways to use up some of these excess foodstuffs floating around. Here are three versions of the must-have summer popsicle.

USES UP juices, dairy, fruit

MAKES 6 popsicles

TOTAL TIME 5 minutes (+ 6 hours freezing time)

KEEPS FOR up to 6 months (popsicles may start to develop ice crystals over time)

THE JUICY

Any combination of fresh juice, iced tea, lemonade, or fruit purée/smoothie you like

Add-ins Chopped mashed fruits/berries, chopped fresh herbs, and liquid sweetener to taste

Examples
- Banana mango
- Lemon and hibiscus iced tea
- Strawberry basil

THE CREAMY

Mix yogurt, coconut milk, sour cream, or kefir into the juicy version above. You can also steep cream with tea for 3 minutes for a signature flavoring, like Earl Grey or matcha.

Add-ins Chopped fruits or berries, shredded coconut, chopped nuts and/or seeds, freshly chopped herbs, chocolate hazelnut spread, nut or seed butters, and liquid sweetener to taste.

Examples
- Cherry frozen yogurt with chocolate shavings
- Chocolate, mint, and raspberry
- Matcha green tea and mint

MAKE IT BOOZY

Since alcohol doesn't freeze, you have to have the right percentage of it in your popsicle mix for it to work. To freeze, 20% or less of the total popsicle mix can be alcohol, which works out to a 5:1 ratio, so for every 5 oz. of liquid you can add 1 oz. or less of alcohol.

Examples
- Coconut, pineapple, and rum
- Lime, avocado, and tequila
- Strawberry, cream, and Campari

Zero–Waste Tip Don't have reusable popsicle molds? Here are some items you probably have on hand that you can use instead. Muffin tins (or other small baking vessels), washed small yogurt containers, paper cups, ice cube trays, or small glass vessels (like shot glasses).

Endless Ice Cream F

I debated whether to include this recipe, as not everyone has an ice cream machine. Then I tested it with a borrowed ice cream machine, and was blown away. Then I tried making it without the machine, and although it sets harder, it was still just as delicious. Now I want to make ice cream all of the time because I can make it just the way I want it, and you can too! Plus it's an incredible way to use up fresh fruits, eggs, dairy, nut and seed butters, teas, spices . . . The list goes on! Here are some general tips to get you started:

BASE An ice cream base just takes 5 to 10 minutes to make. Then all you have to do is wait until it's frozen. Depending on your ice cream flavor and preference, the recipe below can be adjusted quite easily by using these tips.

RICHNESS For richer ice cream, add more yolks (no more than eight) and use heavy cream (35%) in the base recipe. For lighter ice cream, use no less than two yolks and increase the milk, decreasing the cream by the same amount, in the base recipe.

SWEETNESS Experiment here: Decrease the amount if you want something less sweet. Or vary your sugar flavor profile with honey, brown sugar, and maple syrup.

Note that if you're adding fruit, fruit adds water content, which leads to ice crystals, so adapt the base by decreasing the milk and upping the cream (fat) by the same amount.

> **USES UP**: egg yolks, dairy, fruit, berries, spices, teas
>
> **MAKES** about 3–4 cups
>
> **TOTAL TIME** 30 minutes (+ about 15 minutes churning time)
>
> **KEEPS FOR** Up to 2 weeks with good texture; after that it may become more icy
>
> **CAN SUBSTITUTE**
> - A portion of the cream and milk with buttermilk, or replace the dairy with coconut milk

2 cups heavy cream (see substitutions)
1 cup whole milk (see substitutions)
⅔ cup sugar (see Sweetness, above)
Pinch salt
6 egg yolks (reserve whites for egg white recipes (see page 224) or store for later use)

Flavor Variations

Berries and/or Bananas Omit the milk. Use 3 cups of cream in the base. Purée 1 lb of berries and/or bananas with a few Tbsp of sugar and stir into the ice cream base before chilling.

Chocolate Reduce the sugar to ⅓ cup and add 2 Tbsp unsweetened cocoa powder with the sugar to dissolve in the milk or cream in step 1. Once the base is thickened, add 1 tsp Pure Vanilla Extract (page 212) and 6 oz chopped milk or semi-sweet chocolate in step 4. Whisk until the chocolate is melted and smooth. Chill.

Citrus Blend citrus zest with sugar in a food processor and use citrus sugar instead of plain sugar.

Fruit Omit the milk. Use 3 cups of cream in the base. Dice 1 to 2 lb of fruit and simmer with ½ cup sugar until the fruit is tender, 5 to 10 minutes. Add this to the warm base after straining.

Nut or Seed Butters Whisk 1 cup butter + 1 tsp Pure Vanilla Extract

(page 212) into the warm strained base in step 4.

Spiced In step 1, add ground cinnamon, nutmeg, anise, cardamom, etc. with the sugar, or steep whole spices in the milk and cream base as you would tea in step 2.

Tea Whatever flavor you like, just steep the tea in the milk and cream base in step 2.

Vanilla In step 2, steep the milk and cream base with the scraped seeds and/or pods of 1 or 2 vanilla beans. You can use recycled pods as well.

Continued . . .

1. In a small pot, bring the cream, milk, sugar, and salt to a low simmer until the sugar completely dissolves, about 5 minutes.

2. If you are steeping aromatic flavor infusions into the milk and cream base, you can add them now and steep, covered, for 10 minutes.

3. In a separate bowl, whisk the yolks. Then, while whisking, very slowly pour about a third of the hot cream into the yolks to prevent them from curdling. Then whisk this mixture back into the pot with the remaining milk and cream mixture.

4. Over medium-low heat, heat the base, while stirring, until the mixture is thick enough to coat the back of a spoon (about 170°F), about 4 minutes.

5. Immediately strain the mixture through a fine-mesh sieve into a clean bowl and chill in the fridge for at least 4 hours, preferably overnight. You can speed up the process by placing the bowl in another large bowl of ice.

6. If using an ice cream machine, after chilling, churn according to the manufacturer's instructions. No machine? Freeze in a sealed container until hard enough to scoop.

100% Pure Vanilla Extract L

Did you know you can make pure vanilla extract at home? It's true—I haven't had to buy pure vanilla extract in over seven years, which saves money in the long run, and it's the easiest thing to make. Double the recipe if you bake with vanilla often.

About 4 fresh vanilla beans and/or previously used and rinsed vanilla beans, cut lengthwise to expose seeds

½ cup unflavored vodka (see substitutions)

1. Add the split vanilla beans to a clean bottle. Cover with vodka, using a funnel if necessary, and seal shut.

2. Store in a cool dark place and shake daily for a minimum of 14 days.

3. Use when needed, adding rinsed leftover pods from previous recipes and topping up with more vodka as it depletes.

Food 911 You know how recipes always say to add vanilla extract last, away from a heat source? Well, it's because the flavor is held in the alcohol, and when alcohol is burned off, the flavors diminish. Pure vanilla extract is pricey, so the last thing you want to do is just burn it off.

USES UP (recycled) vanilla pods, vanilla beans, vodka

MAKES ½ cup

TOTAL TIME 2 minutes (+ 14 days of steep time)

CAN SUBSTITUTE
- Vodka with gin, brandy, rum, or bourbon, or even a little splash of one of these mixed in (just remember you've got to like the taste of the alcohol you use)

CBZ Cake with a De–Lightful Cream Cheese Frosting F P S

CBZ. Carrots. Bananas. Zucchini. This is what happens when you love carrot cake just as much as banana and zucchini bread.

4 Tbsp melted butter or oil (+ extra for greasing)

4 eggs

1 cup white or brown sugar

2 mashed overripe bananas (if adding peels, see This Bread Is Bananas on page 217 and blend with banana)

2 tsp Pure Vanilla Extract (page 212)

3 cups flour

2 tsp baking powder

1 tsp salt

3 tsp cinnamon

1 Tbsp grated fresh or 1 tsp ground ginger

½ tsp ground or freshly grated nutmeg

2 cups grated zucchini with skins

1 cup grated carrots

Optional Add-Ins

½ cup chopped nuts or seeds

½ cup chocolate chips of choice

1. Preheat the oven to 350°F. Grease the cake pan(s) with melted butter or oil and lightly dust with flour or line with cut parchment rounds.

2. In a large bowl, whisk together the eggs, melted butter, sugar, mashed bananas, and vanilla. I use a blender for this, as it's faster.

3. In another large bowl, whisk the flour with the baking powder, salt, cinnamon, ginger, and nutmeg.

4. Stir the wet ingredients into the dry ingredients until combined. Fold in the zucchini, carrots, and if desired, the nuts and chocolate chips. Divide the mixture if making a layer cake and pour the mixture into the prepared pan(s).

5. Bake for 20 minutes or until a cake tester comes out clean. Layer cakes will be thinner, so may bake more quickly. Place on a cooling rack for 10 minutes, remove from the pan(s), and continue to let cool on racks. Once completely cooled, you can frost if desired with De-Lightful Cream Cheese Frosting (see below).

USES UP carrots, bananas, zucchini

MAKES one 9-by-12-inch cake or 8-inch round double or triple (thinner layers) layer cake

TOTAL TIME 50 minutes

KEEPS FOR up to 3 days on the counter, 1 week in the fridge, or 3 months in the freezer

DE-LIGHTFUL CREAM CHEESE FROSTING

2 cups whipping cream

8 oz cream cheese, at room temperature

½ cup icing sugar

1 Tbsp Pure Vanilla Extract (page 212)

1. Using a stand mixer with the whisk attachment, whip the cream until stiff peaks form. Set aside.

2. In another bowl, whip the cream cheese with the icing sugar and vanilla until fluffy, about 5 minutes.

3. Fold the whipped cream cheese into the whipped cream until incorporated. Keep refrigerated.

USES UP whipping cream, cream cheese, icing sugar

MAKES about 5 cups, enough for a double-layer cake; double the recipe for a three-layer cake

TOTAL TIME 15 minutes

KEEPS FOR the day of is best but can be stored for up to 3 days in the fridge before using

This Bread Is Bananas F P S

Yep, the whole banana, peel and all. This version is also insanely better than regular banana bread—denser and more moist. Also, check out the Banana Peel Chutney recipe (page 198) for all the reasons why we should be eating more banana peels.

2 overripe bruised bananas, peels and all
½ cup butter, at room temperature
¾ cup sugar
1½ cups flour
1 tsp baking soda
1 tsp baking powder
Pinch salt
2 eggs
½ cup buttermilk
1 Tbsp Pure Vanilla Extract (page 212)

Optional Add-Ins
½–1 cup chocolate or dark chocolate chips
½ cup chopped nuts and/or seeds

Optional Add-Ons
The Only Crumble You Will Need (page 227)

1. Preheat the oven to 350°F and line or grease a loaf pan. Bring a large pot of water to a boil.

2. Peel the bananas and roughly chop the peels. Simmer the peels in boiling water for 5 minutes and then drain, rinse under cold water, and set aside.

3. Using a hand mixer or a stand mixer fitted with the paddle attachment, mix the butter and sugar together until incorporated, light, and fluffy.

4. In a medium-size bowl, mix the flour with the baking soda, baking powder, and salt.

5. Using a blender or food processor, blend the bananas, peels, eggs, buttermilk, and vanilla.

6. Slowly beat the banana mixture into the butter mixture until incorporated. Beat in the flour mixture until combined. Stir in any optional add-ins and evenly spread with the crumble if using.

7. Pour the mixture into the prepared pan and bake for about 1 hour or until a toothpick comes out clean.

Food 911 Apple slices can keep your baked goods and breads moist, just cozy up a few slices in a sealed container with any extra baked goods you have to prevent them from going stale too quickly.

USES UP bananas

MAKES 1 loaf

TOTAL TIME 1 hour, 20 minutes

KEEPS FOR up to 3 days at room temperature, 1 week in the fridge, or 6 months in the freezer

Guilt–Free Cookies `F` `P` `L`

I have no idea where I came across this recipe using cooked sweet potato, but I was very skeptical of it until I tried it . . . so skeptical that as I was putting them in the oven, I was telling myself there is no way these are going to work. My timer went off, they came out of the oven, I let them cool, and yes, success! I love these as a post-workout snack or afternoon pick-me-up.

1 cup mashed cooked sweet potato

2 Tbsp coconut oil, melted

2 eggs, whisked

1 Tbsp Pure Vanilla Extract (page 212)

1 scoop favorite protein powder (can be flavored, like vanilla or chocolate)

½ tsp salt

2 tsp cinnamon

½ cup unsweetened shredded or flaked coconut

¼ cup dark chocolate chips

¼ cup raw nuts or seeds, chopped if necessary

Optional Add-Ins

¼ cup dried fruits

¼ cup kasha (buckwheat groats)

¼ cup amaranth

1 Tbsp ground flax

Sprinkle of cacao nibs

1. Preheat the oven to 375°F. Lightly grease a baking sheet or line with a silicone mat.

2. In a large bowl, mix the sweet potato with the melted coconut oil, eggs, vanilla extract, protein powder, salt, cinnamon, shredded coconut, chocolate chips, nuts, and any optional add-ins until incorporated.

3. Drop the dough by the tablespoon, about 2 inches apart, onto the baking sheet.

4. Bake 10 to 12 minutes or until lightly browned and cooked through. The dough will be very loose but the cookies bake up and cool perfectly.

USES UP cooked sweet potato, flaked coconut, nuts and seeds

MAKES 12–14 cookies

TOTAL TIME 20 minutes

KEEPS FOR up to 3 days at room temperature, 1 week in the fridge, or 6 months in the freezer

Zero-Waste Tips from Anna Olson

Meet Anna Olson, a professionally trained chef and pastry chef who lives in Ontario, Canada. You might know her as the host of the Food Network's Bake with Anna Olson, Fresh with Anna Olson, *and* Sugar, *or as the bestselling author of several cookbooks on baking and cooking.*

Q. You have been a pastry chef and in the food business for over 20 years. What has changed when it comes to food waste and food waste awareness?

A. In my mind, the most unfortunate change is the decline of home economics programs, where high schools teach the "business" of running a household, which includes food cost awareness and food waste prevention. We need these programs back, desperately!

Q. Does being a pastry chef change how you shop and/or cook at home? If so, how?

A. I plan my meals just one to two days ahead and buy what I need. I like to shop seasonally and locally, and I tend to shop three to four times a week but in small increments. I find if I do the "big shop" I forget what I have purchased and risk it going to waste.

Q. Can you list a few storage tips when it comes to pastry and baking ingredients?

A. Store dry goods in airtight jars (not in their original paper packaging) on open shelves so the items that need to be used up are on display.

If you aren't consuming nuts or dried fruits within 3 months, freeze them in an airtight container.

Store chocolate, vanilla, and spices in a cool, dark place, but do not refrigerate or freeze.

Freeze unused egg whites (I do this if I've used the yolks for a custard or conversely, I'll plan a custard if I used egg whites to make a meringue).

If you have a big bag of lemons, zest and freeze the zest, then juice and freeze the lemons—I use so much lemon zest in my baking, it comes in handy!

Butter and even cream can be frozen and thawed in the fridge before using (you'll need to give the cream a shake).

Q. What are your top three food items that typically get tossed, but can easily be baked into something delicious?

A. Overripe pears. You can purée overripe pears and use them in place of juice or water in a baking recipe to add a subtle sweetness and flavor. I also love adding a bit to a parsnip or squash soup.

Buttermilk. It tends to be sold in a one-liter carton, but many baking recipes only call for a cup. I use my buttermilk in baking even a week after its best before date (it's soured anyhow, and the baking cooks it through) or else, I make ranch dressing with fresh buttermilk. This also applies to yogurt and sour cream.

Bloomed chocolate. Many people think that the white dust on chocolate is mold. Don't throw it away! This is not mold but a bloom of cocoa butter, a sign that at some point the chocolate went through a slight temperature shift. The chocolate is perfectly good, and you don't need to scrape the bloom off—just chop and bake as usual.

Q. Where do you look for inspiration when it comes to zero-waste cooking?

A. We can take inspiration from pre-industrialized times, when we couldn't waste any food because we were responsible for feeding our families from what we could raise, grow, process, and preserve ourselves. I cherish recipes from my grandmother's time, because they make use of humble ingredients in innovative ways. My background is Slovak, so I love that a single cabbage can make dozen of cabbage rolls, using tomatoes that were canned in peak season and minimal meat stretched with barley or rice. I'm a big fan of "putting up" preserves, and I use homemade preserves in my baking regularly.

Q. What do you think our biggest challenge is in reducing food waste globally?

A. We can't look at food waste without considering how our food is produced, how it is transported, and how it is processed and packaged. I've always been a fan of shopping at my local markets to buy in-season produce, but I'd also rather buy a local, non-organic apple than an organic apple from New Zealand.

Bostock P L

This easy-to-make pastry has become a regular weekend breakfast treat in our house. Day-old bread is toasted and topped with jam and a frangipan filling. When baked and served warm, it smells and tastes like a French pastry, almost croissant-like.

5 Tbsp unsalted butter, at room temperature

⅓ cup granulated sugar

1 large egg

Dash vanilla & almond extract

¾ cup ground almonds

6 thick slices of day-old brioche or egg bread, toasted

⅔ cup strawberry jam

¼ cup sliced almonds

Icing sugar, for dusting

1. Preheat the oven to 350°F and line a baking sheet.

2. In a mixing bowl, cream the butter and sugar together by hand. Beat in the egg and extracts and stir in the ground almonds. Set aside.

3. Lay the slices of toasted bread onto the prepared baking tray. Spread each generously with strawberry jam. Dollop the almond paste over each piece and spread (no need to be fussy and make it perfect, it spreads as it bakes). Sprinkle sliced almonds on each piece and bake for 15 to 20 minutes, until the almond paste is a rich golden brown. Dust generously with icing sugar and serve (but be careful—the jam is really hot right out of the oven!).

The bostock is best served warm or at room temperature, on the day it is baked.

(Recipe contributed by Anna Olson)

USES UP stale bread

YIELD Serves 6

PREP TIME 35 minutes

KEEPS FOR day of

Dried Plum Brownies P

Dried plum brownies . . . doesn't that sound better than prune brownies? I should have called them "Healthy Brownies," since they pack a good punch of fiber. Not only should we be eating prunes more regularly for their soluble and insoluble fiber, but they also have potassium and boron, which is great for bone health. These are decadent, moist, and super chocolaty, and you don't even taste the prunes! They are also relatively inexpensive for their unique nutritional value.

Brownies

1½ cups pitted prunes

⅓ cup chopped (or chips) semi-sweet or dark chocolate

¼ cup neutral-flavored oil or melted butter

⅓ cup sugar

Pinch salt

1 Tbsp Pure Vanilla Extract (page 212)

2 eggs or 1 Tbsp + 2 tsp Aquafaba (page 102)

⅔ cups all-purpose flour or all-purpose gluten-free flour with xanthan gum added (see note on page 224)

¼ cup cocoa powder

½ tsp baking soda

Chocolate Ganache Icing

¼ cup milk

⅔ cup chopped (or chips) semisweet or dark chocolate

1. For the Brownies: Preheat the oven to 350°F and line or grease an 8-by-8-inch square baking pan.

2. Place the prunes in a medium-size bowl. Cover with 2 cups of boiling water and let sit for 10 minutes to soften.

3. In a small heavy-bottomed saucepot over medium heat, melt the chocolate with the oil, sugar, and salt, stirring occasionally. Once melted, remove from the heat and stir in the vanilla. Let cool for 5 minutes.

4. Drain the prunes and place in a blender or food processor along with the cooled melted chocolate mixture. Blend until puréed.

5. Whisk the eggs in a small bowl. With the blender running on low speed, slowly add the eggs and blend until fully incorporated.

6. In a large bowl, whisk together the flour, cocoa powder, and baking soda. Stir in the chocolate purée and mix until incorporated. The batter will be quite thick.

7. Drop the batter into the prepared pan and spread out evenly. Bake for 25 minutes or until set. Let cool in the pan.

8. For the Ganache Icing: While the brownies are cooling, make the ganache icing by heating the milk in a small saucepot over medium heat until steaming.

9. Place the chopped chocolate in a separate bowl. Pour the hot milk overtop of the chocolate and let sit for 1 minute. Whisk until you have a silky icing. Pour the icing evenly over the brownies. Let cool, cut into squares, and enjoy!

USES UP prunes, eggs

MAKES 16 brownies

TOTAL TIME 35 minutes

KEEPS FOR up to 4 days at room temperature, 1 week in the fridge, or 6 months in the freezer

Raspberry Financiers F P

Heavy, dense, rich-tasting rectangular little cakes named for their close resemblance to bars of gold. These financiers are sure to give some orphaned egg whites a good home, and save some fresh raspberries (or really any fruit) from their expiry date.

¾ cup butter

¾ cup sugar

1¼ cups almond flour

¼ cup all-purpose flour or all-purpose gluten-free flour with xanthan gum added

Pinch salt

4 egg whites or ½ cup Aquafaba (page 102) (reserve egg yolks for later use)

1 cup fresh or frozen raspberries (see substitutions)

1. Preheat the oven to 350°F.

2. In a small saucepot over medium heat, heat the butter until it just starts to turn golden around the edges. This is called making browned butter and can take up to 10 minutes, depending on the heat source. Brush the molds with some of the melted butter.

3. In a large bowl, combine the sugar, almond flour, flour, and salt. Stir in the egg whites until combined and fold in the remaining brown butter. Let cool.

4. Spoon the batter into the greased molds, filling them about three-quarters full, then press the raspberries into the batter.

5. Bake 12 to 14 minutes until golden and cooked through. Let cool for 5 minutes in the molds and then transfer to a cooling rack. Best eaten as soon as possible.

Food 911 These do not have to be rectangular in shape, so use any small oven-safe ramekins, tart tins, muffin tins, silicone, or even madeleine molds. Just make sure to brush your mold with melted butter.

Zero-Waste Tip A clean pillowcase dusted with flour is the best thing to roll out pastry on. The flour gets into the weave of the fabric, avoiding an over-floured surface (so no flour goes to waste!) and too much handling of the pastry. All you have to do is rotate the pillowcase and the dough rotates with it. Genius.

USES UP raspberries, eggs

MAKES 10–12, depending on the size of molds

TOTAL TIME 30 minutes

KEEPS FOR batter can be stored up to 2 days in the fridge. Best eaten ASAP but can be stored for up to 3 days on the counter.

CAN SUBSTITUTE
- Raspberries with any other berries or chopped fruit

Pie Crust: 3 Ways F P

Pies are possibly one of the best and tastiest ways to use up an abundance of fresh or frozen fruit. Here are three classic crusts to fill your pie cravings. The first is made with dough using flour that you have on hand—be sure to freeze the butter first! The second is a perfect crumbly pie crust using goods found hidden in the back of your pantry— and not just graham crackers—be sure to melt the butter first! And then make your desired pie, such as my Vinegar Pie (page 230) or Pucker Pie (page 229). The third is a crumble. Crumbles are great as a pie topping (particularly for fruit pies) in place of a top crust or sprinkled as a topping for loaves, muffins, or cakes, such as my This Bread is Bananas (page 217).

THE ONLY PIE DOUGH YOU NEED

2½ cups all-purpose flour, or half all-purpose flour and half whole-grain flour, or gluten-free flour of choice

1 tsp salt

1 cup cold or frozen butter (see substitutions)

6 Tbsp ice-cold water, divided

Flavor Variation

Sweet Crust In step 1, add 3 Tbsp sugar

Chocolate Crust Replace ¼ cup of the flour with ⅓ cup cocoa powder and add 3 Tbsp sugar

Vanilla Crust In step 1, add 3 Tbsp sugar + in step 3, add 1 Tbsp Pure Vanilla Extract (page 212)

Citrus Crust In step 1, add the zest of 1 citrus fruit

Spiced Crust In step 1 add 3 Tbsp sugar + 1 tsp cinnamon, nutmeg, and/or ground ginger

Savory Crust In step 1, add 2 Tbsp fresh (or 2 tsp dried) hardy herbs + 1 to 2 Tbsp ground spices like curry powder, fennel, smoked paprika, and/or turmeric

1. In a large bowl, whisk the flour with the salt. With a box grater, coarsely grate the cold butter into the flour. Mix and fold in with your fingers, coating the grated bits of fatty goodness with flour.

2. Add 5 tablespoons of the cold water to the pastry and mix with your hands until the dough starts to come together, adding more liquid if needed. It is better to have the pastry a little more on the moist side than dry.

3. Transfer the dough to a lightly floured surface and give it a good knead until the dough comes together. Divide it in half and form into 2 round disks. Wrap each disk in plastic wrap and chill in the fridge for at least 30 minutes, though resting for 24 hours can really help with handling and rolling the dough.

4. Lightly dust a work surface and rolling pin with flour. Have your pie plate nearby and roll out one disk of dough to fit the plate with a ½-inch overhang. Roll away from you, and from the center out. Rotate the pie dough and flip it over a few times to keep it from sticking. Overhang is great and can be trimmed or folded to create a nice crimping.

USES UP flour, seasonal fruit, or any other food items you want to stuff into a pie

MAKES 2 single or 1 double 9-inch pie crust

TOTAL TIME 10 minutes (+ at least 30 minutes rest time)

CAN SUBSTITUTE
- Butter with ⅔ cup butter + ⅓ cup frozen grass-fed lard, or ½ cup butter + ½ cup cold cream cheese

5. Once the dough is rolled out, gently roll it around the rolling pin for easier transfer to your pie plate. Leaving a ½-inch overhang, trim any excess with scissors. Tuck the overhang under and crimp away. Add the desired filling, and bake as directed in the recipe. If making a double-crust pie, top with the second crust, trim away any excess, crimp, and score the top a few times to let the steam escape, then bake as directed.

THE ONLY CRUMB CRUST YOU NEED

1½ cups graham cracker crumbs (see substitutions) or ground nuts and/or seeds

1 Tbsp sugar, if crumbs are unsweetened (optional)

6 Tbsp melted butter or coconut oil

Flavor Variation (Add in Step 2)

Lemon Ginger Lemon zest + 1 tsp ground ginger

Summer Vanilla 1 tsp Pure Vanilla Extract (page 212) + 1 Tbsp fresh thyme leaves or lavender buds

Winter Spiced 1 tsp cinnamon + ½ tsp nutmeg

USES UP cookies, graham crackers, wafers, pretzels, nuts, seeds

MAKES one 8- or 9-inch pie shell or the bottom layer of an 8- or 9-inch square baking pan

TOTAL TIME 17 minutes

KEEPS FOR up to 6 months, frozen, if not using right away

CAN SUBSTITUTE
• Graham cracker crumbs for gingersnaps, chocolate wafers, gluten-free vanilla wafers, pretzels, or any other crunchy cookie combination

1. Preheat the oven to 375°F.

2. For a crumb crust, in a medium-size bowl, mix together all of the ingredients until incorporated. For a seed or nut crust, pulse them in a food processor with the sugar, then add the melted butter and pulse until you have a moist sandy texture.

3. Using your fingers or the back of a spoon, press the mixture evenly into a pie plate or square baking dish and bake for 7 minutes or until the edges start to brown. Let cool before layering or filling. Add the desired filling, and bake as directed in the recipe.

THE ONLY CRUMBLE YOU NEED

½ cup oat flour or ground oats

½ cup all-purpose flour or gluten-free flour of choice

1 Tbsp ground cinnamon

½ tsp ground nutmeg

½ tsp ground ginger or 2 tsp grated fresh ginger (optional)

¾ cup packed brown sugar

2 cup rolled oats

Pinch salt

⅔ cup cold unsalted butter

Variations

Cardamom Spice: 1 tsp cardamom

Citrus: 2 Tbsp citrus zest

Coconut: ½ cup coconut flakes

Crunchy: ½ cup chopped nuts or seeds

USES UP Rolled oats, flour, herbs

MAKES about 3 cups of crumble, scant amount for two 8- or 9-inch pies, or a generous amount for one 8- or 9-inch pie. Scale up or down as needed.

TOTAL TIME 5 min

KEEPS For up to 3 days in an airtight container in the fridge, or up to 6 months in the freezer. To bake from frozen, thaw first and break up with your hands if clumped together

1. In a large bowl, combine the flours, cinnamon, nutmeg, ginger (if using), brown sugar, oats, and salt. With your hands or a pastry cutter, mix in the cold butter until the mixture has a crumbly texture. Store in sealed container in fridge or freezer until ready to use, then bake as directed in the recipe.

Pucker Pie F P

Who says lemon meringue pie has to be all lemon? What did limes ever do to you? Here we combine lemons and limes in a puckery pie, which uses egg yolks in the curd and the leftover egg whites in the cloud-like meringue.

Meringue

1 Tbsp cornstarch

⅓ cup water

5 egg whites (reserving yolks for the curd)

¼ tsp cream of tartar

½ cup sugar

1 Tbsp Pure Vanilla Extract (page 212)

Lemon/Lime Curd

1¾ cups cold water

¾ cup sugar

⅓ cup cornstarch

Pinch salt

5 egg yolks

2 Tbsp fresh lemon and/or lime zest

1 cup fresh lemon and/or lime juice

2 Tbsp butter

Pie Assembly

1 blind-baked pie shell (page 226) or 1 Crumb Pie Crust (page 227)

1. For the Meringue: Preheat the oven to 350°F. In a small saucepot, stir together the cornstarch and water, then place over medium heat until it begins to thicken. Set aside to cool.

2. In a large bowl with a hand mixer or a stand mixer fitted with the whisk attachment, whip the egg whites with the cream of tartar until foamy. Slowly pour in the sugar while whipping until soft peaks form. Then, while whipping, add the cooled cornstarch mixture by the tablespoon until stiff peaks form. Whisk in the vanilla.

3. For the Lemon/Lime Curd: In a medium heavy-bottomed saucepot over medium heat, combine the water, sugar, cornstarch, and salt and cook, stirring occasionally, until the mixture begins to thicken.

4. Lower the heat and very slowly ladle ½ cup of this hot mixture into the egg yolks, while whisking, to prevent the yolks from curdling. Then pour this mixture back into the pot.

5. Turn the heat up to medium, bring to a low simmer, and add the zest and juice and continue to simmer until thickened, about 3 minutes. Remove from the heat and whisk in the butter until melted and combined.

6. For Assembly: Pour the hot curd into the cooled prebaked pie shell. The heat from the curd helps cook the bottom of the meringue.

7. Dollop meringue onto the curd, starting at the outermost edges. You want it to touch the edges of the pie shell to prevent it from shrinking while cooking. Use the back of a spoon to fill it in and make some cool-looking whips.

8. Bake for 20 minutes or until the top is golden brown. Cool completely on the counter. If not eating immediately, chill in the refrigerator until serving.

USES UP lemons, limes, eggs, pie crust

SERVES 8

TOTAL TIME 50 minutes

KEEPS FOR up to 3–4 days in the fridge

CAN SUBSTITUTE
- Lemon or lime juice and zest with any other citrus

Vinegar Pie ▪F ▪P

A humble pie truly made out of desperation, this old-school favorite is great for when you are craving a fruit or citrus pie and have none available. This recipe is inspired by the Vinegar Pie at Raymonds (page 123) and it is especially great with homemade Tetley tea ice cream and partridgeberry compote. Though, you can pair it with any flavor of ice cream (page 211) or any fruit compote (page 241)—it's that good!

1 single 9-inch pie crust (page 226)

3–4 eggs

1 cup sugar (see subsitutions)

Pinch salt

4 Tbsp butter, melted

3 Tbsp apple cider vinegar
   (see subsitutions)

1 Tbsp Pure Vanilla Extract (page 212)

1 tsp cinnamon

½ tsp ground nutmeg

1 cup currants, raisins, or other
   chopped dried fruit (optional)

1. Preheat the oven to 350°F. Roll out the pastry to fit the pie plate. Crimp the edges and line the inside of the crust with a cut round of parchment paper. Fill the lined crust with dried beans, rice, or pie weights. Bake for 15 minutes, remove the lining and weights, and prick the bottom of the crust with a fork a few times to prevent air pockets. Bake the pie shell for an additional 10 minutes or until the bottom of the crust looks dry. Remove from the oven and set aside to cool.

2. Increase the oven temperature to 375°F.

3. In a large bowl, whisk together the eggs with the sugar and salt. While whisking slowly, pour in the melted butter. Then whisk in the vinegar, vanilla, cinnamon, and nutmeg.

4. If using currants or raisins, sprinkle them into the pie shell now. Pour the filling into the cooled pie shell and bake for about 25 minutes or until evenly browned and set. Let cool completely before serving. Serve at room temperature or chilled.

USES UP pie crust, sugar, eggs

SERVES 8

TOTAL TIME 50 minutes

KEEPS FOR up to 4 days in the fridge

CAN SUBSTITUTE
- Sugar with brown sugar
- Apple cider vinegar with white vinegar

Zero–Waste Tip   When buying parchment, look for a brand that is labeled certified compostable. All other brands are just garbage. Also, make sure to reuse the dried beans and rice that you use for blind baking. Once completely cooled, I store mine in a container in the pantry.

Coconut Mango Panna Cotta F P

Panna cotta is an easy five-ingredient dessert that starts by steeping cream or milk and finishes with silky smooth jiggly spoonfuls of wonder. Yes, I did say easy, because it is easy to make and adapts to whatever fruit you have on hand. It also keeps well in the fridge for up to 10 days, so that's dessert for a week, at least.

¾ cup coconut milk

¾ cup heavy cream

⅓ cup sugar

2 tsp Pure Vanilla Extract (page 212)

3 tsp unflavored gelatin

3 Tbsp cold water

1½ cups mango purée, divided
  (see subsitutions)

1. In a heavy-bottomed medium-size saucepot over medium-low heat, bring the coconut milk, cream, and sugar to a bare simmer, stirring until the sugar is dissolved. Remove from the heat and stir in the vanilla extract.

2. In a small bowl, sprinkle the gelatin into the cold water and let sit to bloom, 5 minutes.

3. Whisk the gelatin mixture into the warmed milk until the gelatin dissolves. Whisk in ½ cup of the mango purée.

4. Pour into dessert ramekins, little glasses, or custard cups. Place in the fridge until set, a minimum of 4 hours depending on the size. Once set, portion out the remaining mango purée over top of each panna cotta. Cover and place back in the fridge.

Food 911 When puréeing certain fruits or berries, like raspberries for instance, some will need a good straining through a fine-mesh sieve after blending to get rid of all those tiny seeds or bits. This helps keep your panna cotta silky smooth.

USES UP fresh or frozen fruits

SERVES 8

TOTAL TIME 15 minutes
(+ 4 hours set time)

KEEPS FOR up to
10 days in the fridge

CAN SUBSTITUTE
• Mango purée with any other fruit purée, strained if necessary (see note)

CocoRose Pudding F P

I love pudding. I was the kid that ate those tin cans of milk chocolate Nestlé pudding in my lunchbox almost every day. Then I went to Paris with my mom when I was 14, and I tasted pastries filled with pastry cream (real vanilla pudding) for the first time. I was in heaven. At 17, after moving away from home to Toronto, I tasted pastéis de nata (baked custard tarts) from a local Portuguese bakery around the corner, and they blew my mind. Then I went to chef school and learned how to make pastry cream (or real pudding, as I like to call it), and it still rocks my world. Not to mention, it's a great way to use up egg and milk staples.

4 egg yolks (reserve whites for egg
  white recipes (see page 224) or
  store for later use)
¼ cup cornstarch
1 cup light or table cream
One 14 oz can coconut milk
⅓ cup sugar

Pinch salt
1½ cups sweetened flaked or shredded
  coconut
1 Tbsp Pure Vanilla Extract (page 212)
2 tsp rose water (see subsitutions)
2 Tbsp butter

USES UP egg yolks, coconut milk, shredded coconut

MAKES 4–6 servings, or fills one 9-inch pie

TOTAL TIME 20 minutes

KEEPS FOR up to 1 week in the fridge

CAN SUBSTITUTE
• Rose water with orange flower water

1. In a medium-size bowl, whisk the egg yolks with cornstarch until well incorporated. Set aside.

2. In a heavy-bottomed saucepot, combine the cream with the coconut milk, sugar, and salt. Place over medium heat and bring to a bare simmer until the sugar has dissolved. Remove from the heat.

3. Very slowly whisk 1 cup of the hot milk mixture into the egg yolk mixture to prevent curdling. Then add this back into the saucepot.

4. Place back over medium heat, stirring occasionally to avoid burning on the bottom, until mixture starts to simmer and thicken.

5. Remove from the heat and whisk in the coconut, vanilla, rose water, and butter. Transfer to a bowl to cool on the counter.

6. Eat warm and creamy or transfer to small ramekins to cool in the fridge as pudding, or use as a pudding/custard filling for a cream pie, doughnuts, fruit tarts, etc.

Rugelach F P

These little twists of heaven are made with two common ingredients you have lurking in your fridge: jam and cream cheese. The potential flavor combinations are endless. I especially love combining raspberry jam with lavender buds from my garden.

Dough
1 cup flour (+ more for dusting)
½ tsp salt
8 Tbsp cold butter, cut into cubes
8 Tbsp cold cream cheese, cut into cubes

Jammy Filling
¾ cup jam or marmalade (page 243)
½ cup finely chopped seeds or nuts
    (optional)

Optional Add-Ins
¼ cup currants or chopped dried fruit
1 Tbsp citrus zest
Sprinkle of any dried herbs or spices
    that may pair with jam, like cinna-
    mon, thyme, or lavender
Sprinkle of mini chocolate chips or
    crumbled marzipan

Glaze
1 egg whisked well with a splash of
    cold water

Optional Garnishes
Sprinkle of cinnamon, ground nutmeg,
    and/or sugar
2 Tbsp citrus zest

1. For the Dough: In a food processor or stand mixer fitted with the paddle attachment, mix the flour with the salt. Then beat in the butter until the cubes break down into a crumbly, sandy mixture.

2. Beat in the cream cheese until the dough starts to come together, about 1 minute.

3. Dump the dough onto a floured surface and form into a 5-inch disk shape. Wrap in plastic wrap and chill for at least 1 hour. Can be frozen for up to 3 months; just thaw in the fridge overnight.

4. For the Jammy Filling: In a bowl, combine all of the filling ingredients, including any optional add-ins.

5. Preheat the oven to 375°F and line a baking sheet.

6. Roll out the dough onto a floured surface until you have a 10-inch circle. Spread the filling evenly overtop, leaving a ½-inch border.

7. Cut as you would a pizza, into 16 equal wedges. Roll each up, starting at the outside edge.

8. Transfer to baking sheet, 2 inches apart and place in the freezer for 20 minutes (not necessary but better if you've got the time).

9. For the Glaze: Brush each twist with the egg wash. Sprinkle with garnishes if desired.

10. Bake for about 20 minutes or until the tops are golden brown and the jam has gotten all sticky and caramelized. Let cool.

USES UP cream cheese, jam, seeds and nuts, dried fruits,

MAKES 14–16 twists

TOTAL TIME 20 minutes (+ chilling and freezing)

KEEPS FOR up to 3 months if you freeze unbaked assembled twists on a tray until hard and then place in smaller freezer-safe containers. Defrost in the fridge overnight before baking.

Pumpkin Pie Lost Bread Pudding `F` `P` `L`

All the flavors of pumpkin pie baked into moist bread pudding. I always find that bread pudding tastes better when the bread is chopped into small cubes that soak up more of the yummy custard. This, and the recipe on page 221, are both excellent and delicious ways to use up stale bread.

Bread

Butter or oil, for greasing

6–7 cups stale bread or pastry, sliced or torn into 1-inch pieces (see substitutions)

Optional Add-Ins

1 cup chocolate chips

1 cup chopped dried fruits or fresh or frozen berries

½–¾ cup chopped nuts or seeds or shredded coconut

1 Tbsp citrus zest

Pumpkin Pie Custard

1 cup milk or cream

½ cup sugar

1 Tbsp Pure Vanilla Extract (page 212) (see substitutions)

2 eggs

2 tsp pumpkin pie spice (see substitutions)

1 cup pumpkin purée (see substitutions)

Pinch salt

Flavor Variation

For chocolate bread pudding, omit the pumpkin and spices and increase the milk to 1½ cups. Whisk ½ to ¾ cup chopped chocolate or chocolate chips into the hot milk mixture until melted.

1. Preheat the oven to 325°F. Grease a 9-by-9-inch square or medium-size baking dish with butter or oil.

2. For the Bread: Place the bread pieces into the baking dish. Toss with additional ingredients, if desired.

3. For the Pumpkin Pie Custard: In a heavy-bottomed pot over medium heat, bring the milk and sugar to a low simmer. Cook until the sugar is dissolved. Remove from the heat and whisk in the vanilla extract. Set aside to cool slightly.

4. In a medium-size bowl, whisk the eggs with the pumpkin pie spice, pumpkin purée, and salt. Add the warm milk in a slow, steady stream while whisking to prevent the eggs from curdling.

5. Pour the mixture over the bread, toss to coat, and let sit for 10 minutes. This can also be done up to 24 hours in advance and left to soak in the fridge.

6. Bake until the pudding is set and the bread is nicely browned on top, about 20 minutes.

Zero-Waste Tip There are many ways to serve bread pudding. Serve it warm with whipped cream, ice cream, or vanilla custard, layered in a parfait with yogurt and berries, or do what I do, which is to slice it thick, toast it, then slather it with butter and jam.

USES UP stale bread or pastries, pumpkin purée, dried and/or fresh fruit, nuts, seeds, shredded coconut

SERVES 6

TOTAL TIME 30 minutes

KEEPS FOR 2 days at its best, but good for up to 4 days in the fridge. Just reheat, covered, at 350°F for 5 to 15 minutes, depending on amount.

CAN SUBSTITUTE
- Bread with panettone, croissants, rolls, leftover cake, or stale doughnuts
- Pumpkin pie spice with 1 tsp cinnamon + ½ tsp nutmeg + ½ tsp ginger + ¼ tsp allspice
- Pumpkin purée with squash or sweet potato purée
- Vanilla extract with vanilla bean pod and scraped seeds simmered in milk, removed from heat, covered, and steeped for 10 minutes

Leftover Rice Pudding `F` `L`

Pudding has a rich history dating back to medieval times where meaty savory puddings were made with cheap local grains in an eggy broth custard. Then they gained grandeur as rice became a hot commodity. Expensive sugary sweetened puddings were served, only to royalty, studded with gemmy preserved fruit. Now, almost every culture has its version of this classic comfort dessert. With all the many variations of rice pudding around the world, it's almost as if leftover rice was destined to be slowly simmered into a subtly sweetened creamy custard.v

1 vanilla bean

2 cups cooked rice

2–3 cups whole milk (see substitutions)

3 Tbsp sugar

Pinch salt

½ cinnamon stick

¼ ground nutmeg

Handful of dried fruit, chopped if necessary (optional)

Optional Garnishes

1 cup chopped nut brittle

1 cup chopped fresh fruits

½ cup toasted coconut

¼–½ cup nuts or seeds

4–6 Tbsp fruit jam

Drizzle of caramel sauce

Flavor Variation

Orange Ginger Sub ½ tsp ground ginger + 2 Tbsp citrus zest for the cinnamon and nutmeg (especially good when adding dried or chopped fresh fruits)

Rose and Cardamom Sub a few cardamom pods for the cinnamon and nutmeg, omit the vanilla, and add 2 tsp rose water (add when stirring in the sugar)

1. Split the vanilla bean lengthwise. With the back of a knife, scrape out the teeny paste-like seeds and transfer the seeds and pod to a medium-size saucepot.

2. Add the rice, 2 cups of milk, sugar, salt, cinnamon, nutmeg, and dried fruit, if using. Bring to a low simmer and cook, stirring occasionally, until it reaches the consistency of oatmeal, about 6 minutes. Add more milk if needed.

3. Discard the vanilla pod (and save it for another use). Transfer the rice pudding to a bowl. Serve hot, warm, cool, or cold and garnish as desired.

USES UP cooked rice

SERVES 4–6

TOTAL TIME 15 minutes

KEEPS FOR up to 4 days in the fridge

CAN SUBSTITUTE
- Milk with cream, evaporated milk, or 1 cup coconut milk + 1 cup non-dairy milk

Pancakes: 3 Ways P L

With pancake batter, you have a lot of wiggle room for substituting ingredients, which makes it a great zero-waste recipe. For instance, a ¼ cup buckwheat flour to replace ¼ cup of all-purpose flour or any of the variations below. You can even take it up a notch by stacking the pancakes shortcake-style with berries and whipped cream in-between.

The Classic

6 Tbsp butter

2 cups flour

Pinch salt

4 tsp baking powder

4 eggs or ¾ cup Aquafaba
 (page 102), at room temperature

1½ cups milk, at room temperature

1 Tbsp apple cider vinegar
 (see substitutions)

1 Tbsp Pure Vanilla Extract (page 212)

2 Tbsp sugar (optional)

Butter or oil, for frying

Pumpkin Spiced Pancakes

6 Tbsp butter

2 cups flour

Pinch salt

4 tsp baking powder

1 tsp cinnamon

1 tsp ground ginger

½ tsp ground nutmeg

¼ tsp ground allspice

4 eggs or ¾ cup Aquafaba
 (page 102), at room temperature

1 cup milk, at room temperature

½ cup pumpkin, squash, or sweet
 potato purée

1 Tbsp apple cider vinegar
 (see substitutions)

1 Tbsp Pure Vanilla Extract (page 212)

2 Tbsp sugar (optional)

Butter or oil, for frying

Blueberry Porridge Pancakes

6 Tbsp butter

1½ cups flour

Pinch salt

4 tsp baking powder

4 eggs or ¾ cup Aquafaba
 (page 102), at room temperature

1 cup milk, at room temperature

1 cup cooked oatmeal or grainy
 porridge

1 Tbsp apple cider vinegar
 (see substitutions)

1 Tbsp Pure Vanilla Extract (page 212)

2 Tbsp sugar (optional)

½–1 cup frozen (wild) blueberries

Butter or oil, for frying

1. In a small saucepot, melt the butter over medium-low heat and set aside to cool.

2. Mix all of the dry ingredients (except the blueberries, if using) together in a large bowl.

3. Combine all of the wet ingredients together in a separate large bowl, mixing well to incorporate the eggs and stirring in the cooled melted butter last.

4. Pour the wet ingredients into the dry and whisk until combined. The batter should have a thick consistency that just slowly pours from a ladle, instead of plopping. Small lumps are completely normal. Adjust the consistency if needed by adding a little more milk or even water. Fold in the blueberries, if using.

5. Preheat a large nonstick skillet or cast-iron frying pan over medium heat. Add just enough butter to thinly coat the pan. Once hot, start ladling in the batter to form pancakes of your desired size and shape. When bubbles begin to form on the surface, flip over. Continue to cook on the other side for an additional few minutes until cooked through. Transfer to plates and enjoy.

USES UP blueberries, porridge or oatmeal, pumpkin purée

MAKES about 16

TOTAL TIME 30 minutes

KEEPS FOR up to 2 days in the fridge or 3 months in the freezer (just partially freeze on a baking sheet, then transfer to a container; toast them on low heat

CAN SUBSTITUTE
- Apple cider vinegar with citrus juice for a citrusy taste

Fruit Compote 365 🅵

Compote is simply whole chopped fruit cooked with water and sugar to a desired consistency, so you can easily customize this recipe according to whatever fruit is in season. I make compotes year-round, since they are my go-to for when fruit is getting just past its prime. Serve for breakfast over pancakes, for an afternoon snack with chia seeds and yogurt, or for dessert on a little cake or ice cream.

1 vanilla bean (see substitutions)

6 cups fruit, pitted and chopped if necessary (see substitutions)

½ cup sugar

2 Tbsp water

1 Tbsp freshly squeezed lemon juice

Flavor Variation

Cinnamon Spice ½ cinnamon stick + ½ tsp ground nutmeg + ¼ tsp ground allspice

Orange, Ginger, and Anise 1 Tbsp orange zest + 1 star anise + 3 slices fresh ginger (optional)

1. Split the vanilla bean lengthwise with a knife and use the back of the knife to scrape out the vanilla seeds from the inside. Place the scraped seeds and pod in a large saucepot.

2. Add the fruit, sugar, water, lemon juice, and any optional flavor variations and bring to a boil. Lower the heat and simmer, stirring occasionally, until the fruit softens to the desired consistency, 8 to 10 minutes. I like mine chunky and not too soupy so I tend to undercook my compotes.

3. Remove from the heat.

4. Remove the vanilla pod (wash it and use for another recipe, see tip) and remove and discard any other whole spices. Serve warm or cold.

Zero-Waste Tip Vanilla beans aren't exactly budget friendly, but neither is pure vanilla extract. The pods holding the vanilla seeds can be reused easily, making them worth it for me. Simply rinse the pod well with water, leave it to dry on the counter, and reuse. I like to add them to sugar or salt to make it vanilla flavored or even better, try making your own homemade vanilla extract. Check out the recipe for my 100% Pure Vanilla Extract (page 212).

USES UP fresh fruit

SERVES 8–10

TOTAL TIME 15 minutes

KEEPS FOR up to 1 week in the fridge or 6 months in the freezer

CAN SUBSTITUTE
- Fresh fruit with 3 cups dried fruit and increase the water to just enough cover the fruit, simmer for about 15 minutes or until the fruit is soft and the liquid is reduced to syrupy
- Vanilla bean with 1 Tbsp Pure Vanilla Extract (page 212) added in step 3

This Is My Jam

Let's look at how one humble jar of jam can really spread.

1. **ADDING FLAVOR** Stir jam into plain yogurt, vanilla ice cream, whipped cream, oatmeal, or porridge for an added flavor.

2. **JAM AND CHEESE?** If you have yet to try it, spread some jam in your next grilled cheese or add a small bowl of jam to a cheese and charcuterie board. Think baked brie smothered in wild blueberry preserves wrapped in flaky puff pastry.

3. **SUGAR ALTERNATIVE** Use it in place of sugar for a fruity vinaigrette or marinade.

4. **SYRUP ALTERNATIVE** Make homemade granola? Use jam in place of sugar in your syrup.

5. **BREAKFAST STUFFING** If you're making French toast with thick slices of day-old bread, why not stuff that sucker with a layer of jam?

6. **SWEETNESS IN SAVORY** Next time you are making a pan sauce or gravy, add a dollop of jam for added sweetness and tang. Flavors like currant, blueberry, and peach are especially good in savory recipes.

7. **DRINK UP!** Jam can also be added to some fancy flavorful cocktails or mocktails.

8. **BAKE WITH IT** From jam tarts to fancy macarons, you can swirl, spread, dollop, and whip jam into something delicious. Like Rugelach (page 235).

Any Way Marmalade F

This classic, old-school preserve has quite a following. Folks who love it, like me, are passionate about their marmalade. Making a jar of it is quite possibly the best way to use up a bunch of random citrus fruits rolling around in the bottom of my crisper. Here you have two methods for making it. One uses what remains after juicing the fruit, the other uses the whole fruit. So you can have it any way, every day.

1½ lb citrus fruits, washed well

2½ cups water

3 cups sugar

Flavor Variation

Coconut Lime Use lime for all the citrus and add ½ cup grated coconut in step 5

Ginger Stir in 1 Tbsp grated ginger in step 5

Vanilla Stir in 1 Tbsp Pure Vanilla Extract (page 212) at very end

Method 1

1. Place a small plate in the freezer.

2. Cut the citrus fruits in half and juice, reserving the juice in a heavy-bottomed saucepot.

3. With a metal spoon, scrape out all membranes and seeds and wrap them up in a double layer of cheesecloth. Tie this up with some kitchen string to form a pouch. Add the pouch to the saucepot to add more pectin to your marmalade.

4. Slice the peels into the desired thickness until you have about 1½ cups of peels and place them in the saucepot with the juice and pectin pouch.

5. Add the water, bring to a boil, reduce to a simmer, and cook for 1 hour. With a fine-mesh sieve, lift out the pouch and carefully press as much juice out of it as you can with the back of a spoon. Discard the pouch.

6. Stir in the sugar and bring to a boil again, stirring frequently, until it reaches a "gel" stage (225°F), about 10 minutes. Remember that plate in the freezer? You can test the marmalade by placing a small spoonful on the cold plate and putting it back in the freezer for 1 minute. If it wrinkles lightly when pressed with your finger, it is ready.

7. Transfer to clean jars. Seal and label the jars, and once cooled, store in the fridge.

Method 2

1. You want to use the whole fruit? Flesh, juice, and all? With a vegetable peeler, remove all of the citrus rind, leaving as much of the pith behind as possible. Slice the rind until you have about 1 cup. Add this to saucepot.

2. Remove as much pith on the fruit as you can, discard it, and chop all the flesh into chunks. Place all the chunks in the saucepot with the rind. Add the water, bring to a boil, and then simmer for 1 hour.

3. Continue to step 6 in method 1.

USES UP citrus fruits

MAKES about three 1-cup jars

TOTAL TIME 2 hours, 10 minutes

KEEPS FOR up to 3 months in the fridge (be sure to label and date)

Beyond Meals

I have always been that person who reads all the packaging labels thinking there must be a way to make this product at home. I tried everything from homemade salicylic acid moisturizers for acne (made with crushed-up aspirin which I highly recommend NOT trying) to chemical-free green cleaners. Through my experiments, I found how easily food can be used in other innovative ways. From cleaning your kitchen to having a DIY spa day (with a nice homemade steeped tea in hand), here are some outside-the-box ideas for those odd bits and pieces that have yet to find a home. And the bonus is there are no added chemicals!

Teas: 2 Ways `F` `L` `S`

Tea has value beyond being a popular, comforting beverage. Think of it as your next flavor base when cooking or baking. The tannins in tea make it perfect for tenderizing or marinating protein. Tea also infuses effortlessly into your sauces or vinaigrettes, cakes, custards, or cookies and even ice cream or sorbets. Or maybe an Earl Grey pudding? The possibilities are endless.

Here are two versions of the many teas I make at home with bits and pieces of foodstuff I want to use up. My weekly steep is great to drink hot in the winter and is lovely iced in the summer. The Agua Fresca (a Mexican drink that translates to "cool water") is a summertime refresher that can be made with whatever variety of produce that needs using up. These both work well in boozy cocktails, and if you have a home carbonation system, try it as a fizzy drink.

MY WEEKLY ICED STEEP

6 cups water

2 tsp dried hibiscus flowers (see substitutions)

1 recycled vanilla pod

Zest of ½ citrus fruit

3 slices fresh ginger

2 tsp lavender buds

½ cup citrus juice

Liquid sweetener or a few drops liquid stevia (optional)

Optional Add-Ins

1 Tbsp dried fruits

1 bag or 1 tsp loose black or green tea

USES UP citrus rinds, ginger, dried fruits, used vanilla pods, dried herbs, spices and petals

MAKES about 4 cups

TOTAL TIME 5 minutes

CAN SUBSTITUTE
- Recycled vanilla pod with 1–2 tsp Pure Vanilla Extract (page 212), add in step 2
- Dried hibiscus for dried lavender or rose

1. Bring the water to a boil. Take off the heat and add everything except the juice and sweetener. Add any optional add-ins. Let steep for at least 5 minutes.

2. Strain, cool, and add the citrus juice and the sweetener, if using. Refrigerate.

Past their prime teas or gifted teas you just don't like? Here are some ideas for upcycling them:

1. **SCENT MAKER** Tea bags can be used as natural potpourri sachets for your home, car, or closets. Loose teas can freshen up a kitty litter box or carpet (sprinkle it on the carpet for a few hours then vacuum it up).

2. **BODY PRODUCTS** Steep your body in a homemade DIY tea-infused soap or herbal bath salt (page 249).

3. **GET SOAKING** Use old herbs, herbal tea bags, or loose-leaf teas in your next bath or foot soak. Steep 1 ounce of dried herbs or tea with 1 quart of boiling water for 20 minutes and add to a hot bath. Try infusions like lavender and chamomile, sage and lemon balm, or peppermint and calendula. Maybe even toss in some Epsom salts.

4. **PLANT FOOD** Gardening is made easier when you use tea bags as absorbent pot liners and loose tea leaves for plant food.

STRAWBERRY CUCUMBER HIBISCUS AGUA FRESCA

2 cups water

2 Tbsp dried hibiscus or 2 hibiscus tea bags

2 cups chopped strawberries

1½ cups chopped cucumber

1 Tbsp honey, maple syrup, or agave

1 Tbsp fresh lime juice (about ½ lime)

Optional Add-Ins

1–2 Tbsp chopped fresh basil or mint

Optional Garnishes

Chopped strawberries

Lime wedges

Fresh basil or mint

1. Bring a large pot of water to a boil and add the hibiscus. Take off the heat and let steep for 5 to 10 minutes. Once tea has finished steeping, strain or remove the tea bags. Let cool to room temperature or place in the fridge or the freezer to cool quickly.

2. Add the strawberries, cucumber, honey, lime juice, and basil (if using) to a blender along with the cooled tea. Blend until smooth. Taste and adjust by adding more honey to make it sweeter or more lime juice to make it more tart. Strain before serving if you prefer a clearer tea.

ৢ. Fill glasses with ice and add the agua fresca. Garnish as desired.

Zero–Waste Tip   Leftover steeped tea can be easily frozen into ice cubes and added to any summertime drink for added flavor.

Food 911 Different teas have different steep times, herbal teas needing the most time. When in doubt, steep black or herbal teas for 3 minutes. If using green tea, the hot water needs to be at a lower temperature of 160°F, whereas most teas are best steeped at 203°F. Your basic loose tea brewing ratio is 1 teaspoon of tea to ¾ cup water.

USES UP strawberries, cucumber, hibiscus, fresh herbs

MAKES 4 small or 2 large glasses

TOTAL TIME 5–10 minutes (plus chill time)

KEEPS FOR up to 2 days in fridge or freeze into flavored ice cubes or popsicles

Foody Beauty `F` `L` `P`

Having a teenage daughter means it is not uncommon for me to find small jars of experimental DIY beauty concoctions scattered in the bathroom, while my virgin coconut oil jar and local farmers' market coffee bag lie empty. Here are some beauty regimen recipes easily made with odd foody bits and inspired by my daughter.

THE FACE MASH-K

Slip on those pajamas, pour yourself a stiff drink, and mash up a relaxing after-dinner face mask with some of tonight's leftovers.

½ cup mashed cooked pumpkin or
    squash (see substitutions)
2 tsp raw honey

Optional Add-Ins
1 Tbsp lemon juice (clarifying)
1 Tbsp ground turmeric + a spoonful
    of yogurt (glowing)
1 tsp baking soda (acne-fighting)
1 tsp cinnamon (calming)
1 tsp rose and/or orange flower water
    (reduce redness)

> **USES UP** cooked pumpkin or squash, honey
>
> **TOTAL TIME** 2 minutes
>
> **MAKES** 1 facemask
>
> **CAN SUBSTITUTE**
> • Pumpkin or squash with mashed avocado or leftover oatmeal from breakfast

1. In a bowl, combine all of the ingredients, including any optional add-ins.

2. Apply an even layer over clean face and neck, avoiding eyes, and let sit for 10 to 15 minutes before washing off.

THE SUGAR SCRUB

This all-natural skin exfoliant will not only leave your skin super soft but also smelling sweet.

1 cup brown or white sugar (see sub-
    stitutions)
½ cup coconut or olive oil

Optional Add-Ins
2 Tbsp raw honey
1 Tbsp citrus zest
1 tsp Pure Vanilla Extract (page 212)
½ tsp cinnamon
A few drops essential oil
2 Tbsp yogurt or kefir

> **USES UP** sugar (or coffee or oatmeal), oil, honey
>
> **TOTAL TIME** 2 minutes
>
> **MAKES** 1 face scrub
>
> **CAN SUBSTITUTE**
> • ½ cup sugar with ½ cup ground coffee or ½ cup oatmeal

1. In a bowl, combine all of the ingredients, including any optional add-ins.

2. Apply an even layer over clean face and neck, avoiding eyes, and let sit for 10 to 15 minutes before washing off.

THE SOAK

There is nothing better than a long hot bath, except a long hot bath steeped with soothing herbs and fragrances easily found in your own kitchen.

1 cup Epsom salts or 2 Tbsp sea salt
½ cup baking soda
¼ cup dried loose herbs, teas, or
    2–3 tea bags

Optional Add-Ins
½ cup coconut milk
½ cup leftover oatmeal
¼ cup dried petals (e.g., as lavendar,
    rose, or calendula)
2 Tbsp coconut oil
Good knob of ginger, sliced
A few drops of essential oils
Fresh rose petals or white sage
Raw honey
Cacao powder (albeit messy)

USES UP baking soda, tea, coconut milk. tea, herbs

TOTAL TIME 2 minutes

MAKES 1 bath soak

1. In a bowl, combine all of the ingredients, including any optional add-ins.

2. Add to a warm running bath and allow yourself to soak for at least 20 minutes.

BEAUTY PRODUCTS

In a pinch, here are some other food ideas for your skin. As with food, the better the quality of these ingredients, the better they are for your skin.

MAKE-UP REMOVER Sunflower seed, olive, and canola oil

ROSE FACIAL TONER MIX ¼ cup steeped rose tea, 2 teaspoons of witch hazel, ½ teaspoon of raw honey, and ¼ teaspoon of baking soda. Transfer to a dark glass bottle and use as a daily facial toner.

MOISTURIZER Coconut oil

BEST MASSAGE OIL (EVEN FOR BABIES) Any food-based, organic, and cold-pressed cooking oil can be used (stay away from any oils that may cause sensitivities or allergies, like nut or seed oils). My personal favorites are avocado and grapeseed.

Foods to Keep Your Home Spick and Span

Yes, certain foods, odds, and ends can make your home very clean!

BAKING SODA From tubs to toilets, baking soda can be used as an all-purpose cleaning solution. Here are just a few suggestions:
- For carpet or furniture stains or odors, sprinkle with baking soda, let sit for an hour, then vacuum.
- To deep-clean items known to build-up gunk, like oven-hood exhausts or hanging pot racks, take superhot water with equal parts dish soap and baking soda and use to clean.
- To make your silverware sparkle, place your silverware in a very large pot of hot water with a piece of aluminum foil and a couple of tablespoons of baking soda. Let sit for a few minutes depending how tarnished things have gotten.

BROWN SUGAR Have some brown sugar going hard? Mix it with some salt and use it to scrub pots and metal surfaces.

CITRUS There are so many uses for these fruits that are antiseptic, antibacterial, acidic, and smell great!
- For a natural freshener, throw some citrus rinds in the bottom of your garbage can.
- To freshen the dishwasher, pour the juice of one lemon in the bottom of dishwasher and run a rinse cycle.
- To clean your microwave, add juice of one lemon to a cup of water and microwave for 3 minutes, let it stand and steam for 5 minutes and wipe away all the gunk.
- To make your cutting boards glisten, just rub them with half a lemon and a sprinkle of baking soda to fizz away dirt and odor.
- To make a multipurpose citrus cleaner, fill a canning jar one-quarter full with white vinegar, adding citrus peels and scraps until the mixture is halfway full, and topping it off with more vinegar. Let stand for two weeks in a cool dark place before transferring to a spray bottle and clean.

COFFEE GROUNDS AND FILTERS As well as being a great option for composting, coffee grounds can also be used as a natural, abrasive cleaner for things like pots and pans. Do not use them on anything porous though, since they may leave a stain. And filters can be used as a lint-free way to polish your home monitors and screens.

RICE If you get water on your cell phone, dry it off as best you can, then place it in a bowl of rice overnight. The rice may help absorb any remaining water. Good luck!

VINEGAR To make an awesome glass cleaner, mix 1 tablespoon of vinegar and 1 quart water of water.

For the Pets F L P

In the making of this book I learned how shockingly easy it is to bake over 100 homemade dog treats with one leftover sweet potato. Then I thought, there have to be cat treats too! And so I came up with these recipes, which are also easy ways to sneak in some healthy ingredients like cinnamon for circulation no matter how stubborn your pet is. Customize these dog and cat treats to your furry best friend's palate or any allergies and sensitivities.

DOG TREATS

2–3 cups flour (if dog is sensitive to wheat, see tip on page 252)

1 tsp salt (or less)

½ tsp cinnamon

1 cup cooked sweet potato, squash, pumpkin, carrots, or any combination

1 egg, beaten

½ cup water

Optional Add-Ins

½ cup grated cheese

¼ cup applesauce

¼ cup chopped leftover bits of protein, rinsed

¼ cup grated carrots

1 Tbsp dried parsley (freshens breath)

1 Tbsp ground flax seed or oil

1 Tbsp peanut butter

1 Tbsp turmeric

1 Tbsp coconut oil

½ mashed banana

1. Preheat the oven to 350°F. Line a large baking sheet.

2. In a bowl, mix together the flour, salt, and cinnamon plus any optional add-ins.

3. In a separate bowl, mash together the sweet potato with the egg and water.

4. Add the dry ingredients to the wet ingredients. Using your hands or with a hand mixer or a stand mixer with the paddle attachment, mix until you have a dough that is not sticky and that you can roll out. You can always add more flour or water if needed.

5. Roll out the dough onto a floured surface until ¼ inch thick. Use a floured cookie cutter or a knife to cut into small shapes. Reroll all scraps.

6. Bake for 20 to 25 minutes until completely cooked though. These are hard treats, not soft. Cool and store in an airtight container.

USES UP sweet potato, protein, grated cheese, cooked carrots

NEVER ADD onions, garlic, chives, grapes, cherries, avocado, mushrooms, tomatoes, chocolate, nuts, xylitol

MAKES about 100 tiny treats

TOTAL TIME 40–45 minutes, depending on size

KEEPS FOR up to 2 weeks at room temperature or 6 months in the freezer

CAT TREATS

10 oz drained canned or leftover
    cooked fish, finely chopped (reserve
    drained water from can if using)
1 egg
2 cups whole-grain flour

Optional Add-Ins
Chicken or turkey, finely chopped
½ cup oats
1 Tbsp bacon grease
Sprinkle of catnip
Small handful of blueberries

1. Preheat the oven to 350°F and line a baking sheet.

2. In a stand mixer fitted with the paddle attachment, blend the fish, egg, and flour until a dough forms. If the dough is too dry, add a little reserved canning liquid or water. Add any optional add-ins. If it is too wet, add more flour.

3. Roll out the dough on a floured surface. Cut or shape to your kitty's desires and place on the baking sheet. Bake for 20 minutes or until slightly browned. Cool before serving.

Food 911 Gluten-free fur family? Use a gluten-free flour mix. Start with 1½ cups gluten-free flour, adding more as needed. Other gluten-free flours you can use are rice, potato, corn, millet, barley, coconut, and oat flour.

USES UP fish

NEVER ADD onions, garlic, chives, grapes, cherries, dog food, chocolate, milk or other dairy, peanut butter, xylitol

MAKES about 100 tiny treats

TOTAL TIME 40 minutes

KEEPS FOR up to 2 weeks at room temperature or 6 months in the freezer

Resources

WEBSITES

GLOBAL:

www.lovefoodhatewaste.com/portion-planner

www.stopfoodwaste.org

www.thefoodwasteatlas.org

www.fao.org

www.davidsuzuki.org

www.arcgis.com

CANADA:

www.lovefoodhatewaste.ca

www.csafarms.ca

www.notfarfromthetree.org

www.foodrescue.ca

www.inspection.gc.ca/food
/information-for-consumers/fact
-sheets-and-infographics/date
-labelling/eng/1332357469487
/1332357545633

www.nzwc.ca

www.vancouverfoodrunners.com

UNITED STATES:

www.dumpsters.com

www.eatbydate.com

www.endfoodwaste.org

www.foodtank.com

www.thefoodtrust.org

www.recyclenation.com

www.preserve.eco

www.usda.gov

APPS

GLOBAL:

Winnow

Earth Hero

UN Climate Change

CANADA:

Waste Wizard

Flash Flood

Food Hero

UNITED STATES:

iRecycle by Earth911

Food Resuce US

BOOKS

What Can I Do? by Jane Fonda

Bread is Gold by Massimo Bottura

The Substitutions Bible by David Joachim

The Flavor Thesaurus by Niki Segnit

The Uninhabitable Earth by David Wallace-Wells

Bibliography

Beef magazine. 2019. https://www.beefmagazine.com.

Burns Rudalevige, Christine. "Salt Cod Lands Back on Mainers' Dinner Plates." *Portland Press*, December 2018. https://www.pressherald.com/2018/12/23/baccala-is-back.

Clark, Melissa. "The Only Ice Cream Recipe You'll Ever Need." *New York Times*, July 2014. https://www.nytimes.com/2014/07/02/dining/the-only-ice-cream-recipe-youll-ever-need.html.

"Cod." Marine Stewardship Council, 2019. https://www.msc.org/what-you-can-do/eat-sustainable-seafood/fish-to-eat/cod.

"Dry vs. Canned Beans: Which Is Better?" The Bean Institute, 2019. https://beaninstitute.com/dry-vs-canned-beans-which-is-better.

Grundig. Respect Food. 2019. https://www.respectfood.com.

Krcek Allen, Nancy. *Discovering Global Cuisines: Traditional Flavors and Techniques*. Pearson, 2014.

"Napes." *Government of Canada's TERMIUM Plus*. 2019. https://www.btb.termiumplus.gc.ca/tpv2alpha/alpha-eng.html?lang=eng&i=1&srchtxt=napes&index=alt&codom2nd_wet=1#resultrecs.

Ontario Bean Growers. 2019. http://ontariobeans.on.ca.

Richards, Gwendolyn. *Pucker: A Cookbook for Citrus Lovers*. Whitecap, 2014.

Statistics Canada. Table 13-10-0472-01 Household food insecurity. DOI: https://doi.org/10.25318/1310047201-eng "The Serious Eats Guide to Beans." Serious Eats, 2019. https://www.seriouseats.com/2016/10/beans-legumes-pulses-varieties-recipes-cooking-tips.html.

"7 Reasons Why You Should Be Eating the Banana Peel, as Well as the Banana." *Runner's World*, September 2018. https://www.runnersworld.com/uk/nutrition/diet/a776150/7-reasons-why-you-should-be-eating-the-banana-peel.

Acknowledgments

My thanks to:

Robert McCullough, Katherine Stopa, Lindsay Paterson, Lindsay Vermeulen, Kelly Hill, Michelle Arbus, Erin Cooper, and the Penguin Random House Team for having as big of an appetite as I do for conquering food waste. You never let me down with your passion and commitment working on this book.

Chris Casuccio at Westwood Creative Artists agency for being my sounding board and having my back.

My super cool photography team: Reena Newman, Andrea McCrindle, Lindsay Duncan, Ryan Hegarty, and Megan Vincent, who, amidst ever-changing hectic schedules, set aside their time and expertise to truly make these photos super spectacular.

The contributors: Carson Arthur, Jason Cox, Todd Perrin, Jeremy Bonia, Anna Olson, Joanne Gauci (Love Food Hate Waste Canada), Nick Liu, Bob Blumer, and Allison Day for thinking this book was important enough to share your ideas and thoughts about food waste with all of us.

Matt, for forcing me to take a vacation even though I am a constant pain and . . . I know we have hardly eaten out anymore because of me writing this book. I promise I will take you out for dinner again . . . at some point.

My friends for telling me that everything tasted great when I know it sometimes didn't—and for coming when called for dinner when I have too much food left over from work.

My kids, who have never hesitated in telling me how my cooking really is. I know, deep down inside, you think I am still super cool. I love you and thank goodness I have my small little family to share meals with. Please always come home for dinner.

To Rhubarb, our mini but mighty schnauzer, for your consistency in keeping the kitchen floor clean and rinsing the dishes as they go in the dishwasher.

Index